MEASURES OF ASTONISHMENT

Oskana Poetry & Poetics
BOOK SERIES

Publishing new and established authors, Oskana Poetry & Poetics offers both contemporary poetry at its best and probing discussions of poetry's cultural role.

Advisory Board
Roo Borson
Robert Bringhurst
Louise Bernice Halfe
Tim Lilburn
Randy Lundy
Daniel David Moses
Gary Snyder
Jan Zwicky

For more information, please contact:
Karen May Clark, Acquisitions Editor
University of Regina Press
3737 Wascana Parkway
Regina, Saskatchewan S4S 0A2 Canada
karen.clark@uregina.ca

Measures
of Astonishment

POETS ON POETRY

presented by the League of Canadian Poets

Copyright © 2016 The League of Canadian Poets

All rights reserved. No part of this work covered by the copyrights hereon may be reproduced or used in any form or by any means—graphic, electronic, or mechanical—without the prior written permission of the publisher. Any request for photocopying, recording, taping or placement in information storage and retrieval systems of any sort shall be directed in writing to Access Copyright.

NOTE: Every effort has been made to contact copyright holders. Any copyright holders who could not be reached are urged to contact the publisher.

Owing to limitations of space, permission to reprint previously published material may be found at the end of the book.

Printed and bound in Canada at Friesens. The text of this book is printed on 100% post-consumer recycled paper with earth-friendly vegetable-based inks.

COVER AND TEXT DESIGN: Duncan Campbell
PROOFREADER: Kristine Douaud
COVER IMAGE: "Aurora Borealis over Trees" by Justin Reznick Photography

Library and Archives Canada Cataloguing in Publication

Measures of astonishment : poets on poetry / presented by the League of Canadian Poets.

Most of the essays in this volume were previously presented as lectures as
    part of the Anne Szumigalski lecture series.
Includes bibliographical references.
Issued in print and electronic formats.
ISBN 978-0-88977-371-4 (pbk.).—ISBN 978-0-88977-373-8 (html).—ISBN 978-0-88977-372-1 (pdf)

    1. Canadian poetry (English)—21st century—History and criticism.
I. Lilburn, Tim, 1950– . Poetry's practice of philosophy. II. League of Canadian Poets, editor

PS8155.1.M42 2015   C811'.609   C2015-901671-1   C2015-901672-X

10 9 8 7 6 5 4 3 2 1

University of Regina Press, University of Regina
Regina, Saskatchewan, Canada, S4S 0A2
tel: (306) 585-4758 fax: (306) 585-4699
web: www.uofrpress.ca
email: uofrpress@uregina.ca

The University of Regina Press acknowledges the support of the Canada Council for the Arts for our publishing program. We acknowledge the financial support of the Government of Canada. / Nous reconnaissons l'appui financier du gouvernement du Canada. This publication was made possible through Culture on the Go funding provided to Creative Saskatchewan by the Ministry of Parks, Culture and Sport.

 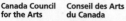 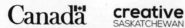

*To Jennifer Boire and Jacques Nolin—
whose generous support and vision turned
our Anne Szumigalski Lecture Series
from a wonderful idea to a respected annual tradition.*

contents

ix   Preface—*Glen Sorestad*

xiii   Acknowledgements

1   2002: Poetry's Practice of Philosophy
Tim Lilburn

11   2004: Every Exit Is an Entrance (A Praise of Sleep)
Anne Carson

33   2005: Frederick Ward: Writing as Jazz
George Elliott Clarke

69   2006: Why Poetry?
Margaret Atwood

79   2007: The Angel of the Big Muddy
Mark Abley

99   2008: Ediacaran and Anthropocene: poetry as a reader of deep time—*Don McKay*

113	2009: Re-Discovering Ancient Springs: a consideration of metaphorical space—*Marilyn Bowering*
129	2010: Poetry and Community *Anne Simpson*
139	2011: Pristine and Startled: Ways of Seeing *Glen Sorestad*
155	2012: Coming (back) to Poetry *Robert Currie*
169	2013: A Garden Is Not a Place: Poetry and Beauty *A. F. Moritz*
191	2014: Black Voice: Context and Subtext *Lillian Allen*
207	2015: Conversation with the Poet / *Who didn't know my aunty*—*Gregory Scofield*
227	Contributors
231	Permissions & Acknowledgements

Preface

GLEN SORESTAD

ANNE SZUMIGALSKI CLAIMED THAT AS A VERY YOUNG GIRL she knew that she was going to be a poet, that it was to be her goal in life and, indeed, that even at an early age she knew that she *was* a poet. By the time of her death in 1999, Anne Szumigalski was one of Canada's most widely respected poets, a Governor General's Award winner, an active force in the Saskatchewan and Manitoba writing communities, a strong influence on and a tireless mentor for a great many writers. Her home in Saskatoon became literally a poetic drop-in centre. Szumigalski, as one of the founders of the Saskatchewan Writers' Guild, was a strong champion of writing organizations and was also a long-time member of the League of Canadian Poets. How fitting then that the League should choose to name after Anne Szumigalski its inaugural lecture series by Canadian poets about the art and craft of poetry by Canadian poets, the Anne Szumigalski Lecture Series. This was done as a lasting recognition of the stature that Szumigalski held as a poet among her colleagues across the country.

Each of the lectures was initially given as an address to a poetry-friendly audience; however, the idea soon emerged of having the entire series to date appear in print in a single volume. It seemed the logical next step towards giving these valuable insights and reflections the largest audience possible. Only one of the lectures does not appear in this volume: Dionne Brand was the second Szumigalski lecturer and apparently she gave her well-received address from a series of note cards and never did write a complete address that could later be published.

The first of the Anne Szumigalski Lectures was given in 2002 by Tim Lilburn to an enthusiastic audience of members of the League and guests in Saskatoon. Lilburn reminded us all that poetry "is the theatre of feeling" and that "poems are an amorous pull, a being in love, that plush, mine-shafty chaos, and sometimes this being in love feels like a sickness." Lilburn, with his lecture, got the series off to a rousing start and established the tone of lectures to follow. Since every poet views poetry through his or her own unique lens, Lilburn, by presenting *his* distinctive view of his art and craft, paved the way for successive poets to offer their own perspectives on poetry. So the lectures to follow are as individual in their approach as the poets who delivered them. They range in style from a more formal academic approach to a more casual and deeply personal approach. But what they all share and what readers will soon discover as they read the voices included here is that all of them deeply love the "sullen art" of which they have become practitioners and that all of them are also very deeply committed to poetry and its craft.

The Lilburn lecture was financed by the Saskatchewan Arts Board to honour Szumigalski's passing the previous year. This lecture was so well-received that the League determined to find a way to make the lecture an annual event, part of the gala evening at its yearly festival. Thanks to a generous donation from League member Jennifer Boire and her husband, Jacques Nolin, the Anne Szumigalski Lecture Series became a reality, with its second lecture delivered by Dionne Brand.

George Elliott Clarke reflected on how we must be very careful in our judgment of the true worth of a poet's work, especially poets who are part of an entirely different cultural milieu, warning his fellow poets that "the world is perverse in its bestowal of recognition and non-recognition," and that we all harbour misconceptions regarding popular culture, misconceptions that can obstruct our own understanding and appreciation of some poets. Margaret Atwood took a broad perspective of humanity and reminded us that "a society without poetry and the other arts would have broken its mirror and cut out its heart." She saw poetry as an "uttering, or outering of the human imagination."

Mark Abley, who grew up in Saskatoon and who knew Szumigalski well, having been one of those young writers who regularly visited her home and who was influenced by her, speculated that had Szumigalski been forced to study poetry in school the way so many Canadians have experienced it, she would not "have loved poetry so fervently." Abley called upon his fellow poets to "not be afraid to demonstrate the energy of language and the sterling power of the human imagination." Both the energy of language and the human imagination are recurrent motifs throughout the lectures. Another common motif when poets discuss poetry is sleep and dreams; Anne Carson subtitled her address "A Praise of Sleep" and she delivered to her audience a classical and most erudite treatment of sleep, or as she put it, "to burrow like a mole in different ways of reading sleep and different readers of sleep."

Don McKay introduced his audience to the concept of "geopoetry," where he thought materialism and mysticism "finally come together, have a conversation in which each hearkens to the other, then go out for a drink." McKay reminded us that poetry is always subversive and political because it turns the tool of language against itself. Marilyn Bowering spoke of the form and nature of poetry making connections and of how each poet finds shapes and relationships that will be recognized as part of that poet's voice. Anne Simpson talked of how poetry begins in a concern for what is, but that it usually proceeds beyond to the world of the possible. Robert Currie discussed the role chance had played in his life and the lives of other poets, then spoke of what kept them coming back to poetry once they had begun to write; he felt it was the actual joy of working on a poem that brings us back again and again. A. F. Moritz used the image of the garden for the poem and told us, "It is a human beauty, part of a human garden, one that we carry within and manifest in poems." Lillian Allen presented an impassioned insight into the origins and nature of dub poetry in North America, its considerable contribution to the development and success of spoken word poetry from the 1970s to the present and its many contributions to poetry in general. By telling us the story of his aunt,

Gregory Scofield illustrated the sheer power of storytelling in First Nations cultures and revealed how his own poetry is a natural result of this need and this desire to create and to share in the forms of poems those stories, past and present, that must not be forgotten.

Each Szumigalski lecturer has brought something of his or her uniqueness as a person and as a poet to the act of sharing his or her thoughts about poetry. Reading this series of presentations will give any lover of language and poetry an amazingly diverse number of ways to view what poetry is, what it does and why it matters to us all.

Acknowledgements

"NO ONE GROWS RICH BY WRITING POETRY, BUT THAT WONderful struggle to write the poem does enrich our lives," Robert Currie said during his 2012 Anne Szumigalski Lecture in Saskatoon. And every year, since the inception of the lecture series in 2002, members of the League of Canadian Poets have had our lives enriched during our annual Poetry Festival and Conference by brilliant poets sharing their wisdom about, and passion for, the art of poetry during the eloquent delivery of the annual Anne Szumigalski Lecture. The League of Canadian Poets is deeply grateful for the exuberance and hard work of all of our members who worked collaboratively to create and maintain the Anne Szumigalski Lecture Series and to publish this rich anthology.

Dave Margoshes championed the idea of the League having its own lecture series, in the manner of the Writers' Union of Canada with its Margaret Laurence Lectures. Paul Wilson suggested that our series be named after renowned Saskatchewan poet Anne Szumigalski.

Jennifer Boire and Jacques Nolin continue to be our dedicated financial sponsors for the lecture series. None of this would have come to fruition without their constant and much-appreciated support.

ACKNOWLEDGEMENTS

Andris Taskans, editor-in-chief of *Prairie Fire*, should be singled out for his splendid support of the Anne Szumigalski Lectures by seeing them into print each year, and for sweetening the compensation for the Lectures.

All the lecturers featured in this anthology have foregone any compensation for their work, and therefore all royalties shall go to the League of Canadian Poets to help continue to fund our various initiatives, including future lectures. Thank you to Gregory Scofield, Lillian Allen, A. F. Moritz, Robert Currie, Glen Sorestad, Anne Simpson, Marilyn Bowering, Don McKay, Mark Abley, Margaret Atwood, George Elliott Clarke, Anne Carson, and Tim Lilburn for inspiring us each year with your beautiful, thoughtful lectures, and for sharing your work in these pages.

The lecture anthology committee included Mary Ellen Csamer, Glen Sorestad, and Jenna Butler, who cheerfully dreamed, schemed, compiled, proofread, lobbied, and badgered despite their busy schedules, and finally found a home for our manuscript.

We are delighted that Bruce Walsh and Dave McLennan at the University of Regina Press were so enthusiastic about becoming that home, and appreciate the diligent editorial work of Donna Grant.

As always, the League is grateful for the continued support of the Canada Council for the Arts, as well as for the commitment and ingenuity of our staff, especially Joanna Poblocka and Ingel Madrus, who gamely helped the committee with the cat-herding involved in turning thirteen lectures into a cohesive submission for a publisher.

Dymphny Dronyk, Past President, League of Canadian Poets

Poetry's Practice of Philosophy

TIM LILBURN

Anne Szumigalski Lecture • Saskatoon, Saskatchewan • June 8, 2002

    How dear to her is the journey of the mind,
    flying from dwelling to dwelling,

    Her feet scraping the tops of the
    forest trees as she floats on by,

    Exchanging one language for another,
    never quite sure of her bearings,
    counting the chimneys on unfamiliar roofs.
                —Anne Szumigalski, "Theirs Is the Song"

SOME WOULD SAY ANNE SZUMIGALSKI SAW IT WRONG: THE life of the mind simply is not livable in the poem. And some of those saying this would be poets. The poem is the theatre of feeling; the poem is the pool of light where passion stands and sings its termagant songs. They might concede that intuition could sit snug and happy in the poem, imagining this as a sort of feral knowing, somatic, far closer to empathy than dialectic. So not thinking, never thinking: the poem is where you go for haven from the tyranny of abstraction. The people who say this might be surprised to find they had what looked like allies among the philosophers, who would declare that poetry is subjectivity to its very bottom. But they shouldn't be fooled by this appearance of alliance: there will be no free meals for them from this source. Philosophy doesn't love the poem construed as the house of subjectivity: it holds it in the same contempt as it holds metaphysics, while recognizing its utility: here is the isolation ward of hysteria.

While philosophers may have such private views of poetry, they almost never have gone on record with them. I can think of two exceptions to this near total silence. Martin Heidegger, of course, seems to refuse the norm, offering poets priestly status in the temple of being, but the even more famous example is Plato's expulsion of the poets from kalipolis, the beautiful city, the city of philosophy. I think we misunderstand these two philosophical utterances on poetry, Heidegger's and Plato's, well-known though they may be; and I further think that by unravelling these misunderstandings, especially the one concerning Plato, we'll come to a fresh comprehension of poetry that will show it not antipodal to philosophy, but sitting alone in front of philosophy's hearth, tending the fire.

Poetry and philosophy. I can imagine few prominent, mainstream philosophers who seriously think *Leaves of Grass, Lyrical Ballads,* or even the *Divine Comedy*—to say nothing of *Life Studies* or *The Beauty of the Weapons*—are philosophical books, places where you might look for light into the darkness philosophy explores. In fact, to so believe is to accept marginal status in the world of professional philosophy. It is now far from obvious that poetry, religion and philosophy are linked in any way—their split is virtually an article of faith: one way of thinking of the last four hundred years of European thought is to see it as a focussed effort to detach these three endeavours, and to denigrate two of them, poetry and religion. But Homer didn't see things this way, nor did the person or persons who wrote the long poem of the descent of the goddess Inanna to the underworld, nor did Haida poets Ghandl and Skaay—in the work of all of these, the three undertakings go on simultaneously; indeed, they make a single doing powering the poetry. I think Ghandl and the others were right: poetry, philosophy, religion come from and return to the same place in the psyche: contemplative attention.

Listen now, for a moment, to Julian of Norwich on prayer. This is from some middle chapters in her *Revelations of Divine Love*. The religious language may be a shock to the ear, but try to hear the form of what she says, try to take in with the seeing ear its erotic shape.

> For prayer is the means by which we rightly understand the fullness of joy that is coming to us: it is true longing and sure trust too. Lack of the happiness which is our natural lot makes us long for it. Real understanding, love, and the recollection of our Saviour enables us to trust. Our Lord sees us constantly at work at these two things. It is no more than our duty, and no less than his goodness would assign to us. It is up to us to do our part with diligence, yet when we have done it, it will seem to us that we have done nothing...

> But when our Lord in his courtesy and grace shows himself to our soul we have what we desire. Then we care no longer about praying for anything, for our whole strength and aim is set on beholding. This is prayer, high and ineffable, in my eyes. The whole reason we pray is summed up in the sight and vision of him to whom we pray. Wondering, enjoying, worshipping, fearing... and all done with such sweetness....

So, prayer as desire, as, more specifically, erotic passivity, a doing nothing with implacable resolve, the what-is-not-the-self stippling in. Waiting, and something coming into the waiting that is not molded by anything, not even anticipation. Here is the doppelgänger of the poem that is mere obedience to what presses the tongue, in which one writes best by doing the least with a strenuous, an elegant, commitment.

Let me stray back to Plato. I'd been saying that we don't really understand what he says in the *Republic* about poetry. We read it usually, as Iris Murdoch did, as sharp-toothed antipathy between Plato's cerebral puritanism and sensuality of all kinds, poetry's in particular. We're wrong, I think, to come at it this way. Another reading of what's going on in the *Republic* around poetry shows that poetry and philosophy are one.

Bear with me; let's walk down the basement steps of the dialogue into the cavern of the book; it's badly lit with a poor fire; you smell mouse shit and wax from guttered candles as you dip your head and enter. It is, of course, night. People are talking; the room floats on a living wave of talk; the talk is sometimes rhythmic, sometimes jerky, like the movements of a large, possibly dangerous, animal. There are, say, ten people in the room: some are in love with one another, some soon could be in love. Socrates, Plato's teacher is here, so is Glaucon, Plato's brother. They're in a room in a seaport not far from Athens—the rotting sexual smell of the sea enters and falls apart around them. The air, if we could see it, would be darkly green, slowly growing. Socrates and Glaucon have just taken in a religious festival, horses ridden hard on the beach by men carrying fire; the room twitches with noumenal energy. Dionysus is on patrol here; be careful, keep your eyes open.

Glaucon is the man of the hour; the talk all eventually flows toward him. He's an interesting specimen: he likes disputation and has a taste for political grandeur—if he were alive today he perhaps would have a job in the Bush White House; he's imperial, eristic; he loves war. His name might be David Frum. He's a rather dangerous personality: charming, ruthless, charmed by his own limitations. He got all of this from poetry. Poetry's ruined him: the erotic deformity of his soul comes from an entranced reading of a particular poem, the *Iliad* of Homer—the giddy ferocity of the assault has stained him—and when Socrates hammers away at poetry in Book III and later in the dialogue, he's trying to free him from this book and the fascism it's nudging him into. Suppose he succeeds—he doesn't, but suppose he does—and Glaucon suddenly feels the ax-cleave of shame for his political hubris, what's left for him? Well, aside from mathematics and astronomy, there's that other book, about one of the fighters at Troy and his return home. In the ruin, the kenosis, the romance with the celestial lover, the descent to the dead, the apokatastasis found in the *Odyssey*, Glaucon would read of the shamanic path of Odysseus and the pattern of philosophy, and he might even internalize and begin to enact this pattern. His eros then would unbend.

Just what is philosophy? I'm not that great a fool that I would attempt to provide a full answer to this question. But I can chatter away for a while about what it roughly is in the *Republic*: there, philosophy is a particular unfolding of desire: a sorrow awakens eros in the non-desiring man; a lavish self-emptying goes on; there are tears, a perpetual disposition to tears; there is the travel below the ground and a final homegoing. A turning around of the soul, as Socrates puts it, entirely erotic, entirely resisted, entirely desired, utterly refusable; it is a turning of the soul so that it finds itself loving the things that return it to itself. The work of philosophy here is a close version of the ceremonial work of Odysseus—intensely private, yet altruistic; psychic, political. This is what is advertised as philosophy in the dialogue; no one really takes it up there, but it's on view in the shop window. It is a journey replicated in foundational poems from many places, as I've said—"The Descent of Inanna," Skaay's "The One They Hand Along"—and it's reproduced, in the ancient and medieval world, in contemplative philosophy in dialogue after dialogue, and in tract on mystical theology after tract on mystical theology.

This same sort of erotic unfolding happens in certain sorts of contemporary poems too—not necessarily long poems either, though it doesn't fear length. The work is partly about the long walk of unsatisfiable longing—epektasis, the endlessness of desire, as Gregory of Nyssa called it. The poetics of the poem I most admire and which I wish to write are really a philosophical therapeutics, an ascesis.

I've said it comes down to contemplative attention: this is what's at philosophy's heart, at the heart of poetry, the centre of religion. Philosophy, of course, doesn't do this sort of thing any more, and religion, for the most part, is transfixed by cosmology and television. Poetry alone, as I've said, still visits the old fire site. But what is contemplative attention? It is what happens to you when you are knocked to the ground by some astonishment. You go very still at some point in yourself and become entirely eye. What can do this to us, hold the attention in such a way that the Odyssean transformations are required, quickened, that the interior travel—the tears, the descent—begins? Lovers, sex, landscapes, God (I think of Pier Giorgio Di Cicco's new work), great horror (I think of the work of Peter Dale Scott, especially *Coming to Jakarta* and *Minding the Darkness*). And when you look hard at such things (at political horror, at sex, at God)—as you must if you truly see them—your life comes apart, just as it begins to drift together. You are entering the cloud. And not only do you break up, but language begins to do so as well. It becomes besotted like you, woundedly drunk.

Here are two sections from a long poem called "Kill-site." The man you will meet in the first section, Henry Kelsey, was the first European on the plains. He took a two-year walk in the last decade of the seventeenth century from Hudson Bay that brought him as far west as the Touchwood Hills, about 250 kilometres east of Saskatoon.

Kill-site

> The animal dreamed of me,
> a brown gust separating above its head;
> this was below snowhumps on the creek,
> ice fog up the towers along
> the valley sides, blood on the snow,
> estrus marks, the water frozen a yard down.
>
> When Henry Kelsey died or left
> Hudson Bay, there's a rumour he continued
>   walking under the ground
> in the highest part of his voice, down the west hip
>   of the Porcupine Hills,
> a pythagorean thrum in his eyes.
> Because all this was a new music, uncooked ratio,
>   a machine of smoke.

And he thought *Let the will sleep here 400 years.*
Let the will sleep here 400 years.
Only some song would turn the lock.
He was looking for the deeper Crees, Naywattame, the Poets,
    people sleeping
      along the rock ledges behind their eyes, someone to put
      something
          in his mouth.

And because he was under the ground, everything came to him—he
saw a face of wheat, a face
of mineral beam, nipples of stones, a face
of winter in things, face of what is
at the back, the watery, the alto part of the mind,
showing through skin.
(It rose to the skin
      for its hump to be seen, then moved back into the trees.)
Only a song would turn the lock.
He kept walking, wanting and fearing
      the freezing of rivers.

Sandhills in a light, likely-daylong rain, looking off
   to the left, grass that's not going anywhere, September—
   everything walks
toward you; it undresses and comes
              toward you with its small bright hands
and the downwind smell of your father's mind
and his shoulders in the early summer of 1964,
he's working two jobs, post office, moving company; right
now he's not wearing a shirt, a hundred and forty-five pounds,
but still less under the name of his lower-in-the-throat citizenship,
where he's not saying a thing, living in a cave two
thirds up a cliff line, how
did he get there, swallows heaving in front of his face, the hole
trench-shovelled into clay sides lifting over the Milk River, north of
the Sweetgrass Hills, cattle clouding off infinitely

to the east, feathers
and bones hung from string at the mouth of the cave,
pale green feathers smooth out long and speechless from his tailbone.
Things climb out of the elms of their names and themselves
and they come forward, moving their tattoed, Fulani hands.
They smell of your father's voice, his
    one
      black
        suit.

Martin Heidegger said ontology was first philosophy; all thinking grew from an account of Being. Emmanual Levinas, his student, sensing a threatening Hitlerian inflation in the tone of this project, nearly losing a wife and daughter in the Holocaust, losing relatives, said no, no, ethics was the originary thinking: everything grows from the dumfounding before the other; a profound courtesy is the residue of this astonishment. I have an idea for a third possibility—erotics, mystical theology, as first philosophy. I suggest this standing before the spectacle of the failure of dogmatic theology, the mammoth racial arrogance it has underwritten, the hubris of a particular culture. What is elemental, quintessentially desirable, is beyond knowing, speech—to presume to know is to begin a colonization of the feral world, to pay the world the great compliment of likening it to yourself. Who can say the large thing which desire wants, wants, wants? But we can watch eros as it cranes for it, see the poses it takes in this reaching: these shapes are adequate ideograms for what cannot be said, and reading them doesn't ossify behaviour, but builds it, plucks it.

    I'll come right out and say it, the thing that roils beneath all this attempt at explanation: poems are an amorous pull, a being in love, that plush, mine-shafty chaos, and sometimes this being-in-love feels like a sickness. So poetics is erotics, is mystical theology. Where's the poet in this? He's keen and useless; he's passive, ready for anything; he's ignorant and busy with the heavy labour of opening, which is, in part, a refusing, a divesting.

    A word of caution. One given over to eros's doings likely will become what those who followed Socrates called atopos; that is, unlike, discreditable, laughable, possibly feared, significantly weird—her eye is caught helplessly by, sequestered by, the out-of-range. But then this liminality draws a certain darkness, slant, commodiousness into the poem that is otherwise not available to writing.

In Heidegger, or at least in the essay "The Origin of the Work of Art," the poet is the passageway through which the world speaks its truth, the poet is the single priest of Being. If the heroism of high Romanticism, the heroism of the Heideggerian poet, strikes you as implausible; if the narcissism of this figure seems repellant, what can you think happens as the poem appears? The way I see it, the poem is far more than the writing of it, and the best language to talk about this far-more comes from contemplative philosophy or ascetical theology. You fall apart before some arresting thing, some terrible beauty, and you empty. If you stay low, this thing may come toward you like an animal from the forest. This permeability before astonishing otherness, and what this astonishment makes you do, is also philosophy. Such language—the language of rapture, of psychagoguery—has no standing, though, in modern philosophy, as I've said throughout this talk; it has not had for many, many years. It appears there as delusion, the betrayal of the four-century, pan-cultural project of reason which has brought us democracy, the MRI machine and more television than you can shake a stick at. Poetry conceived this way, as contemplative attention and availability—a life given to this—seems a dangerous backsliding in relation to this project. Poetry isn't marginal; it must be made marginal: it speaks heterodoxy—just by the way it goes about its business. Good for it.

I want to return, finally, to Anne Szumigalski. Here is the whole of the third section of "Theirs Is the Song."

> How dear to her is the journey of the mind,
> flying from dwelling to dwelling,
>
> Her feet scraping the tops of the
> forest trees as she floats on by,

Exchanging one language for another,
never quite sure of her bearings,
counting the chimneys on unfamiliar roofs.

One day she hopes to understand progression
how it has no end and no beginning,
how nothing precedes or succeeds,
how time is a disc that wobbles
as it spins.

The melody is an old one
played again and again.
All night she's aware that it scuttles
over the pilllows like a louse on a holiday.

Waking she hears it emerge from her nose,
a hum like paperwasps.

"But that's just the tune," she says,
"tomorrow on my way I'll write the words."

How lucky we were to have Anne Szumigalski's mind, her eye, with us for a while. Her life was a rare visitation, one of the few things we can hold up to someone who might step from the horror Europe has inflicted on the New World, who might step from capitalism's eating of the planet and demand an accounting, one of the few things we might be able to present to a possible survivor and say, here, this was done well.

Every Exit Is an Entrance
(A Praise of Sleep)
ANNE CARSON

Anne Szumigalski Lecture • Montreal, Quebec • June 5, 2004

I WANT TO MAKE A PRAISE OF SLEEP. NOT AS A PRACTITIONER —I admit I have never been what is called "a good sleeper" and perhaps we can return later to that curious concept—but as a reader. There is so much sleep to read, there are so many ways to read it. In Aristotle's view, sleep requires a "daimonic but not a divine" kind of reading.[1] Kant refers to sleep's content as "involuntary poetry in a healthy state."[2] Keats wrote an "Ode to Sleep," invoking its powers against the analytic of the day:

> O soft embalmer of the still midnight!
> . . . .
> Then save me, or the passéd day will shine
> Upon my pillow, breeding many woes;
> Save me from curious conscience, that still lords
> Its strength for darkness, burrowing like a mole;

Turn the key deftly in the oiléd wards,
And seal the hushéd casket of my soul.[3]

My intention in this essay is to burrow like a mole in different ways of reading sleep, different kinds of readers of sleep, both those who are saved, healthy, daimonic, good sleepers and those who are not. Keats ascribes to sleep an embalming action. This means two things: that sleep does soothe and perfume our nights; that sleep can belie the stench of death inborn in us. Both actions are salvific in Keats's view. Both deserve (I think) to be praised.

My earliest memory is of a dream. It was in the house where we lived when I was three or four years of age. I dreamed I was asleep in the house in an upper room. That I awoke and came downstairs and stood in the living room. The lights were on in the living room, although it was hushed and empty. The usual dark green sofa and chairs stood along the usual pale green walls. It was the same old living room as ever, I knew it well, nothing was out of place. And yet it was utterly, certainly, different. Inside its usual appearance the living room was as changed as if it had gone mad.

Later in life, when I was learning to reckon with my father, who was afflicted with and eventually died of dementia, this dream recovered itself to me, I think because it seemed to bespeak the situation of looking at a well-known face, whose appearance is exactly as it should be in every feature and detail, except that is also, somehow, deeply and glowingly, strange.

The dream of the green living room was my first experience of such strangeness and I find it as uncanny today as I did when I was three. But there was no concept of madness or dementia available to me at that time. So, as far as I can recall, I explained the dream to myself by saying that I had caught the living room sleeping. I had entered it from the sleep side. And it took me years to recognize, or even to frame a question about, why I found this entrance into strangeness so supremely consoling. For despite the spookiness, inexplicability and later tragic reference of the green living room, it was and remains for me a consolation to think of it lying there, sunk in its greenness, breathing its own order, answerable to no one, apparently penetrable everywhere and yet so perfectly disguised in all the propaganda of its own waking life as to become in a true sense something *incognito* at the heart of our sleeping house.

It is in these terms that I wish to praise sleep, as a glimpse of something *incognito*. Both words are important. *Incognito* means "unrecognized, hidden, unknown." Something means not nothing. What is *incognito* hides from us because it has something worth hiding, or so we judge. As an example of this judgment I shall cite for you two stanzas of Elizabeth Bishop's poem "The Man-Moth." The Man-Moth, she says, is a creature who lives most of the time underground but pays occasional visits to the surface of the earth, where he attempts to scale the faces of the buildings and reach the moon, for he understands the moon to be a hole at the top of the sky through which he may escape. Failing to attain the moon each time he falls back and returns to the pale subways of his underground existence. Here is the poem's third stanza:

>   Up the façades,
> his shadow dragging like a photographer's cloth behind him,
> he climbs fearfully, thinking that this time he will manage
> to push his small head through that round clean opening
> and be forced through, as from a tube, in black scrolls on the light.
> (Man, standing below him, has no such illusions.)
> But what the Man-Moth fears most he must do, although
> he fails, of course, and falls back scared but quite unhurt.[4]

The Man-Moth is not sleeping, nor is he a dream, but he may represent sleep itself—an action of sleep, sliding up the facades of the world at night on his weird quest. He harbours a secret content, valuable content, which is difficult to extract even if you catch him. Here is the poem's final stanza:

>   If you catch him,
> hold up a flashlight to his eye. It's all dark pupil,
> an entire night itself, whose haired horizon tightens
> as he stares back, and closes up the eye. Then from the lids
> one tear, his only possession, like the bee's sting, slips.

> Slyly he palms it, and if you're not paying attention
> he'll swallow it. However, if you watch, he'll hand it over,
> cool as from underground springs and pure enough to drink.

To drink the tear of sleep, to detach the prefix "un-" from its canniness and from its underground purposes, has been the project of many technologies and therapies—from the ancient temple of Asklepios at Epidauros, where sick people slept the night in order to dream their own cure, to the psychoanalytic algebras of Jacques Lacan, who understands sleep as a space from which the sleeper can travel in two directions, both of them a kind of waking. If I were to praise either of these methods of healing I would do so on grounds of their hopefulness. Both Asklepiadic priests and Lacanian analysts posit a continuity between the realms of waking and sleeping, whereby a bit of something *incognito* may cross over from night to day and change the life of the sleeper. Here is an ancient account of one of the sleep cures at Epidauros:

> There came as a suppliant to the god Asklepios a man who was so one-eyed that on the left he had only lids, there was nothing, just emptiness. People in the temple laughed at him for thinking he would see with an eye that was not there. But in a vision that appeared to him as he slept, the god seemed to boil some medicine and, drawing apart the lids, poured it in. When day came the man went out, seeing with both eyes.[5]

What could be more hopeful than this story of an empty eye filled with seeing as it sleeps? An analyst of the Lacanian sort might say that the one-eyed man has chosen to travel all the way in the direction of his dream and so awakes to a reality more real than the waking world. He dove into the nothingness of his eye and is awakened by too much light. Lacan would praise sleep as a blindness, which nonetheless looks back at us. What does sleep see when it looks back at us? This is a question entertained by Virginia Woolf in *To The Lighthouse,* a novel that falls asleep for twenty-five pages in the middle. The story has three parts. Parts I and III concern the planning and execution of a trip to the lighthouse by the Ramsay family. Part II is told entirely from the sleep side. It is called "Time Passes." It begins as a night that grows into many nights then turns into seasons and years. During this time, changes flow over the house of the story and penetrate the lives of the characters while they sleep. These changes are glimpsed as if from underneath; Virginia Woolf's main narrative is a catalogue of silent bedrooms, motionless chests of drawers, apples left on the dining room table, the wind prying at a window blind, moonlight gliding on floorboards. Down across these phenomena come facts from the waking world, like swimmers stroking by on a night lake. The facts are brief, drastic and enclosed in square brackets. For example:

> [Mr. Ramsay, stumbling along a passage one dark morning, stretched his arms out, but Mrs. Ramsay having died rather suddenly the night before, his arms, though stretched out, remained empty.]

or:

> [A shell exploded. Twenty or thirty young men were blown up in France, among them Andrew Ramsay, whose death, mercifully, was instantaneous.]

or:

> [Mr. Carmichael brought out a volume of poems that spring, which had an unexpected success. The war, people said, had revived their interest in poetry.][6]

These square brackets convey surprising information about the Ramsays and their friends, yet they float past the narrative like the muffled shock of a sound heard while sleeping. No one wakes up. Night plunges on, absorbed in its own events. There is no exchange between night and its captives, no tampering with eyelids, no drinking the tear of sleep. Viewed from the sleep side, an empty eye socket is just a fact about a person, not a wish to be fulfilled, not a therapeutic challenge. Virginia Woolf offers us, through sleep, a glimpse of a kind of emptiness that interests her. It is the emptiness of things before we make use of them, a glimpse of reality prior to its efficacy. Some of her characters also search for this glimpse while they are awake. Lily Briscoe, who is a painter in *To The Lighthouse*, stands before her canvas and ponders how "to get hold of that very jar on the nerves, the thing itself before it has been made anything."[7] In a famous passage of her *Diaries*, Virginia Woolf agrees with the aspiration:

> If I could catch the feeling I would: the feeling of the singing of the real world, as one is driven by loneliness and silence from the habitable world.[8]

What would the singing of the real world sound like? What would the thing itself look like? Such questions are entertained by her character Bernard, at the end of *The Waves*:

> So now, taking upon me the mystery of things, I could go like a spy without leaving this place, without stirring from my chair.... The birds sing in chorus; the house is whitened; the sleeper stretches; gradually all is astir. Light floods the room and drives shadow beyond shadow to where they hang in folds inscrutable. What does this central shadow hold? Something? Nothing? I do not know.[9]

Throughout her fiction Virginia Woolf likes to finger the border between nothing and something. Sleepers are ideal agents of this work. So in her first novel, *The Voyage Out* (a story in which Clarissa Dalloway and six other people travel to South America on a boat), she places her heroine in a remarkable paragraph afloat between waking and sleep:

> "I often wonder," Clarissa mused in bed, over the little white volume of Pascal which went with her everywhere, "whether it is really good for a woman to live with a man who is morally her superior, as Richard is mine. It makes one so dependent. I suppose I feel for him what my mother and women of

her generation felt for Christ. It just shows that one can't do without *something*." She then fell into sleep, which was as usual extremely sound and refreshing, but visited by fantastic dreams of great Greek letters stalking round the room, when she woke up and laughed to herself, remembering where she was and that the Greek letters were real people, lying asleep not many yards away.... The dreams were not confined to her indeed, but went from one brain to another. They all dreamt of each other that night, as was natural, considering how thin the partitions were between them and how strangely they had been lifted off the earth to sit next each other in mid ocean....[10]

I think Virginia Woolf intends us to enjoy the gentle marital experiment in which Clarissa condenses her husband (Richard) with Christ and then Christ with *something*—put in italics to remind us of its proximity to *nothing*. But I am not sure how "natural" it is for dreams to go stalking from brain to brain on an ocean liner, or for ancient Greek letters of the alphabet to be identified with real people. Something supernatural is beginning to be conjured here. Slightly more spooky is a story Virginia Woolf published in 1921 called "A Haunted House," which features a pair of ghosts sliding from room to room of a house where they had lived centuries ago. The ghosts seem happy but their transit through the house is disturbing, not least of all in its pronouns. The narrative voice shifts from "we" to "one" to "you" to "they" to "I," as if no one in the story can keep a stable skin on, and the story ends with a sleeper startled awake by the ghosts leaning over her bed:

> Waking, I cry "Oh, is this *your* buried treasure? The light in the heart."[11]

I don't exactly know what the last two sentences mean. A transaction of some importance seems about to take place. Between the realms of sleep and waking, life and death, Virginia Woolf throws open a possibility of dispossession, and then leaves it standing ajar, as if she isn't sure which side she wants to be on. The story, although light and almost comical, leaves a dark aftertaste. Let us compare the supernatural effects of an earlier author. Homer locates the psychological climax of the *Iliad* in a scene at the start of the 23rd book where Achilles falls asleep and is visited by the psyche of his dead friend Patroklos. Achilles converses with Patroklos and vainly tries to embrace him. As he reaches out his arms in sleep towards his dead friend, Achilles may remind us of poor Mr. Ramsay in *To The Lighthouse*, stretching out his arms in square brackets to his dead wife. Yet Homer's metaphysic of sleep is much less dark than Virginia Woolf's. Ghosts in epic are sad but they are also efficacious. While Patroklos goes gibbering off to his place in the underworld, Achilles jumps out of bed to perform the funeral rites enjoined on him by the dream, with this careful comment:

> Soul and ghost are certainly *something*![12]

Sleepers in Virginia Woolf do not negotiate sublime transactions in this way. Her narrative advises us to place no hope in them:

> ... and should any sleeper, fancying that he might find on the beach an answer to his doubts, a sharer of his solitude, throw off his bedclothes and go down by himself to walk on the sand, no image with semblance of serving and divine promptitude comes readily to hand bringing the night to order and making the world reflect the compass of his soul .... Useless in such confusion to ask the night those questions as to what and why and wherefore, which tempt the sleeper from his bed to seek an answer.[13]

In Homer on the other hand, we find answers, beds and sleepers often intertwined, especially in the *Odyssey*. You could say the *Odyssey* is a saga of who sleeps with whom, in its driving mythic impulse towards Penelope and away from Helen, in its fantastic elaboration of kinds of beds, culminating in the famous "trick of the bed" whereby Penelope and Odysseus prove who they are. Throughout the poem, Homer orchestrates a master sleep plan that pulls all the major characters into a nocturnal rhythm lying just under the surface of the awake narrative. Let's look more closely at how people sleep and where their beds are in this epic.

Telemachos, to begin with, is an insomniac. On the seven occasions in the *Odyssey* when we observe him going to bed, only once does he "take the gift of sleep" in Homer's phrase. Usually he lies awake worrying, as at the close of Book 1:

> There all night long, wrapped in a sheep fleece,
> he deliberated in his mind the road Athene had shown him.[14]

or at the beginning of Book 15:

> Sweet sleep did not get hold of Telemachos but in his heart
> throughout the ambrosial night, cares for his father kept him awake.[15]

Cares for his father include, not least of all, cares for who his father is. When Athene asks him if he is Odysseus's son he gives a tough teenage answer:

> Well my mother says I'm his but I'm dubious
> myself: no one ever knows his own begetting.[16]

Yet he would certainly like to know. Sexual knowledge ripples everywhere in this story just out of Telemachos's reach. He sits amid the suitors "biting his heart" as they cavort before his mother. He travels to the houses of other married couples, Nestor and his wife, Menelaos and Helen, where he passes the night on a couch aligned with the marital bed. Thus pursued by primal scenes and primary doubts he makes his way to the 16th Book and to the hut of Eumaios, the swineherd, where he finally meets and knows his father. Here Telemachos "takes the gift of sleep," lying down in the swineherd's hut beside Odysseus. This idyllic, impossible night as substitute Penelope beside his own father is Telemachos's happiest moment in the *Odyssey*. The very next evening sees him returned to his childhood and to insomnia: back at Penelope's house, as Odysseus plans the rout of the suitors, he sends Telemachos upstairs to bed alone:

Then there Telemachos laid himself down
and waited for radiant dawn.[17]

Meanwhile Odysseus: no question the man of many turns is a master of waking reality, yet his relation to sleep is troubled. He frequently feels the need to force himself awake, as when predatory animals or rapacious humans surround him (5.473; 8.445), or because a roomful of eager listeners wants to hear one more chapter of his adventures (11.379). Whenever he does nod off, catastrophes occur. Sailing from the island of Aiolos, whose king has given him a bag containing all the winds, Odysseus dozes on deck and his companions get curious:

> So they loosened the bag and the winds all rushed out together.
> Storm winds seized them and carried them wailing their hearts
>   out,
> over the sea away from their homes. But I
> awakened from sleep, considered in my excellent heart
> whether to drop from the deck and die right there in the sea
> or to endure, keep silent, go on being one of the living.[18]

Odysseus has another suicidal moment, occasioned by sleep, in Book 12 when slumber overtakes him on the beach of Thrinakia and his companions slaughter the cattle of the sun. Odysseus wakes up and cries out:

> O father Zeus and you other gods who live forever,
> how to my ruin you have lulled me in pitiless slumber![19]

So let's say in general Odysseus and sleep are not friends. Whatever this may mean for the hero's characterization overall, I'm struck by how Homer uses it in subjugating Odysseus to Penelope at the end of the poem. For no one can deny that Penelope is a master of sleep. She goes to bed dozens of times in the course of the story, has lots of sleep shed on her by gods, experiences an array of telling and efficacious dreams and evolves her own theory of how to read them. Moreover, Homer shows us as early as Book 4 that sleep is the deepest contract she shares with her husband. Miles apart, years apart, consciously and unconsciously, they turn the key of each other. So Penelope in Book 4, lying awake in her chamber while the suitors carouse below, is compared by Homer to a lion cornered in a circle of huntsmen. Then she falls asleep, to dream of her husband, "noble Odysseus who has the heart of a lion"[20] and wake up profoundly soothed. Sleep *works* for Penelope. She knows how to use it, enjoy it, theorize it and even to parody it, should need arise. As in her famous "recognition scene" with Odysseus (which occupies Books 19-23 of the poem).

Penelope's purpose in this scene is to seduce and overcome Odysseus, i.e., to seduce *by* overcoming Odysseus. She goes at it from the sleep side, because there she can win. As we have already seen, and as she probably knows, sleep is not his country. Her seduction has two aspects, first a practical one, the bed question: Who sleeps where? This question culminates in Book 23 in the so-called "trick of the bed," which brings recognition between husband and wife based on their knowledge of a bed carved by Odysseus out of an oak tree in the middle of their house twenty years ago. But before Book 23 quite a bit of sleeping goes on, or is prevented from going on, in noteworthy ways.

Let's look at Book 19, which takes the form of a long conversation between husband and wife before they retire to separate beds, on the night before the climax of the plot. After they have conversed, Penelope instructs her maidservants to give Odysseus a bath and prepare a luxurious bedstead for him. Odysseus rejects these arrangements, insists on being bathed by an old woman and being given a place on the bare ground to sleep. So Odysseus goes off, has his bath, then returns and sits down beside his wife. Whereupon, instead of saying goodnight, she launches into Penelope's Interpretation of Dreams (to which we'll return in a moment). Finally they do say goodnight and retire—she upstairs to her chamber, he to the ground in the forecourt. So there they are. In separate rooms of the same house, each lying awake. Athene sheds sleep on Penelope at the end of Book 19, then sheds sleep on Odysseus at the beginning of Book 20. No sooner does Odysseus fall asleep than Penelope awakes, weeping and crying out. Her voice carries through the house to where Odysseus is sleeping, enters his dream and convinces him that his wife is standing over him in the flesh, recognizing and welcoming him home. Odysseus wakes up, receives an omen from Zeus and rejoices in the forecourt. Homer has woven a strange symbiosis between these two people, together and apart in the same night, entering and exiting each other's minds, almost sharing one consciousness—especially at that moment when Penelope penetrates the membrane of her husband's sleep and fills him with joy. I would call that a successful seduction.

For the theoretical aspect of this seduction, let's return to the long conversation of Book 19. It has two parts. First, husband and wife exchange narratives of what they've been doing for the last twenty years; here Odysseus mainly lies, while Penelope tells the truth. Then there is a pause while Odysseus has his bath. Now a bath in epic is often a mechanism of transition to new conditions (and of course this is the bath, made famous by Eric Auerbach, where the old woman Eurykleia knows Odysseus by the scar on his leg—but Penelope doesn't see any of that). After the bath, Penelope takes the conversational initiative and offers a complex (and almost certainly fictitious) narrative about a dream she has had, demanding that Odysseus interpret the dream. Surely this demand is peculiar. The dream is of an eagle who flies down from the sky, slaughters Penelope's twenty pet geese, then announces that he is not an eagle at all, nor a dream, but the real Odysseus returned to save his household. The dream is as blatant as an English movie with English subtitles and Odysseus politely says so. But why does Penelope require his complicity in reading it?

Because it is her game they are playing now: they are reasoning from the sleep side, where she is a master. Look what she does next. Broaches her theory of dreams. Dreams are double, she says, some true, some false. True ones emerge from the gates of horn, false from the gates of ivory. This theory is as bogus as the dream of geese. Penelope is talking through her hat. But all of a sudden, out of her hat, Penelope drops a bombshell. Tomorrow, she announces, I'm going to set up a contest, see which of the suitors can shoot through twelve axes with Odysseus's bow. The winner will take me home as his wife. Here is a sudden practical solution to the whole domestic dilemma. Odysseus hastily agrees it is a great idea. Penelope has orchestrated the conversation so the great idea seems to drop out of a dream—or indeed to shoot out through the very gates of horn. She has involved Odysseus in the interpretive necessity of dreams as he earlier involved her in the autobiographical necessity of lies. She has matched his ambiguities and used her sleep knowledge to wrap him in an act of seduction that he cannot outwit—that he will not wish to outwit. She invites him into the way her mind works. Rather like the moon in the mirror in Elizabeth Bishop's poem "Insomnia":

> The moon in the bureau mirror
> looks out a million miles
> (and perhaps with pride, at herself,
> but she never, never smiles)
> far and away beyond sleep, or
> perhaps she's a daytime sleeper.
>
> By the Universe deserted,
> *she'd* tell it to go to hell,
> and she'd find a body of water,
> or a mirror, on which to dwell.
> So wrap up care in a cobweb
> and drop it down the well
>
> into that world inverted
> where left is always right,
> where the shadows are really the body,
> where we stay awake all night,
> where the heavens are shallow as the sea
> is now deep, and you love me.[21]

As far as love goes, Penelope's only real rival among the female personnel of the *Odyssey* is Nausikaa, the *very* unmarried girl whom Odysseus meets in Book 6 on the island of the Phaiakians. She is asleep when we first meet her:

> ... the girl
> lay sleeping in form and image like to immortals,

Nausikaa, daughter of great-hearted Alkinoos,
and alongisde her two attendants having beauty from the Graces
on either side of the pillars. But the brilliant doors were shut.[22]

Homer shows us the sleeper in all her layers of defense. He shows us the doors, pillars, attendants, behind which the she lies. Then he shows us how to pass through doors, in the person of Athene, who traverses the house as a blast of wind and stands over Nausikaa's bed, whispering:

Nausikaa—how is it your mother bore so slack a girl as you?
Look, your shining clothes lie in a mess.
But for you marriage is near, when you will need beautiful things
to wear yourself and to give to those who attend you.
... let's go do laundry as soon as dawn appears.[23]

Athene puts into Nausikaa a word that condenses laundry with marriage (cleanliness with sex), a word whose dream logic names Nausikaa's perfect purity at the very moment we see it most exposed to violation. For there is another motionless presence on this page. Nausikaa lies sleeping side by side with Odysseus, not in the space of her room but in narrative juxtaposition. Two verses describing Odysseus (who is lying naked in a pile of leaves on the outskirts of Nausikaa's city) immediately precede our view of Nausikaa in her bed:

So there he lay much-enduring goodly Odysseus
overwhelmed by sleep and exhaustion.[24]

Odysseus's exhaustion subtends and embraces Nausikaa's dream (she rises at v. 50 but he does not wake until 117). Their sleep prefigures everything that will occur between the man and the girl in the days to follow—a system of contradictions curving in and out of impossibility without arriving at refutation, oxymoron of male and female—as the old, wild, dirty, naked, married, shelterless, man of many turns coils himself around a girl who lies straight in her nine frames of safety dreaming of laundry.

She is the cleanest girl in epic. And his dirt emphasizes that, not to say the brutal opacity of his sleep—whereas she lies transparent: we watch the dream in her head, we know her action before she does, we see her desire prior to itself. Her desire is to find a pretext and travel far from the city, to where the washing pools lie. But this is precisely where Odysseus lies. The night before, at the end of Book 5, he laid himself down "on the edge of the land" to sleep the sleep of elemental life. Life is all he has left. Wife, child, parents, home, ship, comrades, possessions, clothing, youth, strength and personal fame are all lost. He had to cover himself in a pile of leaves to survive the night:

> And when he saw [the leaf pile]
> much-enduring goodly Odysseus laughed
> and lay in the middle and heaped a big bunch of leaves over himself.
> As when someone hides a firebrand in black embers
> on the edge of the land, who has no other neighbours near,
> preserving the seed of fire, lest he have to kindle a light
> from somewhere else,
> so Odysseus wrapped himself in leaves.[25]

"On the edge of the land" is a symbolic description. "Land" means farmland, cultivated space. Odysseus is stranded at the margin of culture: he has come back in from the wilderness and preserves within himself (just barely) the means to begin civilization again. But no one can begin civilization alone. And the sleep of fire needs careful waking. Homer seems to enjoy assigning this task to a girl whose chief concerns are cold water and aristocratic hygiene.

Once he is awake, Odysseus finds the island of the Phaiakians a perplexing place. Almost everyone he meets presumes he has come there to marry Nausikaa, inherit her father's kingdom and live happily ever after. It is as if he has waked up inside someone else's dream, only to find himself the protagonist of it. For these dreamlike Phaiakians know who Odysseus is, although he withholds as long as possible from them the news that *he* is Odysseus. And as their local poet performs songs from the epic tradition that tell of Odysseus's exploits at Troy, he sits and weeps to hear himself acclaimed in the third person. He has backed into his own heroic persona, like a shadow finding its body.

Or, like Rosencrantz and Guildenstern in Tom Stoppard's play, *Rosencrantz and Guildenstern Are Dead*, where two Shakespearean courtiers find themselves in the midst of the tragedy of *Hamlet* without quite understanding who wrote them into the script. Yet they scramble to play their part, manage to produce the right lines and end up dead in England, as Shakespeare's scenario requires. It is not clear whether they are awake or asleep—they talk about having been roused at dawn yet act like people stuck in a bad dream. It is a familiar dream. Stoppard uses the familiarity of Shakespeare's play to lock us into the badness of the bad dream. He puts us, as audience, on the sleep side of the play, alongside Rosencrantz and Guildenstern, while the other characters of Shakespeare's *Hamlet* wander in and out muttering passages of Shakespeare's text. Stoppard uses Shakespeare's text to capture Rosencrantz and Guildenstern within his own, in somewhat the same way Virginia Woolf used square brackets to capture the Ramsays and their friends in a long night of sleep. As readers we take a guilty pleasure in these arrangements. For we would almost like to see Rosencrantz and Guildenstern escape their predicament, except it would spoil the plot of *Hamlet*. Good sleepers that we are, we do not quite want to wake up. We are not quite ready to sever that pale green link between exits and entrances. Stoppard's play praises sleep, functionally, for its necessity. No other experience gives us so primary a sense of being governed by laws outside us. No other substance can so profoundly saturate a story in compulsion, inevitability and dread as sleep can. Mr. Ramsay in square brackets has no option to snatch his wife back from death, nor Rosencrantz and Guildenstern to rewrite the tragedy of *Hamlet*. It is, as Virginia Woolf says, useless to ask the night these questions. Stoppard allows his character Guildenstern to ask them anyway. Guildenstern is a kind of amateur philosopher; he derives consolation in the middle of the play from a well-known Taoist parable about waking and sleeping:

> Guildenstern: Wheels have been set in motion, and they have their own pace, to which we are ... condemned. Each move is dictated by the previous one—that is the meaning

of order. If we start being arbitrary it'll just be a shambles: at least let us hope so. Because if we happened, just happened to discover, or even suspect, that our spontaneity is part of their order, we'd know we were lost. (*He sits.*) A Chinaman of the T'ang dynasty—and by which definition a philosopher—dreamed he was a butterfly, and from that moment he was never quite sure that he was not a butterfly dreaming it was a Chinese philosopher. Envy him; in his two-fold security.[26]

There is something cheesy about Guildenstern's envy, and about his use of the parable of the butterfly and the sage (traditionally ascribed to Zhuang Zi, who was not of the T'ang dynasty), and about his philosophizing in general, that makes me happy to turn to a different amateur philosopher for my final example of the praise of sleep. Sokrates, arguably the most amateur and the most different of the philosophers of the Western tradition, exhibits, in the Platonic dialogues describing the final days of his life, a certain regard for that sublime residue, the tear of sleep.

Let's consider the *Krito*. Plato begins this dialogue in the dark, with Sokrates starting up sheer from sleep and his dream still wet on its back. Here are the opening lines of the dialogue:

Sokrates: Why are you here? Isn't it early?
Krito: Yes pretty early.
Sokrates: What time?
Krito: Near dawn.
Sokrates: I'm surprised the guard let you in.
Krito: Oh he knows me by now. Anyway I tip him.
Sokrates: So did you just arrive or have you been here awhile?
Krito: Quite awhile. Sokrates: Why didn't you wake me?[27]

And so it emerges that Krito sat watching Sokrates sleep because he looked happy sleeping and Krito had nothing to wake him for but his death day. Perhaps I should call to mind the situation here. The *Krito* is the third of a tetralogy of dialogues concerned with Sokrates's trial, imprisonment and death. Sokrates has by now been judged guilty and is in jail awaiting execution. His death is postponed because his trial coincided with the annual Athenian mission to Delos, during which no prisoners could be executed. Krito has come to announce to Sokrates that the ship from Delos has been sighted and so his death will take place the next day. To which news Sokrates responds:

> Sokrates: You know I don't think so. It won't be tomorrow.
> Krito: What are you talking about?
> Sokrates: I had a dream last night—lucky you didn't wake me!
> Krito: What dream?
> Sokrates: A beautiful woman came up to me, dressed in white, called to me and said: *Sokrates, on the third day you shall reach rich Phthia.*
> Krito: Weird dream, Sokrates.
> Sokrates: Well it seems obvious to me.[28]

Plato has constructed the opening of this dialogue in such a way as to align the realms of waking and sleeping, drawing our attention to an active boundary between them—active because it leaks. Sokrates brings a bit of difference back with him from the sleep side. The words of the woman in white contain a hint of the argument that will carry Sokrates all the way from these sleepy sentences to his death at the end of the *Phaedo*. She tells Sokrates he will reach Phthia on the third day. It is a line from Homer. In the 9th Book of the *Iliad* Achilles receives an embassy of Greeks sent by Agamemnon to persuade him to return to war, promising tons of gifts if he does. He responds with a 114-line denunciation of gifts, war and Agamemnon, including a threat to leave for home at once:

> On the third day I could reach rich Phthia.[29]

Phthia is Achilles's homeland. It is also a name cognate with a Greek verb for death (*phthiein*) but that may be incidental. Let us observe some analogies between these two heroes heading for Phthia on the third day: both Sokrates and Achilles are eccentric gentlemen who find themselves defying the rules of life of their society and disappointing the hopes of a circle of intense friends. For, as Achilles is surrounded by Achaians urging him to resume life as a warrior, Sokrates is surrounded by Athenians urging him to escape prison and take up life in exile. Both of them say *No* to their friends. Both argue this choice on the basis of an idiosyncratic understanding of the word *psyche*, "soul, spirit, principle of life." So Achilles repudiates Agamemnon's offer of gifts in these terms:

> All the gifts and treasure in Troy aren't worth as much as my own soul![30]

And Sokrates explains his choice for death at the end of the Phaedo by saying:

> Since the soul seems to be immortal . . . a man [who has lived a good life] might as well be cheerful as he makes his exit into Hades.[31]

Who knows what either of them means by *psyche* or whether "soul" is a reasonable translation of it. Still we can say they both use this word to indicate some kind of immortal value, some sort of transcendent attractor, that exerts such a strong pressure on their mortal lives and thinking as to pull them into a choice that strikes everyone around them as insane. I reckon that Plato in his dialogues involving Sokrates had somewhat the same literary problem as Homer in his *Iliad,* viz. to convey a hero in his *difference* from other people, a hero whose power over other people arose in part from something *incognito* in his very being. In the dialogues that record his last days, the Platonic Sokrates seems increasingly a person ungraspable in ordinary sentences, a person who is (to use a current expression) *coming from somewhere else.*

Plato shows him coming from the sleep side in the *Krito*. As if he had slept in the temple of Asklepios, Sokrates emerges from his dream "seeing with both eyes." And he does not hesitate to trust what the woman in white has let him see, although Krito dismisses it. The woman in white will turn out to be correct. Sokrates is inclined to trust, and to be correct about trusting, different sources of knowledge than other philosophers do—like his crazy *daimon,* or the oracle of Apollo, not to say the good sentences of sleep. Sokrates also puts a fair amount of faith in his own poetic imagination—his power to turn nothing into something. So in the latter half of the *Krito,* since Krito can think of nothing further to say, Sokrates conducts both sides of an imaginary conversation between himself as Sokrates and a ventriloquized projection of the Nomoi, the Laws of Athens. These ventriloquized Laws are as weird as the ghosts that Virginia Woolf sent rustling and whispering around the rooms of her "Haunted House," looking for their buried treasure. If you recall, that story of the haunted house ends with a spooky moment of dispossession, as the ghosts lean over the sleeper's bed and discover *their* treasure buried in *her* heart. Sokrates also suffers a moment of dispossession at the end of the *Krito.* The voices of the Laws, he says, fill his prison cell and drown out all other sound. He has to stop talking:

> O beloved friend Krito, these voices are what I seem to hear—
> as Korybantic worshippers imagine they hear flutes—and the
> sound of their words is so loud in me, I am deaf to everything
> else.[32]

So Sokrates falls silent, overcome by what Virginia Woolf might call "the singing of the real world."
To sum up.
I shall state my conclusions in the form of an "Ode to Sleep."

Ode to Sleep

Think of your life without it.
Without that slab of outlaw time punctuating every pillow
—without pillows.
Without the big black kitchen and the boiling stove where you
snatch morsels
of your own father's legs and arms
only to see them form into a sentence
which—*you weep with sudden joy*—will save you
if you can remember it
later! Later,
not much left but a pale green *upsilon* embalmed
between *butter* and *fly*—
but what's that stuff he's dabbing in your eye?
It is the moment when the shiver stops.
A shiver is a perfect servant.
Her amen sootheth.
"As a matter of fact," she confides in a footnote, "it was
a misprint for *mammoth*."
It hurts me to know this.
Exit wound, as they say.

Notes

1. Aristotle, *Parva Naturalia*, ed. W. D. Ross (Oxford: Clarendon Press, 1955). Translations are my own unless otherwise noted.
2. Immanuel Kant, *Anthropology from a Pragmatic View*, trans. M. J. Gregor (The Hague: Martinus Nijhoff, 1974), 85.
3. John Keats, *Complete Poems*, ed. J. Stillinger (Cambridge, Mass.: The Belknap Press of Harvard University Press, 1978, 1982).
4. Elizabeth Bishop, *The Complete Poems: 1927–1979* (New York: Farrar, Straus and Giroux, 1979, 1983), 14.
5. *Inscriptiones Graecae*: vol. IV, *Inscriptiones Argolidis*, ed. M. Fraenkel (Berlin: Berlin Academy, 1902), 223–24.
6. Virginia Woolf, *To the Lighthouse* (New York: Harcourt, Brace, 1927), 128; 133; 134.
7. Ibid., 193.

8   Virginia Woolf, *The Diary of Virginia Woolf*, eds. A. O. Bell and A. McNeillie (London: The Hogarth Press, 1980), 3.260: Oct. 11, 1929.
9   Virginia Woolf, *The Waves* (New York: Harcourt Brace Jovanovich, 1931), 292.
10 Virginia Woolf, *The Voyage Out* (London: Duckworth, 1915), 59.
11 Virginia Woolf, *A Haunted House and Other Stories* (London: The Hogarth Press, 1944), 11.
12 Homer, *Iliad*, eds. W. Leaf and M. A. Bayfield (London, 1895), 23.103.
13 Virginia Woolf, *To the Lighthouse*, 128.
14 Homer, *Odyssey*, ed. W. B. Stanford (London: Macmillan, 1947) 1.433–34.
15 Ibid., 15.7–8.
16 Ibid., 1.215–16.
17 Ibid., 19.50.
18 Ibid., 10.47–52.
19 Ibid., 12.371–72.
20 Ibid., 4.514.
21 Elizabeth Bishop, *The Complete Poems*, 70.
22 Homer, *Odyssey*, 6.15–19.
23 Ibid., 6.25–30.
24 Ibid., 6.1–2.
25 Ibid., 5.486–91.
26 Tom Stoppard, *Rosencrantz and Guildenstern Are Dead* (London: Faber and Faber, 1967), 51.
27 Plato, *Krito*, 43a–b, in *Platonis Opera*, ed. J. Brunet (Oxford: Clarendon Press, 1976), vol. 1.
28 Ibid., 43d–44b.
29 Homer, *Iliad*, 9.363.
30 Ibid., 9.401.
31 Plato, *Phaedo*, 114d–115a, in *Platonis Opera*, vol. 1.
32 Plato, *Krito*, 54d.

Frederick Ward
Writing as Jazz[1]
GEORGE ELLIOTT CLARKE

Anne Szumigalski Lecture • Toronto, Ontario • June 11, 2005

For Diana Brebner (1956-2001)[2]

Diagnosis of a Disappearance
ONE OF THE DULL CLICHÉS, ONE OF THE DREARY STEREO-types, one of the drab platitudes, to be spouted by anyone deigning to comment on African Diasporic writing, is that the black author is a would-be or a used-'ta'-be musician or singer. In the popular perception of popular cultures, every black writer is, at birth, swaddled in sheet music, and begins to sing even before he or she can speak. These conceptions also attach to African-Canadian writers, who, already viewed as bizarre exotica by their compatriots, are presumed to have taken up print keyboards because they have eschewed, perversely, the natural, musical ones.

Yet, there is—insidiously—bountiful reason for the common belief. For instance, an entire school of poets—the dub poets—that is, Lillian Allen, Klyde Broox, Afua Cooper, Rudyard Fearon, Clifton Joseph, Ahdri Zinha Mandiela and Motion (Wendy Braithwaite), to name only a Toronto-based and principally Jamaican-born few, perform their works within a musical tapestry, often a form of reggae (the Jamaican influence) or rap (the African-American orientation).[3] Certainly, Ghana-born, Jamaica-raised, Canada-educated poet Kwame Dawes performs reggae and drafts poetry (plus 'lit-crit'). British Columbia-based poet Wayde Compton DJs at his own readings, while Montreal's Kaie Kellough mixes French and English in ways as radical as any Jimi Hendrix guitar solo. Kenyan-Canadian novelist David Odhiambo sketches a novel-memoir of an acid-jazz band leader in skanky East End Vancouver in his *diss / ed banded nation* (1998). Toronto-centred poets Dwayne Morgan and Andrea Thompson release books and records that are recordings of their books. Literary figures like Trinidadian-Canadian poets Dionne Brand and Claire Harris, Tobagan-Canadian M. NourbeSe Philip, Barbadian-Canadian novelist Austin Clarke and the Haitian-Canadian novelist Dany Laferrière refer to African-American jazz and blues singers in their creative writings as well as in their essays. If we add the Canadian poets (black) who often employ jazz in their performances, or as subject matter, then almost every African-Canadian poet may be said to be vested, one way or another, in music.

But the *baddest* (in the 1960s Black English sense), hippest and mos' def' word-composer-arranger in Canada is the least *sounded*, the least *heard*, the least *understood*. I refer here to Frederick E. Ward—or Fred Ward—whose published oeuvre consists only of three novels, two poetry collections and scatterings of stories, plays and poems among anthologies, one of them (edited by Ward himself), now forty years old (see *Anthology of Nine Baha'i Poets* [1966]). African American by birth—in Kansas City, Missouri, in 1937—and resident in Canada since 1970, Ward has received *always* ecstatic acclaim, yet remains as opaquely phantasmal as a ghost writer, save that his obscurity is not chosen. He is excluded from African-American anthologies and omitted from Canadian ones.[4] One cannot find Ward in either *The Oxford*

Companion to African-American Literature (1997) or *The Oxford Companion to Canadian Literature* (1997). All of his books are out of print. He is the Invisible Man of African-American literature and the Sasquatch of English-Canadian literature. That he lays legitimate claim to the attention of two national(ist) literatures explains his rejection by both. His one-time publisher, May Cutler of Tundra Books of Montreal, said, a quarter-century ago when his third novel appeared, "It's just not permissable [sic] for a black American writer to live in Nova Scotia" (Kimber 37).

Cutler has a point: few African-American writers resident in Canada have won sustained attention. (One exception is probably Josiah Henson, the putative real-life model for Harriet Beecher Stowe's 'Uncle Tom,' whose own ghost-written memoirs appeared in 1849.) Cutler's assumption that white Canadians don't want to hear about African America from a writer living here is also probably right. For complex reasons of nationalism, European-Canadians prefer to hear tales about the supposed degradation of African-American life from writers living *there*. Cutler is also depressingly correct to assume that African-Americans, for complex reasons of *their own* nationalism, may shy from expatriate writers (the later Richard Wright, the post-mortem Frank Yerby).[5]

Still, white ethnocentrism also plays a role in apportioning obscurity to black writers—especially those working in non-mimetic modes. This phenomenon transgresses borders. U.S. African-Americanist Aldon Lynn Nielsen, in his important book *Black Chant: Languages of African-American Postmodernism* (1997), registers that "critics of white poetry simply seldom look at black writers while compiling their genealogies of aesthetic evolution" (13). Rather, shamelessly, there exists, he feels, a "disinclination on the part of most critics to discover African-American *literary* precedents for white avant-garde writing ..." (71). In fact, "Historians of avant-garde movements in American poetry have tended to write as if black Americans had little direct involvement, and hence our histories have tended to elide the powerful influence of black poets on American verse in general and 'experimental' verse in particular" (259). Thus, T.J. Anderson III, in his article "Body and Soul: Bob Kaufman's *Golden Sardine*" (2000), argues that

"Writers like Kenneth Rexroth and Jack Kerouac have received more notoriety for their jazz-inspired verse than have innovators like Bob Kaufman, Amiri Baraka and Ted Joans. Why have there been several documentaries done on Jack Kerouac that highlight the importance of jazz to his writing, but few done on Amiri Baraka? Even a recent compilation by Rhino Records called *The Beat Generation* fails to include any work by these three African American innovators" (345, n.1). European-Canadian editors and critics have been no better at chronicling black participation in the construction of either Canadian literature or music. A current, flagrant example is the treatment of the Spoken Word movement. Certainly, discussions of the development of 'Spoken Word' poetry in Canada have focussed, naturally, on supposed white innovators such as the sound-poetry quartet, The Four Horsemen (bp nichol, Steven McCaffrey, Rafael Barreto-Rivera and Paul Dutton), active mainly between 1970 and the mid-1980s.[6] But nothing is said of Brand's work with the Gayap Drummers, or of the championing of dub poetry by Allen, Joseph and others, yet these black creators were disseminating rhythm backed with reasoned dissent throughout the 1970s and 1980s—in Toronto, the capital of English-Canadian, media culture, while Ward was melding poetry and drama in Halifax and Montreal. In his review (1999/2000) of CARNIVOCAL: *A Celebration of Sound Poetry* (1999), a compact disc anthology of Anglo-Canadian sound-poetry edited by Stephen Scobie and Douglas Barbour, Spoken Word poet John Sobol recognizes that the implicit canonization practised by the editors enacts some salient omissions:

> In their liner notes, Barbour and Scobie contend that '[w]hile sound poetry borders on and sometimes overlaps other performance-based genres (song, rap, dub, slam), it is distinguished by its relative nonreliance on syntax and discursive statement.' But wait a minute. If sound poetry at times overlaps with dub, rap or slam poetry, why is there no non-discursive dub, rap or slam poetry on *Carnivocal*? How can the editors claim, as they do, to be representing 'the range of contemporary sound poetry in Canada,' when that range—by their own

admission—encompasses so much more than appears on their CD? ("Anti-Anthrax" 40).

Sobol continues on to ask, with just irritation, "what is gained by creating an almost exclusively white, male, Anglo-Canadian sound poetry canon? And what is lost? Why are the editors manning the aesthetic barricades when the real carnival is underway outside?" ("Anti-Anthrax" 40).[7]

While Eurocentrism—and African-American-centrism—bedevil the acceptance of Ward's work, he is not just relegated to obscurity because he is a minority in two challenging contexts (an African-American expat in Canada; a Canadian relocatee *ex* African America), but also because he is a writer whose texts are profoundly, ambitiously, grounded in music, particularly jazz. His plight is not just one of ostracism from the "national" literatures that should be most accommodating for his work. It is much worse: he is the devotee of a deviant genre, namely, jazz-inflected poetry; jazzy fiction.

Observe that practically every significant *black* jazz-poet or jazz-novelist is, ironically, correspondingly *obscure*—save for Amiri Baraka and Ntozake Shange (who is known, really, for one *great* work: *for colored girls who have considered suicide / when the rainbow is enuf* [1977]).[8] In the Preface, then, to their influential work, *The Jazz Poetry Anthology* (1991), editors Sascha Feinstein and Yusuf Komunyakaa proclaim that they include "a large percentage of lesser-known poets, many of whom deserve more recognition than they have received" (xviii).[9] Avant-garde jazz and avant-garde poetry are both minority discourses. Thus, commentator after commentator speaks of shadowy or forgotten black jazz-poets—as if he or she were conducting a séance. T.J. Anderson realizes that African-American jazz-poet Bob Kaufman (1926-1986), despite receiving awards and prizes, "was to remain fairly anonymous, financially impoverished, and addicted to methedrine for most of his life" (333).[10] Nielsen complains that "Once more [*now*] we see repeated a pattern whereby entire groupings of African-American poets once widely anthologized and seen as contemporary contributors to the innovation of new black poetries are deaccessioned from the steadily constricting canon of black poets available for critical attention and university instruction" (60-61). These 'lost' poets include several jazz-performers of the 1950s and early 1960s. Nielsen goes on to lament, "... the texts of this early period of black postmodernity are mostly fugitive, having passed out of print or never having been printed in the first place" (82). Unsurprisingly then, one review of Ward is headlined, "Halifax's Hot, But Unknown, Author" (Kimber 33). An announcement for a reading series at the National Library in Ottawa, Ontario, in which Ward was a reader/performer in 1988, charges, "It is an undisputed fact that the work of those writers whose inspiration comes from a strong sense of ethnocultural heritage has not as yet achieved full recognition in the mainstream of Canadian literature" (Cayley 11), particularly Ward, whose "musical training never left him and music informs all his writing" (Cayley 11). Ward is just one more jazz-attuned poet to see his offerings fall into the blank, silent Limbo dividing orality and literature.

Founding a Poetics of Jazz Literature

The reception—or non-reception—of Ward underscores the notion that the critical problem for critics is the practical one of 'reading.' In this case, they (we) do not know how to read Ward. One journalist-critic notes, rightly, that Ward has a "sometimes difficult, complex, *avant-garde* writing style" (Kimber 37). But difficulty in poetry is akin to dissonance in jazz, and perhaps just as enjoyable, if we can discern the *beat*. But one dilemma remains: Canadians cannot hear the jazz in our literature. Too often, efforts to appreciate what one reviewer calls "literary jazz" (Kimber 37), either by Ward or by others, dissolve into cranky impressionism or bankrupt silence or skanky dismissal. In a 1996 article contesting various critiques of Miles Davis's trumpet playing, Robert Walser offers this pregnant insight:

> Prevalent methods of jazz analysis, borrowed from the toolbox of musicology, provide excellent means for *legitimating* jazz in the academy. But they are clearly inadequate to the task of helping us to *understand* jazz.... They offer only a kind of mystified,

ahistorical, text-based legitimacy, within which rhetoric and [the African-American vernacular technique of] signifyin'[11] are invisible. (179)

Unable to generate an "analytical vocabulary that [can] do justice to their perceptions" (Walser 180), critics have been unable to articulate convincingly either their approval or their disapproval of Davis's playing. Let us sound Walser again:

> ... Davis's consistent and deliberate use of risky techniques and constant transgression of genre boundaries are antithetical to "classicism" and cannot be explained by formalism; from such perspectives, unusual content looks like flawed form. That is why so many critics have responded to Davis's music with puzzlement, hostility, or an uneasy silence. (172)

In other situations, the paucity of responsible and responsive intellectual apparatus in jazz criticism leads to the most medieval racialism. Hear here Ronald M. Radano's revelation of the treatment of Anthony Braxton by a 1977 *Newsweek* writer: "*Newsweek*'s characterization of Braxton, the 'free spirit,' as the modern version of the antediluvian noisemaker captures the mass of stereotypes of 'the most innovative force in the world of jazz'" (209-210):

> Braxton is a virtuoso on the saxophone, and the instrument has never been subject to such assault. He squeezes out bizarre sounds and clashing, hitherto unheard tone colors. He plays like a man possessed, in a paroxysm of animalistic grunts, honks, rasps, and hollers. He rends the fabric of conventional musical language as he reaches into himself—and back into pre-history—for some primordial means of communication. (Saal 52-53)[12]

Deliciously—or seditiously—Radano opines that, for some critics, "Braxton represented the supreme anomaly: while possessing the 'calculating mind' of an 'intellectual,' he reinforced traditional images of jazz through his blackness..." (208). The promulgations of duplicitous depictions of jazz emphasize, again, the relative lack of a vocabulary that can assess jazz forensically. But if jazz music poses explanatory difficulties for its auditors, jazz-infused writing is just as challenging. Hence, in the article "Jazz" in *The Norton Anthology of African American Literature* (1997), the anonymous author anticipates—hopes—"in the years to come, students of African American culture will find more ways to talk about the elements of jazz—its vamps (or introductory statements), breaks (or solos), riffs (repeated structural phrases), choruses (main themes), bridges (secondary, connecting themes), call/response patterns, improvisations, syncopated cadences and other definitive structures—and the ways in which they operate in the pages of a book" (56). In the meantime, given this absence of critical proficiency, one of the most deft practitioners of the jazzed-up literature genre—Mr. F.E.W.[13]—languishes in *our* deaf illiteracy.

But what do we mean by 'jazz poetry' or 'jazz literature'? Generally, definitions fluctuate between emphasizing styles—such as phrasing or line breaks or a sense of stream-of-consciousness liberty—or just subject matter: a paean for saxophonist Charlie Parker, even if written in strict sonnet form, is a 'jazz' poem according to this criterion.

To go further, however, we need to think about jazz music and the ways in which it can be manifested in print. Significantly, jazz is a vesper of oral African-African culture.[14] The anonymous *Norton Anthology* author provides this *sound* recording of the anthropological origins of jazz in Black U.S. speech:

> ... jazz was primarily an instrumental music strongly impacted by the sound of the African American voice. What this music can sound like more than anything else is the jam-session-like talk and song from the Harlems of America and from its southern roads. In a real sense, the sound of jazz is that of the African American voice scored as band music, with all of black talk's flair for story-telling as well as the dirty dozens, understatement as well as braggadocio, whispery romance as well as loud-talk menace, the exalted eloquence of a Martin Luther King and the spare dry poetry of a pool-hall boast or a jump-rope rhyme. (55)

With this conception in mind, it appears that 'jazz-directed writing' should be focussed on the voice, according it primacy. Ward achieves this poetic: his writing aspires to the condition of jazz vocals—or vocalized jazz. The *Norton Anthology* writer stresses that jazz music and musicians dialogue with speech:

> All of that "talking and testifying" and "speaking and speechifying" boldly make their way into this music, giving it great force and flavor. Once singers got into the jazz act, they tended to follow Louis Armstrong in using their voices as if they were jazz instruments—which meant, ironically, that they were voices imitating instruments that were imitating voices! (55-56)

Ward's work is nothing if not flush and plush—or chock-a-block—with voices. In his key article, "Poetry and Jazz: A Twentieth-Century Wedding," Barry Wallenstein establishes the importance of oral religious performance to the development of a jazz-styled vocal delivery:

> Jazz with poetic elements actually has origins in the church services of plantation blacks, where the preacher was one of the community who had a way with words. Like the poet/priests of ancient times, these preachers were said to have received the "call" from heaven. Their sermons moved emotionally and fluidly from speech to poetry: "to song to dance to moaning and back again," as one ex-slave has said. (598)

Something of this cultural inheritance infuses Ward's depiction of Rev. Mores in *Riverlisp* (1974):

> Rev. Mores come out of th pulpit walked up th ile and stood afore Micah: "Th Lord welcomes every soul in th Kingdom. And th Kingdom here on earth is th church. Let's hear you say amens." (answered) "You, young man been a servant of His for our people with your Bible selling and all. Th community loves you as their own and what better than you show *your people*

[Jews] what th Lord done tol and we here believes—that all th Messengers is one spirit and loves us cause we is one." (40-41)

Lawrence W. Levine argues that "In their songs ..., Afro-American slaves ... assigned a central role to the spoken arts, encouraged and rewarded verbal improvisation ..." (6). However, this dexterity is not easy to translate into print:

> William Arms Fisher warned his readers that his attempts to reproduce the music of the spirituals he heard in the 1920s could not capture "the slurring and sliding of the voices, the interjected turns and 'curls,' the groans and sighs, the use even of quarter-tones, the mixture of keys, and the subtle rhythms." (Levine 159)

Yet, Ward is attentive to the problem and inventive enough to attempt to overcome it (as we will hear). His 'solution' to the problem of 'typing' the voice is to explore fundamental literary adaptations of jazz technique, as identified by Siva Vaidhyanathan: "improvisation, syncopated rhythm, lyrics with such blues-influenced devices as call and response, repetition, and ... the practice of signifying: thoughtful revision and repetition of another's work" (395). By utilizing these devices, the jazz-mused poet enacts an archival-prophetic role, recalling and reformulating mass, vernacular fusions of orality and music and text. Nielsen feels that the practice of such 'recollective' innovation illustrates the truth that "... African-American traditions of orality and textuality were not opposed to one another and did not exist in any simple or simplistic opposition to modernity and postmodernity" (34). For the jazz-bard, then, the emphasis must be on polyphony, that is, the stacking up of a series of different speakers or voices. Arthur Jafa terms this process, in "Black popular culture" itself, as "polyventiality" (253): "'Polyventiality' just means multiple tones, multiple rhythms, multiple perspectives, multiple meanings, multiplicity" (253). According to Eileen Southern, these effects are achieved through "collective improvisation" by jazz band members (qtd. in *Call* 807), or, by extension, by a series of speakers in a text. Hence, Ward's work is also as multiculturally influenced as jazz is itself. In "The Death of Lady Susuma," a prose poem about a black woman, then, Ward inserts a Gaelic lyric:

Ar bidh
Is sinn
Cridhe

Mor
An daimheach

Uidhe agus eadar
A

Ar cridhe bidh mor daimheach
Agus a is an uidhe eadarainn[.][15] (22)

Any truly jazz-auditing poet must attempt to replicate the music's interest in mixing culturally distinctive sounds.[16] The resulting potpourri, derived from the rambunctious, delirious *miscegenation* that must define jazz, licenses, as in Be-Bop, "... the use of nonsensical language. Jazz musicians sing words and phrases such as 'hey Boppa Rebop' for rhythmic effect and/or expression of ecstasy or joy" (Anonymous "Bop" 1101). Ward's penchant for capturing orality, as in the sound of a whisper ("spish spish, spish spish!" [*Riverlisp* 108]), manifests the superficially nonsensical to mandate fresh sense. Associated with the 'freed speech' of the Bop idiom, as it is transferred into print, is the deployment of "tributes, boasts, and slogans ... unified by internal rhymes—the virtuoso single-sound free-rhyming that Stephen Henderson first identified as a hallmark of black vernacular style" (Williams 165). Hear the style in these stanzas from Ward's song, "Around 12 Bars in 3/4 Time":

I made a
Song with your
Name.
Sort of

> Whined it and
> Cried it I made a
> Song with your
> Name—and when I
> Sighed it, I
> Put a spell be-
> Side it what made a
> Song. ("Around" 6)

Nielsen notices that the jazz poetic employs "virtual catalogues of jazzy rhythmic effects, virtuoso free rhyming, hyperbolic and metaphysical imagery, understatement, compressed and cryptic imagery, 'worrying the line,' and . . . black music as poetic reference" (14). Here is Ward's system of 'sound-writing' catalogued and defined. (Examples will follow.) Pertinent particularly is the notion of 'worrying the line.' One explicator senses, ". . . the tendency in Black music [is] to 'worry the note'—to treat notes as indeterminate, inherently unstable sonic frequencies rather than the standard Western treatment of notes as fixed phenomena" (Jafa 254). The effect of 'worrying' is well articulated by African-American novelist Ralph Ellison *via* a character's interpretation of the effect of his social 'invisibility' on his *black* consciousness:

> Invisibility . . . gives one a slightly different sense of time, you're never quite on the beat. Sometimes you're ahead and sometimes behind. Instead of the swift and imperceptible flowing of time, you are aware of its nodes, those points where time stands still or from which it leaps ahead. And you slip into the breaks and look around. That's what you hear vaguely in Louis' music. (8)

Following these precepts, Ward's style is, therefore, one of open-ended closure. Works aren't written or plotted; they're composed and they're improvised. Combined with slang-shaded imagery or homely surrealism, jazz-banded lingo moves toward the condition of 'scat,' the *sine qua non* of improvised vocalization: "In the scat idiom are all of the characteristics of extreme, verbal ritual: special styles and registers, fast delivery, high pitches, broken rhythms, grunts, anomalous, mumbo jumbo words, and prosaically pleasing repetitions" (Leonard qtd. in Wallenstein 600).[17] The logic of scat informs portions of Ward's "Lady Susuma's Dream":

—SPLENDID SPECIALNESS!

She shouted it through her imaginings and greeted
her *impressions* in ancientnesses:

—Woyi bie! Woyi bie! Welcome! Welcome!
O Wedo, calling Wedo, O Wedo there . . ." (56).

If jazz disruptively subverts traditional European musical concepts, Ward's writing makes English speak a new tongue. However, scatting—a type of scansion—is only one aspect of a polyphonic jazz poetic. In his 1995 article, "Purple Passages or Fiestas in Blue? Notes Toward an Aesthetic of Vocalese," Barry Keith Grant insists that jazz also relies on "vocalese" which "involves the setting/singing of lyrics (almost always composed rather than improvised) to jazz instrumentals, both melody and solo parts, arrangement and solos, note for note" (287). Printed "vocalese" must allow odd spacings, irregular keyboard leaps, phrases instead of sentences, typographic shorthand and dingbats, and pages that look as if they had been vetted by Charles Olson in the most subjective episodes of his Projectivist project. Such work "tends to be tempered by a visual intelligibility . . . , a sense of coherence that resides in shape rather than message or paraphrasable statement, a sense impressed upon the reader by the placement of the words on the page" (Mackey 134). Now, Ward is conservative, playing his lines always off the left margin, and rarely venturing into the middle of a page. Nevertheless, he plants unusual spaces between words to separate a particular one or series into a breathing phrase:

*tears sometimes washes th stickeness of love
'way and put a river wall tween*

> *separation bein on th one side and*
> *justice on th other*[.] (*Riverlisp* 92)

T.J. Anderson III views Kaufman as an adept practitioner of both vocalese and scat precisely because he is able "to blend and blur their demarcations. He also emphasizes the 'music' of silence, the rhythms that occur outside our concepts of music" (331). For Anderson, Kaufman exploits a "jazz meter" (335), in which "the improvisatory gesture is a crucial element, rendering his use of regular meter unpredictable" (335). Ultimately, then, says Anderson, Kaufman "managed to apply the rhythmic and tonal techniques of be-bop in order to achieve [his] aesthetic purposes" (331). I believe that Ward is just as proficient in adapting jazz to suit the requirements of poetry. But Kaufman is not the only African-American poet who may be claimed by the jazz genre. Vaidhyanathan reports that Amiri Baraka

> employs jazz devices and his own loud, postmodern style to erase the line between poetry and prose. For example, in his short story "The Screamers" (1963), Baraka fuses syncopated sounds, sights, and speech to paint a powerful yet humorous picture of an urban jazz scene. The climax of the story, when the musicians lead their charged fans into the streets, is more than musical, it is political. The fury of jazz becomes a weapon for the oppressed in Baraka's hands. (396)[18]

Wallenstein praises "the strong imagistic sense, the overwhelming rhythms, and the sophistication throughout" a Baraka jazz poem (612). Gayl Jones tells us that, although "Baraka shares some of the techniques of the Beats—the juxtapositions, 'loose' structure, nonstandard or slang diction, he never shares with them 'valuelessness' but only noncomformity" (112-13). One of Ward's clear influences is another African-American poet closely associated with music: Robert Hayden (1913-80). In a 1999 article on Hayden, Brian Coniff asserts, "[Hayden's] poetry uses improvisation and linguistic heterogeneity as a means of constantly redescribing, and cultivating, human complexity and dignity" (503). Hayden's interest in a humanistic and musical poetic, mastered by Ward, returns revivified in the protegé's verse.

Given Ward's utilization of the elements of a jazz poetic—the inking (blacking) of voices, their multiplication in polyphony and their diversification *via* multiculturalism, the enjoyment of improvisation (surprise—in rhythm and in imagery), the employment of non-standard rhythm (aiding vocalese), the openness to unintelligible speech (scat) and metaphors borrowed from conjure ceremonies (or their like)—render him a jazz poet. He attempts to mimic, to orchestrate, with words, the discordant, but stimulating, conjunctions jazz offers. "But if jazz strives to attain the syntactic logic of what [pianist Bill] Evans calls 'a developmental language' of its own, then poetry, without question, strives that much harder to achieve the emotional complexity and rhythmic drive of music" (Feinstein and Komunyakaa *Second* xi). Frederick Ward's work pursues that end—even if, perilously, by writing *via* jazz, he contributes to his inaudibility, his invisibility in the dull, bland canons of this Northern Confederacy. Now almost 70, he still awaits, with the gracious patience of a martyr, our discovery of his unabated, deathless illumination.

(Re-)Discovering Frederick Ward

The close reader of Frederick Ward will recognize hints of the American modernists e.e. cummings, Wallace Stevens and William Faulkner; the U.S. Black Mountaineer Robert Creeley; the British modernists Gerard Manley Hopkins, James Joyce and Dylan Thomas; but also those royally Romantic rebels—William Blake and John Clare. Skillfully combining words so as to produce a willful, Mallarméan obscurity (mainly in his novels), Ward is also indebted to an African-American assembly of music-tutored, music-touting poets: Jean Toomer, Robert Hayden, Bob Kaufman, Henry Dumas, and, probably, Ishmael Reed. (That European-Canadians are ignorant of these poets does not diminish their importance.) Indeed, Ward has come to his excellent poetic, compositional style not primordially through Canada but through his special past, flamboyantly African-American and flagrantly 'artsy.'

Born in Kansas City, Missouri, in 1937, Ward was the son of Samuel, a tailor, and Grace (née Douglas), who encouraged him to play piano when he was wee. As a youth, following the sudden death of his mother, Ward quit the piano and studied art on a scholarship at the

University of Kansas. Restless, he stayed only one year. Then, he returned to music, trying out composing at the University of Missouri Conservatory of Music at Kansas (graduating in 1957). Following a stint in Hollywood as a songwriter, Ward plunked jazz piano, studying with Oscar Peterson at Toronto's Advanced School of Contemporary Music, 1962-63. Next, he journeyed to Arizona, where he scribed poetry under the tutelage of the major U.S. poets Wallace Stevens and Robert Creeley. Ward's first book, *Poems*, appeared in New Mexico in 1964. His next book, the anthology *Nine Baha'i Poets*, appeared in 1966. This edited anthology included his own verse, but also that of his fellow African-American, the splendid poet Robert Hayden, whose work—with its gorgeous imagery, ecstatic, symphonic lyricism and homage to black culture—Ward's own poetry resembles. Landed in Detroit in 1968, Ward, after watching that city burn in an apocalyptic race riot, left for Ville de Québec, staying for two years. In 1970, *en route*, by ship, to Denmark to scrutinize piano, Ward was stranded by a dockworkers's strike in Halifax, Nova Scotia. Here he met exiles from the recently bulldozed (in the name of 'urban renewal') village of Africville—a once-seaside enclave of Halifax. Bonding with this atomized community, Ward stayed in Halifax, writing and teaching, into the 1980s. During this period, he published the bulk of his extant work: three novels, all inspired equally by Ward's own childhood memories as well by those of ex-Africville residents: *Riverlisp* (1974), *Nobody Called Me Mine* (1977) and *A Room Full of Balloons* (1981).[19] Ward also edited an anthology of pupil-and-teacher verse, titled *Present Tense* (1972). In 1983, he released his second slim collection of poems, *The Curing Berry*.[20] Through the 1970s and 1980s, Ward also wrote plays, staged in Montreal, and three screenplays, all produced. At the end of the 1980s, Ward relocated to Montreal, where he taught, until his retirement, at Dawson College. Ward still lives in Montreal, though he also maintains a home in rural Nova Scotia. His work has attracted honours and prizes—an Honorary Doctor of Laws from Dalhousie University of Halifax, the Best Actor plaque, from the 1987 Chicago International Film Festival, in recognition of his role in a film he helped to write. Ward's odysseys among art, music, film and poetry, along with his steadfast adherence to the pacifism and the universalism of the Baha'i belief, inform his *synesthesiac* aesthetic and his cosmopolitan attitude. Even so, his humanitarian vision is evinced squarely within a black—really, African-American—cultural matrix as well as within a black—usually, African-American—milieu. So, Ward's characters speak, sing and think in a 'black' lingo that is soul food, soul music, and *spiritualistic*.

There is no better place to begin to encounter the jazz-composer poet and the jazz-playing novelist than in his masterpiece, *Riverlisp: Black Memories*. Here Ward sketches a series of aural/oral vignettes of a community. But the overarching idea of "Riverlisp" is merely a fixed point the author "come'd round" (to use a favourite Wardism). That is to say, the idea becomes a melody that the author feels free to explore, to move away from as he wishes, just as the jazz artist may depart from a known melody, pursuing its ghost instead. In this way, music guides philosophy. In this book—only conditionally a novel and not a poem—Ward transfigures Africville, Nova Scotia, rendering the village as Ambrose City, a decidedly phantasmal relative. Indeed, although the back-cover, dust-jacket copy *of A Room Full of Balloons* quotes the *Vancouver Sun* as claiming that "Ward has given us the songs, stories, jokes and other poems of the citizens of Africville [in *Riverlisp*]," the novel really uses Africville as a touchstone for scenes and characters out of African America. After all, for Ward, Africville is not a fixed location. His persona expresses this viewpoint in a poem, "You ain't a place. Africville is us . . . . [I]f we say we from Africville, *we are Africville*" ("Dialogue #3" 19). Thus, Ambrose City is merely an abstraction of Africville.[21] It has the same relation to the actual Africville as Dante's *Inferno*, though salted and peppered with Italians, has to Italy.

This aesthetic distance serves to temper Ward's putative realism.[22] Indeed, Ward is not interested in any serious degree of realist 'clarity.'[23] Rather, the sprightly surfaces of his fiction often gloss nasty subjects. His *recherché* realism borders on *sur*-realism, or *over-the-top* realism: "But some ladies took to hanging clothes lines from [a Japanese bridge over a sewer-pipe stream] and hung up the view" (*Riverlisp* 15). Occasionally, a cliché, a dead metaphor, such as 'knock-kneed,' is recast so as to cast a startlingly new spell: "knot kneed" (*Riverlisp* 56). Practical surrealism combines with jazz-jointed orality to explode any simplistic mimetic mode.[24] In *Riverlisp*, "thot" (to use Ward's orthography) is improvisation. And so is plot.

This jazz sensibility is documentary—a series of oral portraits (reports). The book is a set of musical sketches "to be read with indulgence ... out loud" [n.p.].[25] (Note: Part III of *Riverlisp* is dubbed, illustratively, "Hear-Say" [61].) It is speech—and reports on speech delivered in a spoken way. Here every text must be *heard*. Thus, this masterpiece is replete with agrammatical angst and ecstasy. One *Riverlisp* character—Jimmie Lee—believes

> ... *his dreams and lies* ...
> *my thots and determinations*
> DAMN! *they're musical* ...
> *perfect fourths and bent* ...
> *flated fifths* ... *illusion* ...
> *disillusion* ... (119, ellipses in the original)

Another character declares, "*Joy is a stomp! / For the human race*" (110). *Riverlisp* is a tissue of musical rhetorics, of jazzy shiftings every expressive way possible.

To compose a catalogue of Ward's oral and aural devices—the components of his print aesthetics, his text music, is almost as difficult as playing jazz. Begin with Ward's use of 'verbatim' verbs: yell, shout, scream, holler; spit, snort, hiss; mumble, murmur, moan; giggle; "stutterin and stamerin and double clutchin for breath" (*Riverlisp* 58). These action words invest the text with the gabble of speech and near-speech. But the sonic sensibility of the text is heightened further by Ward's usage of dialogue, interior monologues, repetitions of words and phrases, phonetic neo-orthographies that border on neologisms ("dimentions" [13]; "plup" [22]; "arguring" [24]; "payed" [35]; "'s'pantion" [37]; "zageratin" [80]; "consomtrate" [117]); puns ("MANure" 15); editorial interjections ("He were always singing and whistling 'Savior, Near To Me, Be' a song he made up when he git kicked out of the church for hustling ... 'Th most sanctified of sisters is willing to be tempted ...'" [19, ellipses in the original]; "Mr. Jacobs run'd after him but Pee Dee shot him in the leg—where that child git a gun?!—Pee Dee were so scared he dropped his gun..." [24]); majuscule spellings ("I can imagine heaven CAUSE TH STREETS IS A REFLECTION!" [19][26]); pronunciation guides ("'Savior, near to me-e, be.' (whistle)" [19]); concretely metaphorical namings ("Miss Pillor, Gin Drip and Skippin Daddy (cause he had one leg)" [19]); keyboard spacing ("'O Miss Utah, what MY   CHILD, MY   PEE   DEE   DONE   DONE!'" [25]); dropped-out punctuation (thus, apostrophes vanish from contractions: "didnt"); the spoken-song-form that is poetry—either bluesy rhymes (*"What my baby done done / O LORD! what my baby done done"* [24]) or straight-forward *vers libre* (22); direct invocation of sound ("saw-noise-music" [25]; "somebodies child made a siren sound" [80]); plus oral expressions ("Ooo!" [20]; "huh, huh!" [39]); and excellent onomatopoeia ("murmurous yowlin" [22]; "squinched" [31]; *"crunch"* [55]):

> Then the boy moved in close and b'gins to whisper in French—or some tongue—in her ear: spish spish, spish spish! English: spish; spish spish spish spish ... ah shp spish ... spish ...shp spish? You hip? (108)

The ever-present orality of the text syncopates it; perhaps, it even stutters at times, but Ward's 'stutters' are really episodes of melisma.

Ward's techniques could likely exhaust even Richard A. Lanham's *Handlist of Rhetorical Terms* (1991). Certainly, the jazzy writer tries out aischrologia—or foul speech ("'Damn dumb-ass fool hot damn dumb-ass fool!'" [42]; "'Woman, is this your nigger-boy or just a damn chicken thief?'" [42]; "'Hell naw, it was just a little scared white boy bastard. I tol him to kiss it'" [54]); aphaeresis or ablatio, i.e., omitting a syllable from the beginning of a word ("[a]bove," "[be]tween," [24], "[re]members," "[be]fore" [25]); apocope or abscissio, i.e., omitting the last syllable or letter of a word ("tol[d]," "th[e]" [25]); and aphorisms—or proverbs ("'you'll see that when God turns his head, th *devil* wont forgit'" [55]). An alphabet of rhetorical ornaments is revealed in Ward's unique novel. Poicilogia—"Overly ornate speech" (Lanham 116)—defines preachers like Rev. Mores and Rev. Jubilee Jackson. Polyptoton—"Repetition of words from the same root but with different endings" (Lanham 117)—is an incessant presence in *Riverlisp* ("the only womanly thing about the woman" [55]; "even didnt see things I seen" [63]; "backing back" [89]).²⁷ Parelcon—the usage of two words when only one is necessary (see Lanham 108)—is a rhetorical device Ward employs for *Riverlisp* verbs ("fill-heat" [39], "hiss spit" [55], "touch grab" [88]). Antistasis—the "repetition of a word in a different or contrary sense" (Lanham 16)—is a cousin to parelcon: in *Riverlisp*, "a Mrs. Johnson" delivers a "mess of 'greens'"—or veggies—to "Mr. Ward" who, noticing that the "greens" are buried in a broth of mud, sends his son out to a restaurant to ensure he will "eat no mess" (47). Alliteration doubles as a sonic device: "Bantu Banshee *yell*" (*Riverlisp* 55). Inverted words also appear: "friend-girl" (*Nobody* 47). An army of rhetoricians would find almost an eternity of work in cataloguing Ward's oratorical-musical exploits in print.

An extended example of Ward's expert word-singing and word-painting occurs in the section of *Riverlisp* titled "Purella Munificance." The passage treats the interracial and trans-cultural love affair between a Black Christian woman, Purella, and a Jewish Bible salesman, Micah Koch. Their *amour* is bedevilled by so much anti-white bigotry that the couple disintegrates, Purella goes a 'touch' insane, and Micah accepts to be baptized in the Black church.²⁸ Before these tragicomic events unfold, Ward—through his narrator, Jimmie Lee, produces emphatically epiphanic poetry in prose:

> Dear sweet Purella Munificance   the huckster man on his
> produce wagon, put light to your meaning so we can under-
> stand   huckster man be thinking on your continence [sic]   he
> sing the painter's brush strokes of your mouth; a low soft soothing:
> ahhhh   sound of the sea bird, leaning on the air!   and shout:
>
> 'Oooo, tomatoes's red ripe!
> Cabbage   tender peas from the vine
> Sweet...'
>
> and draws them who wish to buy in a voice that forgits [sic]
> what he be selling. The womens is moved, tho. Huckster man

be so taken he neglec'd and one woman is put to ask for her change: 'Owe up, what you owe me, man!' (36)

Unorthodox orthography, white spaces, quirky but expressive grammar, 'watercolours' and 'oils' from an oral palette, onomatopoeia, interjections and suggestions of extra-textual sound (the sea bird, the vendor's own song[29]) all work together to produce an oral-visual[30] rendering of a moment in cultural and personal time. The passage demands and deserves the recollection of a similar one in the work of Ward's precursor, Jean Toomer and his *Cane* (1923):

> Face flowed into her eyes. Flowed in soft cream foam and plaintive ripples . . . . The soft suggestion of down slightly darkened, like the shadow of a bird's wing might, the creamy brown color of her upper lip . . . . If you have heard a Jewish cantor sing, if he has touched you and made your own sorrow seem trivial when compared with his, you will know my feeling when I follow the curves of her profile, like mobile rivers, to their common delta. (16)

Where Toomer stresses visual imagery, however, Ward prefers to foreground sound. Toomer *shows* us—monologically—a portrait of "Fern"; but Ward *talks about* Purella Munificance, while also letting other voices trade notions about her.[31] In *Cane*, Toomer presents a series of poetic sketches of black life and intraracial and interracial *amour* and its *contretemps*, all dedicated to revealing the existence of a universal Oversoul in Gurdjieffian style; in *Riverlisp*, Ward gives us a series of prose-poem *cum* sound-poetry with the same optimism ("vission pictures of lovers that fill-heat the heart"[39]), save that his concern, being a Baha'i, is to reveal the oneness of humanity and the revelation of this ideal in mumbling songs, loud sermons and screeching poems.[32]

Despite all the beauties of Ward's writing, the author scruples to scrutinize the terrors and horrors that interrupt humanity's odyssey towards Oneness and Truth. On this journey, feelings and beliefs only carry one so far; knowledge and wisdom provide the best passports and the swiftest transports. In *Riverlisp*, then, the character Pause is 'lost' because he attempts to intuit music, but finds it is always beyond his ken: "A musician writer he were, always on the verge of 'THE TUNE' but never done. And life, poor soul, be a promise to himselfs: 'Won't be long'" (21). His existence is stymied. However, to know the "inner" or the "inside" is to know the heart of true truth. Ward's Baha'i faith informs this understanding. Hence, one must ask, "What is a Baha'i?" (Esslemont 83):

> Abdul-Baha replie[s]: "To be a Baha'i simply means to love all the world; to love humanity and try to serve it; to work for universal peace and brotherhood." ... In one of His London talks He said that a man may be a Baha'i even if He has never heard the name of Baha'u'llah. (83)

J.E. Esslemont expands upon these sentiments:

> He who would be a Baha'i needs to be a fearless seeker after truth, but he should not confine his search to the material plane. His spiritual perceptive powers should be awake as well as his physical. He should use all the faculties God has given him for the acquisition of truth, believing nothing without valid and sufficient reason. If his heart is pure, and his mind free from prejudice, the earnest seeker will not fail to recognize the divine glory in whatsoever temple it may become manifest. (85)

Ward articulates these precepts—the spiritual search for Truth and Oneness—in typical down-to-earth, plain-spoken, *plainsong* ways:

> "Son, when I were little I use to play in the mud lots your whole body could git lost in th feelin of mud. I thinks mud and oneness is th same all earth mix with water —that's mud— all peoples mix with the spirit —that's oneness." (*Riverlisp* 118)

To find "oneness" is to find peace (the "music"):

> The tune—I sees it as a questionin voice turnin way from mens to some Essence, askin to join or be join'd—Sanctified!— the answer comin n goin. I were thinking of the sea when I writes it [music]. You is like the sea n maybe you will know the tune. I think its life is inside the line 'n not judged by its course. Git it? (*Riverlisp* 122)

The communion—or confrontation—with "spirit" is triggered by "feelings," moods engendered by hate and love. However, in Ward, one needs introspection—a knowledge of "inner" things, the "insides"—to discover happiness. Only this wisdom can result in harmonious creativity:

> ... if you holds a willow seed in your hand to warm it afore it's planted, the seed will remember your palm print and when the tree grows, its branches will take they direction from the thought. And if it grows to fruition in your lifetime, it will be caused, in its rememberings, to weep fer you throughout all your journeyings to God. (*Room* 68)

(This teaching recalls that of Baha'u'llah: "*Man must show forth fruits. A fruitless man, in the words of His Holiness the Spirit (i.e. Christ), is like a fruitless tree, and a fruitless tree is fit for fire*" [qtd. in Esslemont 83]). Our troubled quest for self-knowledge, the inner or inside wisdom, is indicated by Ward's repeated line, in *Riverlisp*, "Fuss is round all beautiful-ness" (36), followed by "*Fuss is round /all beautifull- / ness*" (38).[33]

In the end, to sound his humanitarian theology, Ward means to make everything—every noun—speak or sing. All's alive: "... the mud sucked song from bout me ankles" (*Room* 85). In Ward's (literary) universe, all is spirit—negative or positive—"come'd round"[34] the flesh.

Nevertheless, Ward's humanitarian vision is rooted in a black (African-American) cultural matrix in much the same way as is that of his influential, Baha'i-brother poet Robert Hayden. Brian Coniff reports that critic Rosey Pool used the example of Hayden to invest "négritude" ... with unusually extended, personal, and religious overtones: "In light half-nightmare and half-vision he speaks of the face of Baha'u'llah, prophet of the Baha'i faith, in whose eyes Hayden sees the suffering of the men and women who died at Dachau and Buchenwald for their specific *Négritude*." (504, n.3)

A similarly specific black humanitarian spirit animates Ward's writing, whereby, like Hayden,[35] he eschews world-besotted politics, preferring to voice his philosophy *via* the 'free' stylings of jazz. The English-Canadian poet closest to Ward in style is, arguably, Jewish Montreal poet Abraham Moses Klein (1909-72),[36] whose powerful fusions of English and French, informed by his profound knowledge of Yiddish, Latin and Greek, plus practice of a Jewish humanitarianism, create texts that approach the style and feel of song—as in "Montreal":

O city metropole, isle riverain!
Your ancient pavages and sainted routs
Traverse my spirit's conjured avenues!
Splendor erablic of your promenades
Foliates there, and there your maisonry
Of pendant balcon and escalier'd march,
Unique midst English habitat
Is vivid Normandy! (42).

Ward departs from Klein in being less formal, less classicist, and the result is poetry that is so superficially simple that its dexterity and complexity is almost invisible.
See—hear—"Blind Man's Blues":

The best thing in my life
was a woman named Tjose.

We never had to sneak for nothing
strong woman

Put you in mind of a lone bird at dawn
standing without panic in the dew.

She kissed me so hard
she'd suck a hum from me

The best thing happen to her
were my own papa.

I found her
he had more experience

I think the hound in me sniffed out something—
something about her

And I caught her sucking that same hum from him.
I went dumb staring . . . and she seen it.

My to God, she tried to wave me off— Papa say:
 —O son
  O son

And I don't think she wanted me
to look on my naked papa like that

She throw'd lye
in my face. (42, ellipsis in the original)

Because I believe in the status of this poem as great art, I beg your indulgence of my repetition, now, of my previously published (in 2000) analysis of its genius:

> "Blind Man's Blues" is simple,[37] almost irritatingly so. Really, its eleven (or, if you split the four-line ninth strophe in half, twelve) unrhymed couplets stage a dramatic monologue about backwoods filial love and violent sexual jealousy. The phrases—or

cadences—are accessibly declarative and appealingly authoritative. The first couplet indicates the general style:

> The best thing in my life
> was a woman named Tjose.

The first line could be Tin Pan Alley cliché. But what redeems it is the piano-note-like—or singing—fall of each word into its cadenced place. The second line polishes the meaning of the first, and the position of "Tjose," as its clincher, accents her position as "the best thing"—even as the word *thing* forces us to ponder the speaker's objectification—though amiable—of this woman. The placement of "Tjose" reinforces the challenge of its pronunciation. Should it rhyme with *rose* or *rosé*? Of course, if pronounced in the first manner, the second line will possess—agreeably—the same number of syllables as the first. If pronounced in the alternative fashion, however, the name will sound more exotic. But how should the dipthong "Tj" be pronounced? To sound like "Ch," "Th," "J," or "H"?

These questions tease out the suave priminery of Ward's music-based poetic.... Ward ... writes with peculiar affinity for the linguistic and tonal music of speech, especially Black English, which he scores more sonorously than any other contemporary writer, whether one reads Toni Morrison or the Africadian poet David Woods. 'Times the *blackness* of the line is sounded in Ward's use of a crisp, rich, vernacular utterance, as in the second strophe of "Blind Man's Blues":

> We never had to sneak for nothing
> strong woman.

(The second line must not be read as a continuation of the first; rather, it is a choral reflection on the first. Crucially too, the empty space after *nothing* must be read as a 'rest'—or 'stop.') Or it is sounded in a haiku-like analogy, as in the poem's third strophe:

> Put you in mind of a lone bird at dawn
> standing without panic in the dew.

(Hear the lush sonic correspondences among Ward's words: the consonance between "nd" in "mind" and "standing"; the alliteration of "d" in "dawn" and "dew"; the inner rhyme between "you" and "dew"; the assonance between "standing" and "panic"; and the near rhyme between "lone" and "dawn.") Or blackness is sounded in the biblical parallelism of the fifth strophe's resonant reprising of the first:

> The best thing happen to her
> were my own papa.

Or perhaps it is sounded in the repetition of details such as the pleasure that the speaker *and* his father derive from coitus with Tjose:

> She kissed me so hard
> She'd suck a hum from me.
>
> ....
>
> And I caught her sucking that same hum from him.

Ward deploys the resources of rhyme and repetition with consummate, breathtaking skill.

"Blind Man's Blues" ends with the revelation that the speaker suspects that Tjose did not want him "to look on my naked papa like that // She throw'd lye / in my face." At the same time, though, it was and is a revelation for African-Canadian literature, for, here, Ward liberates a black accent—and frees it to say what it likes. (Clarke "Reading" 50-52)

Because the world is perverse in its bestowal of recognition and non-recognition, critics and scholars—even jazz-literate Canadian ones—may continue to ignore Ward's stellar prose, poetry and plays. However, no one may legitimately accuse Ward of "failure." Rather, the stewards of canons must address their own failures of vision and failures of nerve.

Coda, or Ode
I commence my conclusion by asserting that Ward resembles Miles Davis, who, as Walser writes, "constantly and consistently put himself at risk in his trumpet playing, by using a loose, flexible embouchure that helped him to produce a great variety of tone colors and articulations, by striving for dramatic gestures rather than consistent demonstration of mastery, and by experimenting with unconventional techniques" (176). In his efforts to sound what had not been sounded before, and to sound like no other sound trumpeter, Davis made mistakes: "Ideally, he would always play on the edge and never miss; in practice, he played closer to the edge than anyone else and simply accepted the inevitable missteps, never retreating to a safer, more consistent performing style" (Walser 176). For Walser, the untouchable, unimpeachable greatness of Davis resides partly in the daring, glorious errors of his playing. Yet, some jazz journalists and music-school musicologists cannot attend to Davis's achievement because their conventional studies cannot analyze his playing technique: "Such methods cannot cope with the problem of Miles Davis: the missed notes, the charged gaps, the technical risk-taking, the whole challenge of explaining how this powerful music works and means" (179). Likewise, meditating on Kaufman's masterpiece, *Golden Sardines* (1967), T.J. Anderson III enthuses, "The collection is ... important because it is the work of an artist who is unafraid to take risks. The inclusion of poetic 'failures' and 'successes' certainly marks a heroic moment in literature" (336). Kaufman's resultant "miraculous unevenness of work" (T.J. Anderson 336) reminds one of the creative power of Davis's 'missed' notes.

Yet, Frederick Ward requires, really, none of these defences (i.e., that miscues and mistakes are essential to his aesthetic). However, he does require deliverance from the misunderstandings and misapprehensions of Canadian critics who feel that only Leonard Cohen is able to marry music and print. Mr. Ward (and, in fact, a *tribe* of

African-Canadian and other oral-heritage poets) needs critics able to understand that the tissue of jazz is so close to bone—to notes, not melody—that the naked ear can't easily 'see.' To 'get' Ward, the reader must combine the sensitivities of musicologist, performer and poet. *Will you hear him?*

Notes

1. This paper has enjoyed two previous incarnations: It was first delivered as the keynote address for Improving the Future: Jazz in the Global Community: The Guelph Jazz Festival Colloquium, University of Guelph, Guelph, ON, on September 7, 2000, and then as the Anne Szumigalski Memorial Lecture for the League of Canadian Poets, at Hart House, University of Toronto, Toronto, ON, on June 11, 2005.
2. I dedicate this essay to the memory of Dutch/English-Canadian poet Diana Brebner.
3. Peter Hudson allows, "the work produced by younger [African-Canadian] poets in the 1990s occasionally has less of an explicit debt to the Caribbean. While the influence of dub and reggae, as well as of dancehall's elaborate, insiderist configurations of patois, can still be heard, often this more recent poetry is indistinguishable in form and content from that of their African American peers" (195).
4. Yet, in a beautiful contradiction, Ward appears in almost every *African-Canadian* anthology.
5. Paul Gilroy avers that the critical "consensus stipulates that as far as [Wright's] art was concerned, the move to Europe [in 1947] was disastrous ... It is claimed that after moving to France Wright's work was corrupted by his dabbling in philosophical modes of thought ["the alien influences of Freudianism and Existentialism" (Gilroy 156)] entirely alien to his African-American history and vernacular style" (156). The result of this dismissive attitude is that the eight books "written or assembled for publication in Europe" have been ignored (Gilroy 155). Wright is celebrated for his early, American-centred writing. Says Michel Fabre, "When Wright's collection of short stories, *Eight Men*, appeared posthumously in 1961, [African-American critics] expressed the view that he had been away [from the United States] too long" (271). An expatriate in Europe from 1952 until his death in 1991, the "successful popular writer," Frank Yerby, who published thirty-three novels "which sold more than 55 million copies" (Hill 797), is now so unremarked that he lacks an entry in the encyclopedia *Africana* (1999), edited by Kwame Anthony Appiah and Henry Louis Gates, Jr. James L. Hill comments, "Too long discounted as an anomaly in African American literature, Yerby deserves more critical attention" (798).

6   John Sobol challenges the idea that any evolutionary connection exists between 'sound poetry' and 'Spoken Word': "... I don't believe that sound poetry as a contemporary art form actually exists ... Sound poetry ... refers to a self-consciously avant-garde tradition of wordless poetic verbalizing whose origins lie in Futurism and Dadaism" ("Anti-Anthrax" 39). Sobol continues on to state, damningly, "... in 1999, sound poetry is history, but the SOUND of POETRY is all around us" (39).

7   One reason for Sobol's poignant and exceptional racial inclusivity is, as he states playfully in *Digitopia Blues* (2002), "You should see my record collection. It's as black as I am white" (xiv). Sobol confesses that "the quality that [draws] me to black music is characteristic of orality, of oral cultures. Collectively, Africans and their diasporic descendants possess an idiomatic musical vocabulary that is remarkable for its breadth, subtlety, and passion" (xiv). Appreciating the *vitality* of the musical-oral linkage is crucial for any critique of Ward, African-Canadian literature, and, for that matter, the development of a non-segregated English-Canadian literary history.

8   In a notable contrast, white *Beat*—and *Hippy*—jazz-poets have been practically automatically documented, remembered, celebrated, from Jack Kerouac to Kenneth Rexroth to Allen Ginsberg to Diane di Prima.

9   For the record, Ward is also absent from this compendium.

10 Vitally, however, Kaufman is an influence for Afro-Jamaican-Quebecois and bilingual poet Kaie Kellough (see his *Lettricity*), who may also know that Kaufman was "held in high esteem in avant-garde Paris circles" (Fabre 268 n.2).

11 Walser is referring to Henry Louis Gates, Jr.'s theory of literary criticism that holds that black—African-American—texts participate in a form "of intertextual revision, by which texts establish their relation to other texts, and authors to other authors" (Mason 665). The relevance of this theory to interpreting jazz performance is clear.

12 Maureen Anderson asserts, "In striving to analyze and to understand the concepts of jazz music, white critics often hid behind black stereotypes ..." (135). In her article, "The White Reception of Jazz in America," Anderson refers mainly to European-American critics of 1917-1930, but, as the attitude of H. Saal exemplifies, the need to 'primitivize' black-originated jazz remained *sound* well into the 1970s—if not until the present.

13 Here it means *Maestro*.

14 John Sobol feels that this oral culture reaches back to Africa, which "was, is, and always will be an oral world" (*Digitopia* 6). In fact, Sobol identifies characteristics of African-originated orality that, he implies, also extend to the African-American variant: Orality is "functional," "public," "communal," "participatory," "interdisciplinary" (involving music, song, dance), "experiential" (based in a sense of eternal *becoming*), "vocal" ("I am the drum. I am a talking drum" [*Digitopia* 7]), and "playful" ("Words open like windows" [8]) (*Digitopia* 6-8). Arthur Jafa adds, "...Black American culture particularly

developed around those areas we could carry around in our heads—our oratorical prowess, dance, music, those kinds of things" (251).

15 Ward provides this translation: "Our are / Is us / Hearts // Great / The friends // Space and between / That // Our hearts / Are great friends / and that / Is the space between / Us." (Clarke *Fire* 27, n.3)

16 Jazz emerged "in the first decades of the twentieth century from the artistic meeting of elements including ragtime, marching band music, opera, and other European classical musics, Native American musics, spirituals, work songs, and especially the blues. No seedbed for the new music was richer than that of New Orleans, where, in spite of separatist racial policies, musicians could tap into the city's spectacularly broad range of musical influences ..." (Anonymous "Jazz" 55). Even avant-garde jazz is aggressively multicultural: "Characterized mainly by African, Asian, and Caribbean musical elements, this form of music emphasizes the importance of the collective ensemble rather than the soloist. Hence, its production, which may sound like chaos and disorder to some, is very Afrocentric in nature" (1393).

17 Sobol points out that, "In scat singing, black oralists found a means of escape, a playful arena where their improvisatory urges could be given free rein and they could explode the restrictive limitations of banal lyrics" (*Digitopia* 36).

18 Ward's *Room Full of Balloons* refutes any connection between jazz and aggression.

19 One must note that the already tenuous Africville connection in the first novel becomes further and further attenuated in the next two.

20 As of 2005, no new, independent book by Ward has appeared in more than two decades, though new work by him surfaces, from time to time, almost always in African-Canadian anthologies.

21 But *Riverlisp* (Ambrose City) is also a locale where the author can test—no, *illustrate*—Baha'i teachings.

22 May Cutler references Ward's "way of making the human connection to poverty that makes you feel it when you read him" (Kimber 36). Stephen Kimber posits that Ward "has ... brought the now long gone community of Africville to life for the rest of the world" (33).

23 "Ward ... maintains he isn't writing [in *Riverlisp*] just about the flesh-and-blood Africville or even about blacks; he is writing, he says, to bring to life the people—black and white—society finds 'insignificant. What I write about,' Ward says, 'isn't black or white. It's universal'"(Kimber 36).

24 Discussing one African-American poet's work, Nielsen finds that it "makes the case for a black vernacular base for African-American surrealism, a jazz-and-blues-based surrealism ..."(70). Ward's work fits this paradigm.

25 This same instruction appears at the debut of *A Room Full of Balloons* (n.p.).

26 Ward uses majuscules—and italics—to register sophisticated concepts, intellectual or religious, or simply to 'pump up the volume' of deserving, vernacular words and sounds. Ward's majuscules and italics embody preacherly

insights or just 'loud' ones. See these *Riverlisp* examples: "orchestra" (25) and "DON'T LIE WOMAN!" (80).

27 *Riverlisp* is characterized by the yokings of similar words, using both polyptoton and antistasis, but *Nobody Called Me Mine* features verb-pairs (the first colouring or illustrating the second), a type of parelcon—or deliberate, verbal redundancy.

28 This event is two-sided: on one side, it *seems* a picture of integration (the black community accepts a white church member); on the other, it is a denial of Judaism. Most damningly, Micah's 'conversion' was unnecessary for him to love Purella—and his acceptance by the church is no remedy for their community-caused, racism-inflected break-up.

29 Here one may flag again the links between black speech, other sounds, and jazz:
> Young [Louis] Armstrong's musical education included a pie man named Santiago who blew a bugle to attract customers, a banana man whose musical cries advertised the virtues of his ripe yellow fruit, a waffle man whose customers enjoyed his mess call as much as his waffles, and the barroom quartets "who hung around the saloons with a cold can of beer in their hands, singing up a breeze while they passed the can around." (Levine 204-05)

30 According to Lawrence Levine, Bruce Jackson maintains, "Negro songs don't tend to weave narrative elements together to create a story but instead accumulate images to create a feeling" (240). I think that Ward adopts/adapts this principal principle. By so doing he achieves what Nielsen, speaking of another poet, terms " the palpable nature of [his] imagery, the insistent physicality of even the most fantastic-seeming imagery" (226). The practice of this blues aesthetic means, as Barry Keith Grant's reading of Samuel Charters insists, "... the blues creates poetry out of daily events and objects surrounding the singers, attempting to achieve in the frequent homeliness and concreteness of its language an articulation of lived experience" (295). The power of Ward's imagery derives from his lyrical concretization of the workaday real and the everyday surreal.

31 *Riverlisp* is a revisiting of *Cane*, with Ward's *Ambrose City* replacing Toomer's Sparta, Georgia, Washington, DC and Chicago, Illinois.

32 Ward's narrative of the shooting-lynching of "Miss Jessups's Boy" employs a poem—"*meet me in th hills / sweet Miss Martha / I bring us a picnic*" (*Riverlisp* 42)—which recalls Toomer's similar narrative, "Blood-Burning Moon." But, just as Toomer is more Gothic than Ward, so is his verse: "Red nigger moon. Sinner! / Blood-burning moon. Sinner! / Come out that fact'ry door" (*Cane* 31).

33 True: Fuss is actually, in this fiction, a cat. But I credit an allegorical intent in the feline's contextually felicitous name.

34 This eccentric construction is practically a *mantra* in Ward's work.

35 "A Baha'i by faith, Hayden was committed to 'the affirmation of independent investigation of the truth' and to abstinence from partisan politics of any kind" (Coniff 489).

36 I do not liken Ward to Leonard Cohen—another obvious candidate, given his success as a musician, singer, songwriter, poet and novelist, because Cohen, although verbally experimental in his novels, is much less so in his poetry. Indeed, Cohen's poetry invests in a medieval mysticism that upholds a linguistic conservatism (a point also true about his songs).

37 But the poem is also fiendishly intricate. This *black* aesthetic understands Amiri Baraka's existentialist statement: "Life is complex in the same simplicity" ("Changing" 162).

Works Cited

Anderson, Maureen. "The White Reception of Jazz in America." *African American Review* 38.1 (2004): 135-145.

Anderson, T. J., III. "Body and Soul: Bob Kaufman's *Golden Sardine*." *African American Review* 34.2 (Summer 2000): 329-346.

Anonymous. "Avant-Garde Jazz." *Call & Response: The Riverside Anthology of the African American Literary Tradition*. Eds. Patricia Liggins Hill, et al. Boston: Houghton Mifflin, 1998. 1393.

Anonymous. "Bop and Cool Jazz." *Call & Response: The Riverside Anthology of the African American Literary Tradition*. Eds. Patricia Liggins Hill, et al. Boston: Houghton Mifflin, 1998. 1099-1101.

Anonymous. "Jazz." *The Norton Anthology of African American Literature*. Eds. Henry Louis Gates, Jr., et al. New York: W.W. Norton, 1997. 55-57.

Appiah, Kwame Anthony, and Henry Louis Gates, Jr., eds. *Africana: The Encyclopedia of the African and African-American Experience*. New York: Basic Civitas Books, 1999.

Baraka, Amiri. "The Changing Same (R&B and New Black Music)." 1967. *Selected Plays and Prose of Amiri Baraka/LeRoi Jones*. New York: Morrow Quill, 1979. 157-177.

[Baraka, Amiri.] "The Screamers." By LeRoi Jones. 1963. *Tales*. New York: Grove, 1967, 1968. 71-80.

Call & Response: The Riverside Anthology of the African American Literary Tradition. Eds. Patricia Liggins Hill, et al. Boston: Houghton Mifflin, 1998.

Cayley, Jennifer. "Uncharted territory." Ethnic Writers Series. [Ottawa] September-October 1988. 11. [newsletter]

Clarke, George Elliott, ed. *Fire on the Water: An Anthology of Black Nova Scotian Writing*. Vol. 2. Lawrencetown Beach, NS: Pottersfield Press, 1992.

———."Reading Ward's 'Blind Man's Blues.'" *Arc* 44 (Summer 2000): 50-52.

Coniff, Brian. "Answering 'The Waste Land': Robert Hayden and the Rise of the African American Poetic Sequence." *African American Review* 33.3 (Fall 1999): 487-506.

Ellison, Ralph. *Invisible Man*. 1947. New York: Vintage International, 1995.

Esslemont, J.E. *Baha'u'llah and the New Era: An Introduction to the Baha'i Faith*. 1923. 3rd ed. rev. Wilmette, IL: Baha'i Books, 1970.
Fabre, Michel. *From Harlem to Paris: Black American Writers in France, 1840-1980*. Urbana, IL: University of Illinois Press, 1991.
Feinstein, Sascha, and Yusuf Komunyakaa, eds. Preface. *The Jazz Poetry Anthology*. Bloomington: Indiana UP, 1991. xvii-xx.
———. Preface. *The Second Set: The Jazz Poetry Anthology*. Volume 2. Bloomington: Indiana UP, 1996. xi-xiv.
Gilroy, Paul. *The Black Atlantic: Modernity and Double Consciousness*. Cambridge, MA: Harvard UP, 1993.
Grant, Barry Keith. "Purple Passages or Fiestas in Blue? Notes Toward an Aesthetic of Vocalese." *Representing Jazz*. Ed. Krin Gabbard. Durham, NC: Duke UP, 1995. 285-303.
Henson, Josiah. *Life of Josiah Henson, Formerly a Slave, Now an Inhabitant of Canada, Narrated by Himself*. Boston: A.D. Phelps, 1849.
Hill, James L. "Yerby, Frank." In *The Oxford Companion to African American Literature*. Eds. William L. Andrews, et al. New York: Oxford UP, 1997. 797-98.
Hudson, Peter. "Primitive Grammars." *Sulfur* 44 (Spring 1999): 193-95.
Jafa, Arthur. "69." *Black Popular Culture*. Seattle: Bay Press, 1992. 249-54.
Jones, Gayl. *Liberating Voices: Oral Tradition in African American Literature*. Cambridge, MA: Harvard UP, 1991.
Kaufman, Bob. *Golden Sardine*. San Francisco: City Lights, 1967.
Kellough, Kaie. *Lettricity: Poems*. Montréal: Cumulus Press, 2004.
Kimber, Stephen. "Halifax's Hot, But Unknown, Author." *Halifax*. [Halifax, NS] (November 1981): 33-37.
Klein, A.M. "Montreal." 1948. In *15 Canadian Poets x 3*. Ed. Gary Geddes. Toronto: Oxford UP, 2001. 42-44.
Lanham, Richard A. *A Handlist of Rhetorical Terms*. 2nd ed. Berkeley: University of California Press, 1991.
Leonard, Neil. "The Jazzman's Verbal Usage." *Black American Literature Forum* 20 (1986): 151-60.
Levine, Lawrence W. *Black Culture and Black Consciousness*. Cambridge, MA: Harvard UP, 1977.
Mackey, Nathaniel. *Discrepant Engagement: Dissonance, Cross-Culturality, and Experimental Writing*. Cambridge: Cambridge UP, 1993.
Mason, Theodore O. "Signifying." In *The Oxford Companion to African American Literature*. Eds. William L. Andrews, et al. New York: Oxford UP, 1997. 665-66.
Nielsen, Aldon Lynn. *Black Chant: Languages of African-American Postmodernism*. Cambridge: Cambridge UP, 1997.
Odhiambo, David. *diss/ed banded nation*. Victoria, BC: Polestar, 1998.
The Oxford Companion to African American Literature. Eds. William L. Andrews, et al. New York: Oxford UP, 1997.
The Oxford Companion to Canadian Literature. 2nd ed. Eds. Eugene Benson & William Toye. Toronto: Oxford UP, 1997.

Radano, Ronald M. "Critical Alchemy: Anthony Braxton and the Imagined Tradition." *Jazz Among the Discourses*. Ed. Krin Gabbard. Durham, NC: Duke University Press, 1996. 189-216.

Saal, H. "Two Free Spirits." *Newsweek*. 8 Aug. 1977: 52-53.

Scobie, Stephen, and Douglas Barbour. CARNIVOCAL: *A Celebration of Sound Poetry*. Red Deer, AB: Red Deer College Press, 1999.

Shange, Ntozake. *for colored girls who have considered suicide / when the rainbow is enuf*. 1977. Toronto: Bantam, 1981.

Sobol, John. "Anti-Anthrax Thorax: Sound Poetry in the Post-Literate Age." Review of CARNIVOCAL: *A Celebration of Sound Poetry*. By Stephen Scobie and Douglas Barbour. MIX 25.3 (Winter 1999/2000): 38-40.

———. *Digitopia Blues: Race, Technology, and the American Voice*. Banff, AB: Banff Centre Press, 2002.

Toomer, Jean. *Cane*. 1923. New York: W.W. Norton, 1988.

Vaidhyanathan, Siva. "Jazz." In *The Oxford Companion to African American Literature*. Eds. William L. Andrews, et al. New York: Oxford UP, 1997. 395-396.

Wallenstein, Barry. "Poetry and Jazz: A Twentieth-Century Wedding." *Black American Literature Forum* 25.3 (Fall 1991): 595-620.

Walser, Robert. "'Out of Notes': Signification, Interpretation, and the Problem of Miles Davis." In *Jazz Among the Discourses*. Ed. Krin Gabbard. Durham, NC: Duke UP, 1996. 165-188.

Ward, Fred, ed. *Anthology of Nine Baha'i Poets*. Detroit: n.p., 1966.

———. "Around 12 Bars in 3/4 Time." In *The Curing Berry*. Toronto: Williams-Wallace, 1983. 6.

———. "Blind Man's Blues." In *The Curing Berry*. Toronto: Williams-Wallace, 1983. 42.

———. *The Curing Berry*. Toronto: Williams-Wallace, 1983.

———. "The Death of Lady Susuma." In *Fire on the Water: An Anthology of Black Nova Scotian Writing*. Vol. 2. Ed. George Elliott Clarke. Lawrencetown Beach, NS: Pottersfield Press, 1992. 21-23.

———. "Dialogue #3: Old Man (to the Squatter)." In *Fire on the Water: An Anthology of Black Nova Scotian Writing*. Vol. 2. Ed. George Elliott Clarke. Lawrencetown Beach, NS: Pottersfield Press, 1992. 19-20.

———. "Lady Susuma's Dream." In *The Curing Berry*. Toronto: Williams-Wallace, 1983. 54-56.

———. *Nobody Called Me Mine*. Montreal: Tundra Books, 1977.

———. *Poems*. Albuquerque, NM: Duende, 1964.

———. ed. *Present Tense*. Halifax, NS: New Options School, 1972.

———. *Riverlisp: Black Memories*. Montreal: Tundra Books, 1974.

———. *A Room Full of Balloons*. Montreal: Tundra Books, 1981.

Williams, Sherley Anne. "Two Words on Music: Black Community." In *Black Popular Culture*. Seattle: Bay Press, 1992. 164-172.

Why Poetry?

MARGARET ATWOOD

Anne Szumigalski Lecture • Ottawa, Ontario • June 11, 2006

THE TITLE OF THIS SPEECH TODAY IS 'WHY POETRY?' I thought I might as well go for the viscera. It probably should be—more pickily—'Why Poetry When?' because the reasons poets have given for doing what they do have varied widely according to the age in which they were doing it. Or it could be—even more pickily—'Why Poetry When and Where?' Because place comes into it, as well. But let's just say "Why Poetry," which is what your mother's friends used to ask the poor woman, behind your back, as a prelude to saying, "He would have made such a good doctor." Or, in my case, "botanist."

It's very nice of you to have asked me to this poets' event. I feel like a fraud at poets' events, because I have several other kinds of writing that I do, and my image of a really pure poet would be one that can barely manage to crank out a Christmas thank-you note to the mailman because it would have to be in prose. (Remember mailmen? Remember when they were men? Remember when you wrote Christmas notes to them?)

I'm not a really pure poet; I'm an impure one, when I'm being a poet at all. My impurity is handy for critics, however: if I've published a novel, they can say, "She's much better as a poet," and if I've published some poetry they can say, "She should stick to novels." The truly refined say that I'm a lousy poet and also a crummy novelist, but my short stories are really quite acceptable. There are some who maintain that I'm not very good at anything, and a rotten human being into the bargain—though I would have made a really excellent botanist, if I hadn't strayed off the true path—but you can't please everyone all the time.

It's a strange feeling to be giving the Anne Szumigalski Lecture for the League of Canadian Poets. Anne Szumigalski and I were connected with the same magazine, long, long ago—in the early days of *Grain*—but even longer ago than that, I was present at the formation of the League of Canadian Poets, way back in the mid-'60s. As I recall, we stood around on a lawn. I can't quite remember what we thought we were doing or why we thought we were doing it, but poetry was arguably the dominant locally grown art form in Canada at that time, if you don't count hockey and politics, so we must have thought that what we were doing was important.

Poetry was top dog *faute de mieux*—there wasn't a film industry in Canada then, and it was hard to get novels published. Canadian publishers would tell you that you needed a foreign publisher too—one in England or the States. (This was at a moment when you were also told there was no such thing as Canadian culture or Canadian literature, only a sort of local backwater pond scum that was a thin, smelly variant on what real writers were doing.) Then, if you were lucky enough to get a publisher in one of those other countries to actually read your novel, you were likely to be told it was "too Canadian." The cognitive dissonance was deafening.

So poetry was more likely to see its way into print back then, because it was short, and you could print it in your cellar, on a flatbed press, or even on a mimeo machine. A lot of people who later wrote novels—or, more accurately, who later published novels—they may have been writing them all along—were first brought to public attention, or at least the attention of the 500 or so people who might read them, if they were very lucky—through poetry. Also, poets got around the country. They took buses and hitched rides and hung out at one another's houses, coast to coast—they constituted a sort of informal communications network, or a posse of circuit rides, if you like. If another poet knocked at your door, you were supposed to let them in. Though I wouldn't necessarily do that now. But we were a trusting lot in those days.

Some people who weren't poets occasionally let poets in as well, out of the goodness of their hearts, and in the belief that they were being patrons of the arts. On one memorable occasion—I remember it although I wasn't, technically speaking, there—Milton Acorn got very drunk and fell into the fireplace. The fire wasn't burning, but the fireplace was full of charcoal and ashes, and Milton, Cinderella-like, went to sleep in it. (That's a euphemism for "passed out.") He then rendered himself vertical in the middle of the night and did something or other in his hosts' pristine all-white bathroom that it must have taken five cleaning ladies to put to rights. This is what "patron of the arts" might have entailed, and might still entail. You should think carefully before becoming one. Poets back then didn't hold down many academic jobs, as such—they were a more raffish and subterranean lot. Also most of them were male. They were living in the afterglow of Dylan Thomas and John Berryman, and self-destructive activities were part of the job description.

In any case, there we were, standing around on a lawn, forming the League of Canadian Poets. F.R. Scott was there. He wrote the Constitution. Most likely it was 1966, the year before Expo 67—we were keen on the National Identity and National Purpose in those days, remember them? Maybe not. Just as well, because I think our present government would like to kiss them both goodbye, along with all of you poets. My advice? Go to plumbing school, there's always a demand for that. Also you can think about poetry better while doing things with your hands than you can if you have to run computer programmes and so forth. It's nice and dark underneath sinks, and nobody bothers you in there. My second choice for you would be cemetery upkeep.

However, back to the lawn. Maybe the League had already been formed, and the lawn event was a sort of party. The line between being formed and not being formed was a thin one in those times. I did go onto the League's website to find out more about this historic thing I was actually at myself, but the website didn't have much history on it. My lord though, it has a lot of other stuff! My mind boggled very quickly. I had to turn the site off because it made me dizzy. An on-line store! Posters! An events calendar! A kiddie programme! Never in our wildest dreams did we think we would have any of those things, but then, we didn't foresee the Internet, either.

The foregoing was a long, circumstantial illustration of the particularity—in terms of space and time—of outbursts of poetry. If anyone had asked us Why Poetry on that lawn, they would have got an answer from most present that would have included not only a batch of statements about the condensed and honed uses of language, or about the articulate uses of the individual and human voice, but also some about the importance of condensing and honing and voicing that language in a uniquely Canadian way—something we felt we had to busy ourselves with because it was thought that every nation worthy of the name needed such a thing, and you couldn't be a proper nation without it, and we wanted to be a proper nation, and not just the aforesaid pond scum.

The answers would be different now. But underneath it, perhaps not all that different. Multicultural Mosaic and Regional might have replaced National; gender might come into it—less now than fifteen years ago, but more now than five years ago. The honing and condensing of the language might be phrased in a different way; the voice as opposed to the written word, or as embodied in it, would be stressed to greater or lesser degrees; but the substratum would—I speculate—have remained much the same, because the same assumptions are still more or less in place.

But let's go back to the original question—which is not, Why poetry here? or Why Canadian poetry? or Why twenty-first-century poetry? but Why poetry at all? Why on earth do human beings excrete poetry, whether in written or in oral form? Because they do do it, and they have done it—to our imperfect knowledge—as long as there have been human beings.

Here are a couple of unproven theories. Let me rephrase that: here are a couple of potentially interesting sidelights.

First, coming to you via the neuroscientists: reading, writing, singing and speaking are located in different parts of the brain. Second, if the speaking part is knocked out, the singing part may remain and, if so, it will include the ability to sing in words—words that you may not be able to pronounce in your non-singing voice. Third, proper names have their own little address book in the brain—apart from other nouns. The brain recognizes that "John Smith" is a different sort of thing than "carrot." There is not a category of John Smiths that share a large number of characteristics, such as orangeness, crunchiness, feathery green tops, phallic symbolism, horrible little whiskers growing out of them in the spring and so on. Thus, for the brain, each John Smith has to have its own set of differing recognition tags—which is why some of us find it hard to remember people's names.

Fourth, music, mathematics and poetry seem to be more closely allied than any of them are to ordinary conversational speech, to prose fiction, or to prose in general. Poetry involves pattern recognition—and so do those other forms of word assembly—but the nature of the patterns appears to be different—closer to those of music and math. (I'm speaking here of the kind of poetry that has either overt or concealed rhyme and meter schemes, not of the kind that is indistinguishable from prose.)

That's one small group of ideas I'd like to throw onto the table. Here's the other one.

It's my belief that the first two technologies that were developed by human beings, and by human beings alone, were fire and grammar. All animals eat, but only human beings cook. Cooking—it has been said—not only increased the varieties of things that people could eat, it reduced the amount of time they had to spend digesting unprocessed foods, thus freeing up—it has been said—five extra hours a day for other pursuits.

Most animals have methods of communication, and the so-called higher animals—those with spinal chords, brains as such, central nervous systems and vocal chords—have systems that can be called languages. Of those languages, only human languages have complex systems of grammar—systems that allow us to formulate thoughts that dogs, for instance, most likely don't bother with. Consider tenses. A dog can and does think in the future tense—"My master is likely coming home soon"—and in the past tense—"That man threw a stone at me yesterday so now I am going to keep at a safe distance." But no dog is likely to think, "Where did the first dog come from?" or "Who or what created dogs?" Nor is it likely to ask, "Where do dogs go when they die?" So how did human beings ever get to the point where they will kill one another and even fight wars over these forever unproveable issues, as they have long been doing?

Picture the scene. There are our ancestors, sitting around the fire, cooking, eating and digesting. Due to the cooking, they've got time on their hands. They may be chipping away at their arrowheads or weaving their baskets, but what are they doing at the same time? They're working on their other big technology—their human languages. They're elaborating subtle shades of meaning, they're memorizing and passing down their origin stories—most oral origin stories we know anything about are in poetry, because poetry appears to be easier to memorize, especially if there's a narrative involved, as there always is with origin stories. They may be reciting genealogies, or handing on wisdom about life, in whatever forms that wisdom has been formulated. They may be singing and chanting this poetry, or reciting it with rhetorical flourishes. It's part of the fabric of their being, because they've been born into it and lived surrounded by it as children, and rhymes and rhythms you learn as a child are available to you all your life. (Think, right now, of a nursery rhyme. *Alligator pie, alligator pie, if I don't get some I think I'm gonna die.* You'll wonder where the yellow went, when you brush your teeth with Pepsodent. And many more.)

Oral cultures swam in a sea of language—rich, aromatic, multiplicitous, exfoliating language.

We on the other hand—as a culture at large—live on a comparatively dry shore.

This is possibly why poets often feel—to themselves—obsolete, archaic, somehow not modern. They're told that what they do is a remnant of something human beings no longer need—that we live by technologies and numbers now, and that these technologies and numbers represent the real world, as opposed to the dream world that poets live in, along with lunatics and lovers—of imagination all compact, each one of them—the implication being that the creatures of the imagination are not real.

But those who tell you this have got hold of the wrong end of the stick. What drives the technologies and the numbers is still, not human reason—that abstract and chimerical creature—but human emotion. If we were giant intelligent spiders, we would have altered the world in other ways—bigger flies, better webs, juicier and slower male spiders to be yummily devoured after copulation—but we aren't spiders. We make what we long for as human beings, we destroy what we fear as human beings, and what we long for and what we fear hasn't changed—in essence—for a very long time. How do we know? We've read the poems—the old poems, the myths and the origin stories and the epics and the tales of supernatural heroes and beings.

Here's a partial list: We want the purse that will always be filled with gold. We want the Fountain of Youth. We want to fly. We want the table that will cover itself with delicious food whenever we say the word, and that will clean up afterwards. We want invisible servants we'll never have to pay. We want the Seven League Boots so we can get places very quickly. We want the Hat of Darkness so we can snoop on other people without being seen. We want the weapon that will never miss, and that will destroy our enemies utterly. We want to punish injustice. We want power. We want excitement and adventure; we want safety and security. We want to be immortal. If we can't have that in the body, we want it in the spirit. We want to go to a heavenly afterlife, and we want those we consider bad to go to a hellish one. We know what should be in Heaven: everything we want, and everyone we love. We know what should be in Hell: everything we don't want, and everyone we hate. Some of the most interesting forms of Planet X, in science fiction, combine the two in unpredictable ways.

We want to have a large number of sexually attractive partners. We want those we love to love us in return, and to be sexually loyal to us. (Do the math on these two conflicting desires. You won't get even scores.) We want cute, smart children who will treat us with the respect we deserve, and who will not die young or become drug addicts or smash up the car. We want to be surrounded by music, and by ravishing scents and attractive visual objects. We don't want to be too hot. We don't want to be too cold. We want to dance. We want to drink a lot without having a hangover. We want to speak with the animals. We want to be envied. We want to be as gods.

We want wisdom. We want hope. We want to be good. Therefore we sometimes tell ourselves warning stories that deal with the darker side of some of our other wants.

An educational system that teaches us only about our tools—the How To of them, their creation, their maintenance—and not about their function as facilitators of our hopes, fears and desires, is, in essence, no more than a school of toaster repair. You can be the best toaster repair person in the world, but you will cease to have a job if toast is no longer considered a desirable food item on the human breakfast menu. "The arts"—as we've come to term them—are not a frill. They are the heart of the matter, because they are about our hearts, and our technological inventiveness is generated by our emotions, not by our minds. A society without poetry and the other arts would have broken its mirror and cut out its heart. It would no longer be what we now recognize as human.

As William Blake noted long ago, the human imagination drives the world. At first it drove only the human world, which was once very small in comparison to the huge and powerful natural world around it. Now we're next door to being in control of everything except earthquakes and the weather.

But it's still the human imagination, in all its diversity, that directs what we do with our tools. Poetry is an uttering, or outering, of the human imagination. It lets the shadowy forms of thought and feeling out into the light, where we can take a good look at them and perhaps come to a better understanding of who we are and what we want, and what the limits to those wants may be. Understanding the imagination is not a pastime or even a duty, but a necessity; because increasingly, if we can imagine it, we'll be able to do it.

So that—in short—is 'Why poetry.' Poetry is part of the way we sing our being. And that is why, dear fellow poets, you are not obsolete leftovers from a more archaic age, unless the whole thinking, feeling, speaking, singing, imagining human being is also a leftover.

But that is another question.

The Angel of the Big Muddy

MARK ABLEY

Anne Szumigalski Lecture • Edmonton, Alberta • June 9, 2007

MY SUBJECT WILL BE THE IMAGINATION: ITS POWER, ITS IMportance, the joy it brings. I want to approach the topic of poetic imagination through one particular writer, the one for whom these lectures are named. A lot of you were acquainted with Anne Szumigalski in her later years, as the author of many collections of poetry and also as a teacher, editor and mentor to dozens of writers on the Prairies and beyond. Every human being is unique—but, I hope you'll agree, few of us are so obviously and so memorably unique as Anne. I want to talk about how she grew into the person you remember: not just a large-scale woman with a girlish voice, a tendency to giggle, and a love of mushrooms, dancing and gardens, but also a large-scale force in Canadian poetry with a passion for language and an uncompromising faith in the value and necessity of this, our chosen art. I also mean to raise the question of whether her belief in the imagination can be sustained in a postmodern age.

When poetry began to play a significant role in the life of Anne Szumigalski—or rather Nancy Davis—she was a girl growing up in rural England in the late 1920s, one of seven children in an unconventional family. "[M]y attitude towards poetry," she wrote near the end of her life, "has hardly changed at all since I memorized and recited … my first childish efforts somewhere between my fourth and fifth birthdays. Later, at about the age of twelve, I decided that if the literary arts can be thought of as a mountain, then poetry is at the very peak. The pointy tops of mountains are no doubt the smallest part. The air is more rarified up here and there is snow under your boots, but then you are as near the heavens as you can get while still having your feet on the ground. Well worth the climb, wouldn't you say?"[1]

That was a posture she always maintained: wherever her eyes were peering, her feet were firmly planted on the earth. But Anne says that she arrived at this image or understanding of poetry at the age of twelve, and that she had memorized her first poems before she turned five. Do you think she was exaggerating a bit? Do you suspect she might have been drawing on what we like to call, in a phrase well worth pondering, "poetic licence"?

I believe her. I don't think she was exaggerating at all. And the reason is that a few years ago, when I was rummaging among the Anne Szumigalski papers that are filed away in the University of Regina Library, I came across a copy of an early poem she had written out by hand. The poem is seventy-nine lines long, and it's called "The Angel of the Woods." This is how it begins:

When the first Spring breeze
Blows through the woodland world
And the first new buds upon the trees
Burst and new leaves are unfurled
When the first thrush trills his notes
On the new Spring air
Then comes the Angel of the Woods
Holy, pure and fair …[2]

Not quite the mature Szumigalski voice, you're probably thinking, even if a few of her best-loved poems do feature the odd angel. Yet the more you look at this poem, the more you notice themes and images that make regular appearances in her later work—angels, of course, but also songs, hair, spring, faith, hunting, love, clothes, and most of all: flowers. The poem evokes an April ecstasy of primroses, bluebells, crocuses, violets, anemones, catkins and daffodils. It ends like this:

> She stands her cross in her hand
> On her bosom the dove
> With spring leaves bound on her brow
> For the Angel of the Woods is love
> And the flowers bow down their heads
> As the bluebells ring
> And the little birds sleep in their nests
> For the Angel of the Woods is Spring [3]

I mentioned this was an early poem, but I didn't say just how early. Anne Szumigalski—I mean, Nancy Davis—wrote that poem when she was nine years old. She was already set on a lifetime's course. Sixty-eight years later, at her funeral in Saskatoon on a damp April day, the brochure that was given out to the congregation in the overflowing chapel included a reproduction of a drawing Anne had done in her last years. The drawing is entitled "Mourning Angels, Morning Doves." As a little girl, she had a pure and ardent faith in the imagination. As an old woman, she had the same faith. The faith was even couched in very similar imagery, although the turtledoves of her childhood had been replaced by North American birds.

In between "The Angel of the Woods" and "Mourning Angels, Morning Doves," many things happened to Anne Szumigalski. Still a teenager when the Second World War broke out, she quickly signed up to be an interpreter, welfare officer and medical assistant for the British Red Cross. At the war's end, travelling with a Red Cross unit across Europe, she faced the horrors of the Nazi concentration camps just after they were liberated. She married a Polish refugee, Jan Szumigalski, and gave birth to several children. She lived in north Wales and then in the Big Muddy wilderness of southern Saskatchewan, falling in love with the land and sky of the Prairies before moving once and for all to Saskatoon in 1956. And, after a period of silence, of being rebuffed if not humiliated when she sent out her work, she entered the public world of poetry and took enormous delight in helping to create a vibrant literary community in Saskatchewan.

I want to pause there and talk for a moment about the sources of her work. The literary sources, I mean, apart from her never-ending delight in nature and apart from the personal experiences, whether joyful or deeply sorrowful, that provided the catalyst for individual poems. Anne was immensely well read—although, or perhaps I mean because, she was educated at home and never attended university.

Whenever she was asked to select her favourite writers, she liked to mention one name before all others: William Blake. "[W]e have," she said, "imagined a God with enough imagination to imagine us";[4] and she associated this heretical idea with Blake. The conventional figure of a jealous, white-bearded, patriarchal God, Blake liked to call "Old Nobodaddy."[5] She followed him too in his conviction that the body is but an emanation of the spirit. He once defined imagination as "the real and eternal world of which this vegetable universe is but a faint shadow."[6] Her Blake was not the laureate of childhood innocence but rather the fiery thinker who imagined the fearful symmetry of tigers. It was energy, not peace, that gave him eternal delight. She loved to quote these lines of his: "Without contraries is no progression. Attraction and Repulsion, Reason and Energy, Love and Hate, are necessary to human existence."[7] Responding to that assertion in her quasi-memoir *The Word, The Voice, The Text*, Anne wrote:

> In fact poetry, art, is power, is energy, is eternal. Perhaps it is all that we are. All other things, all other states are pale shadows flitting in the half-light of half-desire, half-energy, half-joy, half-anger, half-contention too. For William Blake was not only a contentious person; he was a contentious poet.[8]

Of course Anne Szumigalski was very fond of this vegetable universe, and Blake was far from the only inspiration she drew upon. She revelled in the language, if not the doctrine, of the Anglican *Book of Common Prayer*, and she once declared that a major influence on her writing was A.C. Budd's *Flora of the Canadian Prairie Provinces*. I don't think her tongue was up her cheek, although with Anne it was sometimes hard to tell. But I'd now like to mention two other writers whom she didn't tend to single out in interviews: Samuel Taylor Coleridge and Ralph Waldo Emerson.

Anne was, I'm convinced, a latter-day Romantic. It was Romanticism, little more than a century before she was born, that had veered away from the authority of classical form, granting power to the unfettered play of an individual's imagination. A good part of her achievement as a writer was finding ways of translating Romanticism into the landscape of the Canadian west and the history of a Holocaust-ridden age. Where some writers have resorted to cynicism and mockery, Anne refused to give up on the insights and difficult beliefs of writers who meant the world to her. I would argue there's a direct relationship between the two short passages that follow, the first of them taken from Coleridge, the second from Anne's poem "A House With a Tower":

> Weave a circle round him thrice,
> And close your eyes with holy dread,
> For he on honey-dew hath fed,
> And drunk the milk of Paradise.[9]

> the Celt within
> who likes to stand up and sing
> ecstatic and undulating songs
> is the one who opens my mouth
> and lets the lies out [10]

In "Kubla Khan," Coleridge promises that "with music loud and long," the poet will build a sunny pleasure-dome whose shadow will float on the waves. In "A House With a Tower" Anne replaces the dome by a Yeatsian tower, and the ocean by "a muddy puddle-edge / (call it a slough)." She identifies herself as a liar, in opposition to "Angle, that indwelling cousin" who preaches care and who prefers to build rationally, using blocks. Angle is a classicist, if you like; the Celt is a romantic who always renews that poetic licence. What matters for Anne, in this poem and many others, is the passion that allows her to climb up the tower and, as she says, "shape the sky." But while the two poets imagine a very different landscape, they share a sense of art as something ecstatic and dangerous. They share a vision of imagination as a force to be reckoned with. The savagery of the deep and wooded chasm Coleridge describes in "Kubla Khan" can't be separated from either its enchantment or its holiness. *Savage, holy, enchanted*: a revealing trio of qualities.

The equivalent in "Kubla Khan" to Anne's inner Celt is a damsel with a dulcimer—a classic anima figure, in Jungian terms, because the poet says he wants to revive within himself her symphony and song. I'm aware that many women poets have had difficulty with the traditional notion of a female muse whose principal job is to divert, delight and inspire a male author. I never used to think this was much of an issue for Anne, although now I wonder if it begins to explain all those angels who flit through her work. Muses and angels both act as a kind of creative intermediary between humans and the otherwise unreachable divine. In a Hallmark greeting card, angels are soft and feminine; but in Milton and Blake, they are male and often ferocious. In "A House With a Tower," Anne clearly identifies the indwelling Angle as a male hindrance, whereas she leaves the sex of the Celt within unspecified.

There's also a subtle connection, I think, between Coleridge's "Frost at Midnight" and Anne's poem "Our Sullen Art." Both are lyrical pieces that involve minute observation of the outer world—lyrics that seek to define ways in which the fruit of such observations can be translated into the human spirit and voice. "Frost at Midnight" is addressed to the poet's infant son, whom Coleridge imagines in years to come appreciating the sweetness of a variety of natural scenes:

Whether the summer clothe the general earth
With greenness, or the redbreast sit and sing
Betwixt the tufts of snow on the bare branch

Of mossy apple-tree, while the nigh thatch
Smokes in the sun-thaw; whether the eave-drops fall
Heard only in the trances of the blast,
Or if the secret ministry of frost
Shall hang them up in silent icicles,
Quietly shining to the quiet Moon.[11]

For Coleridge, what will give the boy's imagination space to grow and develop is a life in nature. The poet looks forward to the way his son will interpret the divine through the minuscule splendours of the natural world. Nature fused with the imagination will bring him joy.

In "Our Sullen Art," Anne also imagines the birth of poetry through the eyes and ears of a young boy. But in her poem, the child is a rebel who has climbed onto the roof of a shed and called out "ha ha and who's the dirty rascal now?"—an obscure sort of crime, for which he's despatched to his room as punishment. It's not winter, as in Coleridge's poem, but high summer; and as midnight approaches, the boy

leans from his window listening for animals
far away in the woods strains his ears to catch
even the slightest sound of rage but nothing howls
even the hoot of owls in the dusk is gentle

he hears the tiny snarl of the shrew
the rasp of the snail's foot on the leaf
the too-high squeaking of bats...[12]

And so on. Coleridge, in "Frost at Midnight," recalls the wild pleasure he took as a boy in the sound of church bells, "falling on mine ear / Most like articulate sounds of things to come." And then he slept. In "Our Sullen Art" the boy listens to the small, articulate sounds of night before he too falls asleep. At the conclusion of the poem Anne evokes "the day's first traffic," something Coleridge never had to contend with, travelling carefully past the house "so as not to awaken in the child / those savage cries our violent / our pathetic language of poems." But that language will inevitably develop, in just the way that Coleridge says in "Frost at Midnight" his son's spirit will grow, thanks to what the child has seen and heard, the attention he has paid to nature.

So much for Coleridge. As far as I know, Anne never spoke about Emerson, so I'm aware of treading on very thin ice in suggesting there may have been a direct link. But I recently had occasion to read his essay "The Poet," and I was astonished by what I found. The Transcendentalist belief in nature and the imagination, of course, grew straight out of the Romantic movement that had flourished a generation or two earlier. For Emerson, and I hope you'll be willing to forgive the male-centred language that was so widespread in the nineteenth century, "The poet is the sayer, the namer, and represents beauty. He is a sovereign, and stands on the centre."[13] Emerson described language as "fossil poetry" and "a tomb of the muses,"[14] because each of its myriad words started life as a stroke of writerly genius. Without poets, we would have no words.

Emerson also insisted, as Anne would a century and a half later, that "it is not metres, but a metre-making argument that makes a poem,—a thought so passionate and alive that like the spirit of a plant or an animal it has an architecture of its own, and adorns nature with a new thing."[15] And just as William Blake had described the body as an emanation of the spirit, so did Emerson assert that "The Universe is the externization of the soul."[16] To quote a particularly remarkable passage from this essay:

> The poet alone knows astronomy, chemistry, vegetation and animation, for he does not stop at these facts, but employs them as signs. He knows why the plain or meadow of space was strown with those flowers we call suns and moons and stars; why the great deep is adorned with animals, with men, and with gods; for in every word he speaks he rides on them as the horses of thought.[17]

Anne's third book, *Doctrine of Signatures*, derives both its name and its guiding principle from the herbal doctrine that certain plants function as signs in nature so as to resemble organs of the human body. Plants, not just people, have signatures—"a world in the shape of an egg," she wrote, "lies in the palm of the hand."[18] The egg, the world, the hand: all are waiting to be transformed and made sacred by the imagination—because poetry, in another of Emerson's beautiful definitions, is "God's wine."[19] Whether or not Anne was familiar with his great essay (and I suspect she was), I would argue that Transcendentalist beliefs underlie, illuminate and perhaps intoxicate much of what she wrote.

Now, following this lengthy digression, let's return to Anne Szumigalski just after she had immigrated to Saskatchewan in the early 1950s, leaving behind a large family and a promising future as a British poet. For four years she lived with her husband and their young children in the Big Muddy badlands, south of Regina near the US border. Anne remembered it as a land "of salt lakes and desert and rolling boulder-strewn prairie. Only in the green coulees are there songbirds, for that is where the trees grow.... Life was hard and isolated. Some of our neighbours still lived in sod huts or even in basements with roofs of turf. Once we tried to race a prairie fire while we were driving into town; it easily beat our sixty miles an hour."[20]

It was, she said, "wonderful country." One day, "when walking under a sky clear and blue as water, I saw a small white cloud floating rapidly across the emptiness. It slowed down. And as I gazed at it a bolt of lightning came out of the cloud and hit the prairie. I could almost see the hand of Old Nobodaddy throwing down his fiery spear." (You'll notice the Blakean reference.) "I took this to be a command to go on writing my poetry, something I had neglected for the last few years, for though I heard it resonating in my head all the time I had not written it down. I started with a pencil and notebook. Then I bought a crotchety little typewriter from a neighbour who didn't know why he had wanted it in the first place. I was on my way, and my poems with me."[21]

There's something very special and magical about the landscape of that region, even more than many other parts of western Canada. It can provoke the most amazing responses even from casual visitors. One day, a few summers ago, I drove back to a place I'd written about in prose many years earlier: the fading First Nations petroglyphs outside the dwindling town of St. Victor, not far west of the Big Muddy. It's a profoundly evocative site, silent except for occasional fragments of birdsong and for the wind slipping across the ancient, art-encrusted rocks. The park doesn't contain any modern toilets, just a couple of outhouses. And in the men's outhouse, I found the following piece of graffiti: "We use the illusion of time to frighten off the illusion of death—Wittgenstein."

In what I've said so far, I've probably given the impression that the young Anne Szumigalski was a very English writer. So she was, and would always remain, in the sense of having been steeped in the language and the literature of Britain. But as soon as her plane touched down in Montreal and she boarded the train west, Anne was keen to become something different. Thanks to her reading, her imagination had set to work. Leaving Winnipeg behind, she murmured under her breath two lines from Roy Daniells: "Farewell to Winnipeg, the snow-bright city / Set in the prairie distance without bound."[22] Arriving in Saskatchewan, she already knew her Duncan Campbell Scott: "Gull Lake set in the rolling prairie— / Still there are reeds on the shore, / As of old the poplars shimmer . . . ."[23] "I was surprised and disappointed," Anne later wrote, "to discover that this was a country that did not know its own poets. In vain I might cry out names like Smith, Birney, Hertel, Choquette, Livesay. Canadians seemed to have been brought up in the conviction that there were no Canadian poets; they would counter feebly with Wordsworth, Tennyson, and (sometimes) Dylan Thomas."[24]

A country ignorant of its own literature. A spiritual colony. Such was the climate that faced Anne Szumigalski in the 1950s. She was ready for Canada. But was Canada ready for her? She would find the greater challenge to be posed not by her new neighbours on the Prairies but by the gatekeepers of Canadian poetry in distant eastern cities. Once she had settled in Saskatchewan, twenty-three years would elapse before her first book of poems appeared—and even then, that book would be published by Doubleday in New York. Not until Winnipeg's Turnstone Press issued her collection *A Game of Angels* in 1980 would she see a book of her own published by a Canadian firm. Thereafter Anne was loyal to Prairie publishers. Never did she send out a collection of poems to a company based in Toronto—or Montreal, Vancouver or Ottawa.

Going through Anne's papers, I began to realize what a bitter struggle she endured as a poet during those first years in Canada. Living in the Big Muddy, her isolation was extreme; even when she moved to Saskatoon she could not hope to join a literary community, for the simple reason that no such thing existed. Most of the infrastructure of the Prairie imagination, so to speak, had yet to be built. I found the same scribbled note at the top of several unpublished poems: "Sent in for lit. competition. No luck." I also found a few poems that eventually had been published in faraway magazines like *Canadian Forum* and *The Fiddlehead* under the name "A. Szumigalski"—in those days, women stood a better chance of literary success if they didn't announce their sex to editors. One of A. Szumigalski's poems appeared in the same issue of *Canadian Forum* as a youthful lyric by somebody who went by the name "M. Atwood." Most galling, perhaps, were three issues of the magazine *Delta*, edited by Louis Dudek at McGill University in Montreal, where A. Szumigalski published poems in 1961.

On the first two occasions, she did not feature in the contributors' notes at the back. The third time her work appeared in *Delta*, Anne was in the illustrious company of Earle Birney, John Glassco, the late Malcolm Lowry and several other distinguished poets. She would have enjoyed that; but she would not have been happy, I'm sure, to discover that although her poems each had a title, Dudek had added a patronizing overall title: "Two Songs From Saskatchewan." Earle Birney's poems did not receive the label "Songs From British Columbia." In this issue of Delta, some information about Anne did appear on the inside back cover. To quote the note in its entirety: "A. Szumigalski has brought so many enthusiastic comments that more information is in order. She is a woman. Owes her name to a Polish spouse; began life in London, England; has lived the last ten years in Canada's west. No relation to Sarah Binks."[25]

Sarah Binks—the fictional "Sweet Songstress of Saskatchewan," the supposed perpetrator of lines like "I know not what shall it betoken, / that I so sorrowful seem...."[26] Was Dudek being intentionally cruel? I assume he was just trying to be witty. But the effect, from what I can tell, was to silence Anne. She was writing poems, not songs, and I don't expect she liked to see the name of her chosen province used by Dudek as a backhanded insult. She would send no further poems to *Delta*. The ensuing years would bring few if any magazine publications. She was writing, she never stopped writing, yet her first collection still lay more than a decade in the future.

It might come as a surprise, if we pause and look back several decades, to realize just how few outlets then existed for poetry in this country. That first book of Anne's, *Woman Reading in Bath*, appeared in 1974, in the midst of a terrific burgeoning of literary magazines and book publishers. You could make a good argument that we're still living off the interest being earned by the poetic capital that was laid down in a brief and glorious period. A year earlier, in Saskatoon and Regina, the magazine *Grain* had sprung to life, with Anne serving as an associate editor from its inception. Right across the country, there were similar birth pangs. A partial list of the English-language literary magazines that arose in Canada between 1969 and 1976 would include *Grain, Ellipse, Salt, Descant, Antigonish Review, Event, Exile, Dandelion, Matrix, Room of One's Own*, CV/II and *NeWest Review*. Where would we be as poets, even today, without these magazines?

They were born in a spirit of great optimism, great faith in the potential of our literary culture. The future seemed wide open. To take but one example, Volume 1, Number 1 of CV/II was published in Winnipeg in the spring of 1975. Dorothy Livesay was the editor-in-chief. Here is a little of what she said in a long editorial:

> [A]gainst alienation and violence in our society and on the screen ... one positive force has held firm: the growth into maturity of the arts in Canada. Poetry is being nurtured in the outports as in the cities, and the strong flowering of this delight is what gives impetus to a magazine such as CV/II. Old and young alike are tasting its virtue. The response to poetry across Canada today is the response of a people longing for warmth and succour, a sense of community.
>
> So be it. We have our poetry, pushing up from every crack and cranny. What we now lack is sufficient outlets for serious criticism of it.[27]

Livesay's editorial took up page two of the infant magazine. Page three was given over to a glowing review of *Woman Reading in Bath*, in the course of which the reviewer praised what he described as "the tour de force involved in turning the Canada Post Office into an erotic symbol."[28]

But, of course, it wasn't only magazines that were pushing up like wildflowers. If we think of the book publishers that arose in English Canada during exactly the same period, 1969 to 1976, we find the following—and again, I fear this is but a partial list: Black Moss Press, Press Porcepic, Breakwater Books, Véhicule Press, Oolichan Books, Brick Books, The Porcupine's Quill, Coteau Books, Thistledown Press, Red Deer College Press, Turnstone Press and Exile Editions. The work of these publishers has allowed much of the lifeblood to course through Canadian poetry. And, like their magazine counterparts, they emerged at a particular moment in our history. One way of interpreting that moment would be to say the culture had finally caught up with Anne Szumigalski.

I want to go back to something Dorothy Livesay wrote in that first editorial for CV/II in 1975. She took delight in "the response to poetry across Canada today," something she regarded as "the response of a people longing for warmth and succour, a sense of community."[29] That might seem, in retrospect, excessively idealistic. But it strikes me that the institutions I've mentioned—the literary magazines, the book publishers, and also the various writers' guilds and unions and associations that accompanied them into life—were established at a time when poetry enjoyed a significant degree of respect in society at large. There was a confidence behind all these clamorous new journals and publishing firms, a confidence that our poets could speak to and speak for the nation. You might even say that if writers had faith in their dreams of Canada, Canada had faith in the dreams of its writers.

Not long ago I happened to come across an issue of the magazine *Quarry*, published in Kingston in March 1966,[30] a few years before the publishing explosion I've just described. *Quarry* had begun life at Queen's University in the 1950s, so it counts as an oldtimer. But what an astonishing array of talent it contained! The twenty-two-year-old Michael Ondaatje guest-edited the issue, which featured a cover by

Harold Town, three poems by Margaret Atwood, four by Gwendolyn MacEwen, five by John Newlove, and others by Doug Jones, Raymond Souster and Joe Rosenblatt, as well as a superb and fairly harsh review of Irving Layton written by Al Purdy. But, peering back from a span of over forty years, the parade of talent is not the only notable thing about the magazine. What staggers me is the support the merchants of Kingston showed for the written word.

In a magazine like *Quarry*, you might expect to find ads from the local university, a local bookstore and a few poetry publishers. You might not be surprised to find an ad from the local newspaper—although in 2007, given the miserable quality of most of our newspapers, you'd be in for disappointment. All those institutions did, in fact, advertise in *Quarry* in 1966. But so did the Hudson's Bay Company, whose ad took up a back cover and featured a poem by Gwendolyn MacEwen, "This Northern Mouth." Can you imagine Wal-Mart paying good money to advertise in a literary magazine today? Can you imagine Sears or Canadian Tire approving marketing copy with a poem at the heart? Even more impressive, to my mind, are the ads from Kingston businesses: Fashion Lane, Kinnear d'Esterre Diamond Merchants, Dover's Clothing Store, the local branch of Victoria and Grey Trust Company, McCormick's Hair Cutting Place, and so on.

In 1966, evidently, there was nothing odd in the idea that local businesses, from barbers to jewellers, had a responsibility to support literary culture, and that it might even prove economically worthwhile for them to do so. Poets and fiction writers who published in *Quarry* back then would not have suffered from the lingering fear that they were sending their work into a vacuum. The idea of imagining Canada—or, in most of the region where I now live, the idea of imagining Quebec—was nothing esoteric, nothing marginal, nothing academic. In a social and an individual sense alike, the imagination mattered.

To reiterate, I'm suggesting that Anne Szumigalski had her first book of poetry accepted and published at a rare moment of grace. When we compare the situation facing poets in the late 1960s and early '70s with the plight of poets who are starting out now, we realize how lucky today's writers are to live and work in a country where an abundance of literary magazines and book publishers can easily be taken for granted. Those journals and publishers exist in every region and every major city. Women poets no longer face the casual patronization, even discrimination that they used to suffer. The spoken word, not just the written text, is alive and well. The Canada Council for the Arts and many provincial counterparts perform superb work, often without thanks. Besides all of which, the Internet has created virtual communities and made possible new forms of poetry distribution that half a century ago were undreamt of. So far, so good.

The downside is that many of us now feel we're writing into a social vacuum. We are comprehensively neglected by the media, except on those rare occasions when prizes and nominations allow literature to be turned into a competitive sport. We are ignored by business, and we are accepted by the academy only insofar as we can be used for its own purposes. We now suffer a federal government that betrays contempt for the arts. Society in general takes so little notice of literature that we are entitled to wonder, at times, why we make the effort to write anything at all. I think it's fair to suggest that the questions "How can I publish?", "What can I publish?" and "Where can I publish?" that so preoccupied writers emerging in the 1950s and '60s, have diminished over time. What has supplanted them, growing ever louder and more worrying in the inner ear, is the nagging inquiry "Why should I bother to publish?"

I want to dispense with the rose-tinted glasses. Nostalgia for the literary climate of Canada in the late 1960s and early 1970s is no more productive than nostalgia for the acoustic folk-strains of Tom Paxton and Judy Collins. Time has moved on. The arts have fragmented. Above all, we have plunged into cyberspace. Looking to obtain a quick, subjective measure of poetry's place in the multifaceted realm of websites, chatrooms, newsgroups and blogs, I recently googled the name "Anne Szumigalski" and the name "Céline Dion." For the first, there were 848 hits. For the second, there were 3,130,000. That doesn't tell you everything you need to know about society's interest in poetry. But it gives you a pretty good idea. So is there any way to recapture a taste of that shared grace—what Dorothy Livesay called the "warmth and succour" of the wider community; the sense that poetry could matter, not just at gatherings like this one, but also in society at large?

That's far too big a question for me to answer in the few remaining minutes I have. So let me just hint at the response I'd want to develop.

We can't return to a time before the Internet and satellite tv. We can't tell young people to turn off the music on their iPods and listen instead to somebody reciting Coleridge or Emerson or Szumigalski. But we can start, I would suggest, by fostering their own love of words. I'm sure many of you have had the experience of leading a writing workshop in a high school where a well-meaning but burned-out teacher tells you not to expect much—whereupon the students go ahead and produce more work and better work than the teacher had imagined possible. And many of the students take such pleasure in the writing. They respond to a verbal challenge with intensity and shy delight. Yet for the young this can also be a fragile pleasure, and if we greet their work with a tactless "Why didn't you do this?" or "You should have done that," we can cause real harm.

We all know how essential it is to revise our work. But for teenagers, for anyone who is just discovering the joy of writing, revision is a difficult concept to get across. I used to think it was crucial to emphasize the idea that good writing involves hard work. Now I've come to believe it's even more crucial to let students experience the sheer pleasure of allowing language and imagination to roam free, without constraint. You never know how that pleasure will manifest itself and what rewards it might later bring.

When I was a teenager in the early 1970s, I was lucky enough to join the informal poetry workshop that Anne Szumigalski had helped to create in Saskatoon a few years earlier. We were a disparate bunch—a couple of professors, a hematologist, a few students, a few homemakers, a visual artist or two. For a while there was also an old farmer, Alf Bye, who used to drive up with his wife from the Swift Current area, a good three hours southwest of the city, just to attend the workshop meetings. I don't recall if his wife ever said a word. His poetry was the old-fashioned sort that most of us quietly sneered at—or even, I regret to say, not so quietly sneered at. He wrote about the prairies in sonorous rhyming couplets and florid blank verse that Tennyson would have considered old-fashioned.

At the time, I thought Alf Bye was an embarrassment. Now, decades later, I can begin to appreciate the man. He loved the English language, he needed to express his emotions, and he took genuine pride in the outmoded verse he produced. Why else would he have driven for hours to sit through meetings where he and his speechless wife must have felt terribly out of place? He had no understanding of modern literature—for him, T.S. Eliot was dangerously radical. But he loved poetry. Anne Szumigalski never made fun of the man. The rest of us were happy when he stopped coming to the meetings, but I'm not sure if Anne shared our relief. She understood both his isolation and his passion for language.

I think too of another gentleman in Saskatoon, George Porteous, who was serving as the province's lieutenant-governor at the time of his death in 1977. One day, having heard that I aspired to be a writer, he asked me how many poems I could recite by heart. Hardly any, I had to admit. I knew that George Porteous had been among the Canadian troops shipped out to Hong Kong in 1941, and I knew that he'd spent the next three and a half years in Japanese prisoner-of-war camps. But I didn't know that he was sustained there by his love of poetry. Every day, amid the squalor and brutality of the camps, he would recite long stretches of Kipling and Wordsworth and Shakespeare to himself. He told me that poetry was what kept him sane.

When I look back on Alf Bye and George Porteous, it occurs to me that somehow, we poets have lost a fair chunk of our essential story. We've misplaced the plot, if you like. Over the past thirty or forty years we have focused so hard on the desire to make our work perpetually new; we have become so suspicious of stale rhetoric; and we have wanted so much to disconnect ourselves from the styles and tropes of the past, that we've ended up isolating ourselves from the public. True, the public appears more than happy to ignore us; but I think we have colluded in our own abandonment. Now, without for a second retreating into florid blank verse, it's time that we imagined ways to reconnect.

On those high-school visits I mentioned a few minutes ago, I often ask the students who among them knows a poem by heart. It's a trick question, really. Almost never do I find more than one or two embarrassed adolescents lifting a tentative hand, usually thanks to "In

Flanders Fields." But then I ask how many people know the lyrics of a song by heart. And if they're not feeling too timid, most of the class end up raising their arms. What I then say, of course, is that they do know poems by heart, sometimes several dozen poems—they just don't think they do. The power of hip-hop derives from in-your-face rhyming. But teenagers seldom think of hip-hop and poetry in the same breath. They associate poetry with textbooks and exams, not with pleasure. I don't believe Anne Szumigalski would have loved poetry so fervently if she had been forced to study it in school.

Let's return, then, to the joy that lies at the root of our beloved craft and sullen art. Whatever style of writing we prefer, let's not be afraid to demonstrate the energy of language and the sterling power of imagination. Let's be willing to share our pleasure, whenever we can, with the young. And let's not scorn anyone who loves poetry, even if it's a kind of poetry we ourselves avoid. In brief, I would suggest, language still needs our imagining. It's a shame if we allow ourselves to get trapped in the vegetable realm. I wonder how many of us have seriously grappled with Blake's belief that the imagination is the real world, or with Emerson's faith that the universe is the soul externalized. Post-Einsteinian physics appears far more open to such ideas than conventional Newtonian physics, if only we have sufficient daring.

But even if we can't share such convictions, let's not get sidetracked by disputes about poetics, or by disillusionment about what poetry can reasonably be expected to accomplish. I suspect that we—and I include myself in this—have internalized the second part of W. H. Auden's great elegy in memory of William Butler Yeats, the part where Auden reminds us that "poetry makes nothing happen" and that it merely "survives, / A way of happening, a mouth." But we've neglected the third and final part of the poem, in which he declares that no matter how bleak conditions may be in the outer world, a poet can still persuade his or her listeners to rejoice. As the elegy concludes, Auden speaks directly to his fellow poets—speaks directly to you:

With the farming of a verse
Make a vineyard of the curse,
Sing of human unsuccess
In a rapture of distress;

In the deserts of the heart
Let the healing fountain start,
In the prison of his days
Teach the free man how to praise.[31]

Besides, I don't think Anne Szumigalski believed that "poetry makes nothing happen." She knew it had given her the angel of the woods.

Notes

1. "Afterword," *On Glassy Wings: Poems New and Selected* (Regina: Coteau Books, 1997), 209-210.
2. "The Angel of the Woods," lines 1–8. The handwritten text is preserved in the Anne Szumigalski papers, Archives and Special Collections, University of Regina.
3. "The Angel of the Woods," lines 72–79.
4. John Livingstone Clark, "Conversation With Anne Szumigalski," *Prairie Fire* 18.1 (spring 1997), 28.
5. For example in "Poems From the Notebook, 1793," *Complete Writings*, ed. Geoffrey Keynes (London: Oxford University Press, 1966), 185–6.
6. *Jerusalem*, Plate 77, *Complete Writings*, 717.
7. *The Marriage of Heaven and Hell*, Plate 3, *Complete Writings*, 149.
8. "Blake's White," *The Word, the Voice, the Text: The Life of a Writer* (Saskatoon: Fifth House, 1990), 102.
9. "Kubla Khan," *Selected Poetry and Prose of Coleridge*, ed. Donald A. Stauffer (New York: The Modern Library, 1953), 45.
10. "A House With a Tower," *A Game of Angels* (Winnipeg: Turnstone Press, 1980), 9.
11. "Frost at Midnight," *Selected Poetry and Prose of Coleridge*, 64.
12. "Our Sullen Art," *Doctrine of Signatures* (Saskatoon: Fifth House, 1983), 40.
13. "The Poet," *Essays: Second Series*, in *Essays and Lectures* (New York: Library of America, 1983), 449.
14. "The Poet," 457.
15. "The Poet," 450.
16. "The Poet," 452.

17 "The Poet," 456.
18 "Annwfn," *Doctrine of Signatures*, 72.
19 "The Poet," 460.
20 "Beginnings," *Salt* 12 (1974-5), 3.
21 "Afterword," *On Glassy Wings*, 212.
22 "Farewell to Winnipeg," *The Oxford Book of Canadian Verse in English and French*. Chosen and with an introduction by A.J.M. Smith (Toronto: Oxford University Press, 1960), 205.
23 "At Gull Lake: August, 1810," *The Oxford Book of Canadian Verse in English and French*, 98.
24 "Beginnings," *Salt*, 3.
25 The *Delta* issues in question are no. 15 (Aug. 1961), no. 16 (Nov. 1961) and no. 17 (Jan. 1962).
26 Paul Hiebert, "The Laurel's Egg" in *Sarah Binks* (Toronto: Oxford University Press, 1947), 29.
27 CV/II 1.1 (spring 1975), 2.
28 G.V. Downes, review of *Woman Reading in Bath*, CV/II (spring 1975), 3.
29 Livesay, CV/II, 2.
30 *Quarry* 15.3.
31 W.H. Auden, "In Memory of W.B. Yeats," *Collected Shorter Poems 1927-1957* (London: Faber and Faber, 1966), 143.

Ediacaran and Anthropocene:
poetry as a reader of deep time
DON MCKAY

Anne Szumigalski Lecture • St. John's, Newfoundland • June 21, 2008

TWO NEW DEVELOPMENTS IN THE TAXONOMY OF TEMPORALity provide the focus for this discussion. One is the official recognition of a new, and very old, geologic period—the Ediacaran, now understood to occupy the stretch of deep time between 575 and 542 million years ago, directly preceding the Cambrian, with its remarkable radiation of life forms. This recognition has been precipitated by the discovery, dating, and analysis of thirty or so species representing an entirely new biota in the fossil record, the earliest animals on the planet. The other wrinkle in our idea of time involves the proposal to name, or re-name, the current epoch after the species which has been most responsible for its character and style, as well as the content of most of its narratives. "The Anthropocene," if accepted, would acknowledge ourselves as the superstars we have been for some time.

After its artful colon, the title divulges the unusual approach that I propose to take. My inspiration for this notion—reading elements in deep time poetically—comes from an unlikely source. It is in fact a geologist, Harry Hess, who coins the handy term "geopoetry," a term that will certainly serve to identify the path I'm attempting to follow here. Hess was one of the researchers whose work led to the breakthrough understanding of plate tectonics, the crucial concept of a dynamic planet which revolutionized earth sciences in the 1960s. He described his speculations as geopoetry in order to induce his readers (mostly other geologists) to suspend their disbelief long enough for his observations about seafloor spreading, driven by magma rising continuously from the mantle, to catch on. He needed his audience, in the absence of much hard data, to speculate imaginatively, as if reading poetry. Now that so much evidence is in, and no one disbelieves in plate tectonics any more (at least no one who does not also disbelieve in evolution), the term might be allowed to lapse, a marriage of convenience whose *raison d'être* has evaporated. But, as you can see, I don't think it ought to be. I think that Harry Hess, like Charles Darwin, Albert Einstein, or any other creative scientist, enters a mental space beyond ordinary analysis, where conjecture and imaginative play are needed and legitimate, and that this is a mental space shared with poets. But even more than this poetic licence, I would say, the practice of geopoetry promotes astonishment as part of the acceptable perceptual frame. Geopoetry makes it legitimate for the natural historian or scientist to speculate and gawk, and equally legitimate for the poet to benefit from close observation, and from some of the amazing facts that science turns up. It provides a crossing point, a bridge over the infamous gulf separating scientific from poetic frames of mind, a gulf which has not served us well, nor the planet we inhabit with so little reverence or grace. Geopoetry, I am tempted to say, is the place where materialism and mysticism, those ancient enemies, finally come together, have a conversation in which each hearkens to the other, then go out for a drink. This may not lead to marriage or even cohabitation, but I'm guessing it does lead to a series of dates, trysts, rendezvous, and other encounters whose mood is erotic rather than simply disputatious.

First, the Ediacaran period. The first new period to be introduced to the geologic time scale in 120 years, it is, as Dr. Guy Narbonne has said, equal in importance to the discovery of a new planet in the solar system. The International Union of Geological Sciences has taken this measure because the fossils from the period, pre-dating those of the Burgess Shale, open an entirely unread chapter in the history of life. Ediacaran sites are rare, since these animals (or, some suggest, these members of an entirely new kingdom as yet unknown to taxonomy) were soft-bodied creatures without the shells and hard body armour which make arthropods like trilobites common in the fossil record. As is usual in the naming of geologic periods, the name derives from a site where the index fossils or strata are found. So the Jurassic period derives its name from the Jura region in Switzerland, the Permian from the city of Perm in Russia, the Cambrian from Cambria, or Wales. Ediacara is in Southern Australia, where these fossils were first discovered, but some of the world's best examples are at Mistaken Point, on the southern tip of the Avalon Peninsula in Newfoundland. In fact there are a few examples of the species known as *Aspidella terranovica* in downtown St. John's on an outcrop kitty-corner from Tim Hortons. As an aside, I wish to observe, as a would-be geopoet, that it is too bad the Mistaken Point fossils were not discovered, or recognized for what they were, before those in Australia, since it would be a splendid moment in the annals of taxonomies to have a period called the Mistaken Pointarean. The name would carry an implicit awareness of its own instability, a fine thing in a name, if you ask me. Mistaken Pointarean would also be appropriate, perhaps, because these creatures seem to have survived a mere 50 million years, an eye-blink in deep time, and only something like 49 and three quarters million years longer than our own distinguished genus. I intend to circulate a petition asking the International Union of Geological Sciences to make this change in the interests of poeticizing the nomenclature. At the very least, the tourist board of Newfoundland and Labrador should support the move, aiming to reap some of the tourist dollars no doubt enjoyed by the likes of Jura and Perm.

If you were to travel as a geopoet-in-training to Mistaken Point to see these remarkable fossils, you would also see the beautiful barrens of the South Avalon on your hike into the site. These barrens—themselves a candidate for renaming by poetry—are only bare if your idea of flora excludes everything under four feet high. The carpet of vegetation over these windswept heaths is an interwoven mat of crowberry, partridgeberry, cranberry, juniper, sheep laurel, bottle brush and Labrador Tea, with sporadic groves of tuckamore dotted here and there. Horned Larks and Water Pipits materialize out of this carpet, lift over a rise and disappear, an occasional Merlin hunts from the four-foot pinnacle of a stunted fir. Everything knows how to be low, how to hug the rock and hunch against the wind. By the time you get to Mistaken Point, you will have already grown accustomed to looking down and looking closely, especially if it happens to be foggy, which is likely. You will also, probably, have had enough experience being buffeted by wind to appreciate the ecosystem's preference for a horizontal lifestyle.

The fossils are printed (although 'embossed' would be the more appropriate equivalent to the geologists' 'epirelief') on flat tilted beds of sedimentary rock right next to the sea. Some of them resemble ostrich feathers, some resemble elongated spindles, some—*Bradgatia*—are bushy. One of the Ediacarans, an unusually long frond called *Charnia wardi*, has been named after the Ward family from nearby Portugal Cove South. It was Catherine Ward and her son Brad who, having spotted two Americans trying to steal specimens from the fossil beds using a diamond saw, blockaded the road and called the RCMP. And it was Brad (who is now a geophysicist) who found the best example of the species that now carries the family name. *Charnia wardi* has since proven to be the oldest complex organism (that is, multi-celled) in the fossil record, and the tallest of the Ediacarans.

Like all fossils, the Ediacarans are, in Christopher Dewdney's phrase, "pure memory," and seem to call, life form to life form, across 575 million years of evolution and geological transformation. It's as though the usually mute siltstone were sending semiotic signals. These animals (or 'animals') were soft-bodied stalks, connected to the ocean floor by hold-fasts, like kelp, living a life perhaps similar to today's jellyfish. It has been speculated by some scientists that they may have existed in a symbiotic relationship with primitive plants, perhaps as a plant-animal hybrid. They preyed on no other creature and, it seems, were not preyed upon themselves. Because of this, the period has been nicknamed The Garden of Ediacara by Mark McMenamin—apparently existing before predation, when symbiosis rather than predation was the order of the day. And, it also seems, they perished abruptly after 50 million years, when some creatures developed the canny notion—which has held sway ever since—that a quick way to nourish yourself is to eat somebody else. That, for the Garden of Ediacara, would have been the equivalent to the Fall. Enter the era of claws and shells.

Listening in on such geopoetry—as, in the spirit of Harry Hess, I venture to call it—one feels one's thinking stretch as it takes on these remote possibilities. That stretch is, I think, not only epistemological (having to do with knowing) but ontological; it involves wonder at the manifold possibilities of being in general, and these beings in particular. Within a purely rational or analytical context such theories crave closure, desire to resolve into fact. The poetic frame permits the possible (I'm thinking of the sense in which Richard Kearney develops the concept) to be experienced as a power rather than a deficiency; it permits the imagination entry, finding wider resonances, leading us to contemplate further implications for ourselves. For although we are palpably here, our presence is no less a remote possibility in the long accident-riddled course of evolution than is that of the *Charnia wardi* and other Ediacarans embossed on the rock.

Today, at Mistaken Point, you can caress the rock with your finger and read their unreadable lines like Braille. You can trace the line between the fossil-bearing siltstone and the petrified volcanic ash which, ironically enough, both killed and preserved them, their assassin and archivist. These particular creatures were living off the coast of Gondwana when the volcano erupted, sending a cloud of ash high into the air, to be carried over the ocean. (Think of the extent of the fallout from Mount St. Helen's.) Eventually the ash particles settled into the water, smothering the Ediacarans under a soft grey cushion. Here and there in the ash layer (now a thin gritty black film) you can see bits of pink feldspar which crystallized out of the magma in the original eruption. You might have the sense, as I have had, that the fossils have been unveiled, as though some intentional hand were eroding the ash to reveal the beautiful fronds and disks beneath. Heidegger's term for beauty, *unconcealment* or *aletheia*, seems almost literally enacted by geologic forces. It even seems as though the slab on which they appear had been pulled from the other strata on the adjacent cliff like a drawer pulled open in a morgue for the corpse to be identified—an image that no doubt springs to mind due to my unhealthy predilection for cop shows, where it is a mandatory scene. If you're lucky—very lucky—it's sunny, and it's evening, so the slant light emphasizes the slight rise of the figures from the rock (their epirelief) and calls them to special eloquence, along with the deep nostalgia that dusk always lends its subjects. Pure memory. It is 570 million years ago on the other side of the Iapetus Ocean, an ocean that by the end of the Palaeozoic will have closed like a slow gigantic wink, along the continental shelf of Gondwana, the parent continent of both Africa and the Avalon Peninsula. Slim creatures sway at different heights in the tide, giving and taking from the water, existing in a world without predators. It is also, say, a Tuesday in September on the southern tip of the Avalon; the sun is setting; you'd better get going if you want to reach your car before dark.

In a geopoetic experience, like the imagined field trip to Mistaken Point, both elements, the 'geo' and the poetic, give something, and both, I think, inhibit or counteract a tendency in their partner. I am thinking here, as may be obvious, of a simpler version of the complex interrelations between members of a symbiosis. Geology, or broadly speaking natural history of any kind, brings the rigour of the scientific frame; poetry brings the capacity for astonishment and the power of possibility—or, perhaps more accurately, legitimizes them. Geology inhibits the tendency, most common in romantic poets, to translate the immediate perception into an emotional condition, which is then admired or fetishized in preference to the original phenomenon—fossil, bird, lichen or landform. For its part, poetry cultivates the astonishment that naturally occurs in the presence of such marvels. As Adam Zagajewski says, poetry allows us "to experience astonishment and to stop in that astonishment for a long moment or two." By doing so it counteracts the tendency, perhaps most common in scientists in the grip of triumphalist technology, to reduce objects of contemplation to quanta of knowledge. Astonishment, humbling our pride in technique, impedes its progress into exploitation and appropriation. In the astonished condition, the other remains other, wilderness remains wild. Robert Hass, in *Time and Materials*, makes a cogent observation, which speaks to Zagajewski's idea of poetry. Interestingly, for the would-be geopoets among us, Hass writes these lines in response to an old lava field:

> It must be a gift of evolution that humans
> Can't sustain wonder. We'd never have gotten up
> From our knees if we could.

Hass makes a good point here, fine, contemplative nature poet that he is. If we could sustain wonder, we'd probably all have been devoured by sabre-toothed tigers long before *homo erectus* could evolve into *homo sapiens*; we'd be gawking at the marvel of the hairy mammoths and neglect entirely to slip our clever clovis-pointed spears between their massive ribs.

Nevertheless, speaking as a human existing in the outflow of the scientific revolution, living in a period of technological mania, I can't help but feel that we would have benefitted from spending more time on our knees, rapt, attending to the being of the other rather than classifying, analyzing, controlling, exploiting, and generally rendering the world as standing reserve available for our use. This is one of the ways in which poetry—any poetry—is always political and subversive: it uses our foremost technological tool, the ur-tool that is language, against itself, against its tendency to be the supreme analytic and organizing instrument. In poetry, language is always a singer as well as a thinker; a lover as well as an engineer. It discovers and delights in its own physical being, as though it were an otter or a raven rather than simply the vice president in charge of making sense.

Well, perhaps my characterization of the geological and poetic elements as symbionts is more of a hope than an observation, a self-serving attempt on my own part to integrate diverse bits of my cluttered life. But it does seem worthwhile to entertain the possibility that the two elements may, at least in isolated instances, feed, and feed upon, one another, and not just inhibit their respective excesses. When the intense experience of poetry, that momentary lyric peak, diminishes, we can turn to a more empirical attitude with a trace or memory of it persisting in our approach. The afterlife of wonder might well persist as a spirit animating the frame of knowledge. And likewise, the thirst to know, which has since Aristotle been recognized as fundamental to human sensibility, might be understood as an accelerant to poetic attention, rather than—as is usual—an aesthetic turn-off. The impact of the Ediacaran fossils is not diminished by a recognition of their place in the evolution of early life of the planet. In fact, I venture to think that such scientific reflections may serve to extend the condition of wonder from its peak epiphany into everyday existence. We might find it spreading from exceptional instances, like a trip to Mistaken Point, to the nondescript rock in my back yard, which turns out to have travelled here from its birthplace in a volcano on the continent that became today's Africa.

This brings us, with more of a lurch than a glide, to the second time period named in the title, the Anthropocene Epoch. The Anthropocene has been proposed, though not yet officially recognized by the International Union of Geological Sciences, as the name for the epoch in which we are now living, an epoch characterized by the profound effect on the earth's systems of one species—*anthropos*, us. If generally accepted it would succeed the Holocene, the epoch which has extended from the ice ages (the Pleistocene) to the present. The date proposed for its onset differs from thinker to thinker, some placing it at the industrial revolution, others spotting the writing on the wall as early as the discoveries of agriculture or fire. Whatever the starting point, it is judged that the innovative technologies of *anthropos*—levelling forests, making cities, producing networks of roads, eliminating some species and domesticating others—have altered the workings of the planet's cycles in a way analogous to an ice age or a collision with an asteroid. Most tellingly, we've been digging up fossilized organisms and burning them, effectively turning earthbound carbon into atmospheric carbon, drastically altering the climate, as has occurred at other times in the earth's history when a greenhouse effect has come about from other causes. As Dean Young—not someone you might think of as an environmental poet—puts it, "Somehow/ we've managed to ruin the sky/ just by going about our business,/ I in my super XL, you in your Discoverer." Writing, prophetically, in 1973, Christopher Dewdney observed that the effect of all the highways and associated fossil fuel emissions would be a kind of renaissance for the old Mesozoic atmosphere in which the plants originally grew.

The philosopher Emmanuel Levinas has given us a definition of European culture which resonates, in a sinister way, with the naming of the new epoch. "Culture," he says, "can be interpreted as an intention to remove the *otherness* of Nature, which, alien and previous, surprises and strikes the immediate identity which is the same of the human self." As an intention which converts the otherness of nature into the sameness of humanity, Levinas's culture sounds alarmingly like Calgary, eating its way steadily toward the Rockies, converting foothills into dismal suburbs of itself. It is against such reduction to the Same that poetry works, introducing otherness, or wilderness, into consciousness without insisting that it be turned wholly into knowledge, into what we know, what we own. Within poetic attention, we might say, what we behold is always "alien and previous," whether it's an exceptional fossil or an "ordinary" rock or chickadee. In poetry there is no "been there, done that"; everything is wilderness. The arrival of the Anthropocene would be an acknowledgement that the intention of culture, as Levinas sees it, has been all too richly realized, that there is little hope for an other that remains other, for wilderness that remains wild. It implicitly acknowledges that there will be no epoch called the Gaiacene, even though the concept was developed and maintained during the last century. In fact, the author of the concept, James Lovelock, is among the least optimistic of the earth scientists contemplating climate change.

Now, there actually is a way that culture has addressed nature during the last two centuries that is not exploitive or consumptive, at least on the surface, and that is Romanticism. Surely this must be reckoned a good thing, since it does not lead, like technology, to a reduction of the natural to either raw material or product. This is true. But Romanticism (of course, I am indulging in a lavish generalization) preserves the other not by respecting its otherness, but by welcoming it into the Same as a form of humanism. Nature as the kindly, pedagogical nurse in Wordsworth's poetry leads us to hear, not some "alien and previous" harmonies but the "still, sad music of humanity." No less than the technological mindset, Romanticism converts the other into the Same of the human self, but by a soft and seductive path, the generous extension of citizenship rather than violent reduction to utility.

One thinks of certain Americans who praise our national character by announcing, generously, that it is the same as theirs.

I was struck afresh, recently, by the famous stolen boat passage from Wordsworth's *The Prelude*. You probably recall it, but let me summon it to mind in some detail, since it raises, quite insightfully, I think, the issue of wilderness, or the unassimilable otherness of the other. As he remembers it, Wordsworth 'borrowed' a boat one evening and rowed out on Lake Windermere, getting far enough from shore that the perspective altered and a distant peak, occluded when closer in, suddenly loomed.

> ... The huge cliff
> Rose up between me and the stars, and still
> With measur'd motion, like a living thing
> Strode after me.

Panicked, he beat a hasty retreat back to shore and, in the days following, was deeply troubled, for it was not the usual contact with Nature, which, as mentor and pedagogue, guided his development in humanistic ways. He had suddenly experienced wilderness-as-other, remorseless and terrifying. Of course, there is always a touch of terror in the experience of the sublime, but the young Wordsworth had received an overdose, and it would leave him at a loss to bring it into harmony with his earlier understanding of Nature:

> ... and after I had seen
> That spectacle, for many days, my brain
> Worked with a dim and undetermin'd sense
> Of unknown modes of being; in my thoughts
> There was a darkness, call it solitude
> Or blank desertion, no familiar shapes
> Of hourly objects, images of trees
> Of sea or sky, no colours of green fields;
> But huge and mighty forms that do not live
> Like living men mov'd slowly through my mind
> By day and were the trouble of my dreams.

In this wonderful passage, the scrim of humanism is torn aside, to be replaced by unknown modes of being, huge and mighty forms that do not live like living men. The experience has revealed the wilderness lurking, like the distant peak, behind and within the idea of Nature, not only resisting the domesticating power of mind (refusing to become the same of culture) but indeed going on the offensive—pursuing, watching, troubling his dreams. Recall Margaret Atwood's query of the lady beholding the apparently innocent relief map of Canada: "Do you see nothing/ watching you from under the water?"

It is interesting to speculate, from a Canadian point of view, on what might have occurred to the young Wordsworth had he been unable to escape that wilderness experience, but been forced to live within it. What if he'd had to live with the "alien and previous" other rather than a Nature that endorsed human values? Well, I think Earle Birney provides the answer in his classic poem "Bushed," a poem that identifies the psychosis we have come to recognize as the consequence of an overdose of wilderness overwhelming the European consciousness. It is notable not only as a cautionary tale for all crypto-Wordsworthians, and not only because of its toothed imagery and curt music, but also because it articulates a crucial ambiguity at the heart of this breakdown. Is Birney's Romantic protagonist, having had his illusions about the sublime wrecked by the alien wilderness, about to become a nutcase or to enter the state of privileged consciousness that we would call—were we Native Americans rather than displaced Europeans—shamanistic? Birney doesn't say:

>   then he knew   though the mountain slept   the winds
>   were shaping its peak to an arrowhead
>   poised
>
>   And now he could only
>   bar himself in and wait
>   for the great flint to come singing into his heart.

For geopoetry to work, then, it must avoid Romantic humanism, despite its considerable uplift and charm, and acknowledge the alien and previous character of the wilderness up front. The astonishment of poetry is right next door to being petrified—as the young Wordsworth and Birney's protagonist discovered. Wilderness does not endorse us as humans; it includes us as mammals.

Entering the Anthropocene, it seems, places our gifted but difficult species in a spotlight. At one time—the Enlightenment—such a focus seemed the illumination that relieved an oppressive darkness, enabling humankind to know itself and exercise fully its intellectual capacities. Now that spotlight may be more analogous to the headlight in which the deer is caught. But despite the dire events and portents that led to it, news of which assaults us daily, I believe there is a positive side to the nomination of the Anthropocene. All poets take naming seriously, aware that such baptisms into language carry enormous potential power. Language is, as John Steffler observed in his recent E.J. Pratt lecture, the first technology which we, the technological animals, have developed; it is the technology upon which all others depend. Naming might be said to be its first move in the conversation of the "alien and previous" into the familiar, accessible and manipulable Same. But the naming of the Anthropocene differs from others in at least two ways. One is that it is partly a negative recognition. Usually, if you get something named after yourself, or you name an organism, like *Charnia wardi*, after its discoverers and stewards, it's an honour. In the case of the Anthropocene, naming is an acknowledgement of responsibility and, in some measure, guilt. Although I do not rule out the possibility that there are folk out there cheering the advent of the epoch as a victory for our side, maybe even in some perverse way the material triumph of humanism, most will regard it as an act akin to naming atrocity atrocity or genocide genocide. Negative recognition, as with the familiar practice at AA meetings of identifying yourself as an alcoholic when you rise to speak, can become empowering. Among the recent works of Canadian poets in this vein, I would cite Dennis Lee's remarkable books *un* and *yesno*, with their torqued contorted technospeak, as well as Pierre Nepveu's *Mirabel*, which brings poetry to witness the replacement of a pastoral landscape with a useless airport.

The second thing I have to say about the naming of the Anthropocene, and the last item in this *breccia* of an essay, regards its function as an entry point into deep time. If we think of ourselves as living in the Anthropocene Epoch, we realign our notion of temporal dwelling. Generally, time is viewed in relation to humanity's place in it, and consists of a present, where we live, and a recent past called history, which is felt to be important for informing the present and helping us understand ourselves better. When we speak of the past with reverence or chagrin, it is this shallow past we mean. Before history there is a vague distant past called prehistory, comprised of a jumble of relics and catastrophes, dinosaur bones mixed with clovis points, missing links, Lucy and The Flintstones cohabiting in the caves of Lascaux, Australopithecus confused with archaeopteryx, and the whole melange construed as a sort of amniotic stew from which we, the Master Species, miraculously emerged. The name "Anthropocene," paradoxically enough, puts a crimp in this anthropocentrism, making the present a temporal unit among other epochs, periods and eras. If we think backward from the Anthropocene we encounter, like rungs on a ladder, the Holocene, the Pleistocene, Pliocene and Miocene epochs—and by this point there are no humans around, or even representatives of the *homo* genus—and we realize that the ladder extends back through periods and eras to the Ediacaran, and that even at this point we've covered only half a billion of the planet's four and a half billion years. On the one hand, we lose our special status as Master Species; on the other, we become members of deep time, along with trilobites and Ediacaran organisms. We gain the gift of de-familiarization, becoming other to ourselves, one expression of the ever-evolving planet. Inhabiting deep time imaginatively, we give up mastery and gain mutuality.

Some Sources

Atwood, Margaret. "At the Tourist Centre in Boston." First published in *The Animals in That Country* (Toronto: Oxford University Press, 1968).

Birney, Earle. "Bushed." *The Collected Poems of Earle Birney* (Toronto: McClelland & Stewart, 1975).

Bjonerud, Marcia. *Reading the Rocks: The Autobiography of the Earth* (New York: Basic Books, 2006).

Dewdney, Christopher. "Sol du Soleil." *Predators of the Adoration: Selected Poems, 1972–1982* (Toronto: McClelland & Stewart, 1983).

Hass, Robert. "State of the Planet." *Time and Materials: Poems 1997–2005* (New York: Ecco, 2007).
Levinas, Emmanuel. "The Philosophical Determination of the Idea of Culture." *Entre Nous: Thinking-of-the-Other* (New York: Columbia University Press, 2000).
Stanley, Steven M. *Earth System History* (New York: W.H. Freeman, 2004).
Wordsworth, William. *The Prelude* (1805).
Young, Dean. "My People." *Skid* (Pittsburgh: University of Pittsburgh Press, 2002).
Zagajewski, Adam. *Another Beauty*. Trans. Clare Kavanagh (New York: Farrar, Straus & Giroux, 2000).

Thanks to the staff at the Interpretation Centre in Portugal Cove South, especially Richard Thomas and Julie Cappleman, to Paul Dean at the Johnson Geocentre, and to provincial palaeontologist Doug Boyce. All have been very helpful and informative. Such foolish errors and extrapolations as appear are my own doing.

Re-Discovering Ancient Springs
a consideration of metaphorical space

MARILYN BOWERING

Anne Szumigalski Lecture • *Vancouver, British Columbia* • *June 13, 2009*

I

IT WAS SPRING AND IT WAS RAINING WHEN I BEGAN TO WRITE this talk. The creek that runs through the back of my yard on Vancouver Island was swollen, islanding the thin alders that grow along its banks. I'd been listening on the radio to news of the rising of the Red River in Manitoba. The Red River meanders over an enormous, flat, ancient lakebed and when there is heavy rain and snowmelt the river rises and the ancient lake begins to refill. This is a natural and predictable phenomenon but knowing so brings no comfort to those whose houses were flooded this spring, just as it brought none to my parents, in 1950, when eight of the city dikes failed and the region returned to its nature, and our house on the banks of the Seine River, a tributary of the Red, filled with water. When the waters retreated, the first floor was covered in mud, a replication of the process that began with the laying down of sediment when the glacier that created the ancient lakebed and lake first began to withdraw. I have a photograph of the house, taken from the sandbags that failed to protect it, showing the graceful reflections of trees in the water, and the storage shed, on slightly higher ground, in which my mother had gathered her most precious belongings. The shed was flooded, too, and when my father returned, ahead of us, to start the clean up, he had to burn all that remained to my mother of her mother—a chest of documents, photographs, keepsakes—along with my mother's wedding dress. My mother was disconsolate: she felt she'd been left with nothing that was hers, nothing to pass on of the world and people who had made her.

I was very small, a year old, during the flood of 1950, but I remember looking up at my parents as they moved the refrigerator and wrestled it with ropes onto the first floor landing, and I remember looking out the window from the kitchen table and seeing our neighbours outside, near the back door, paddling a canoe. This image stuck, perhaps, because the neighbours landed at our porch and took my father and brother onboard while I, unjustly, was made to remain behind with my mother. We watched them paddle away through the smooth waters towards the faster moving current of the river itself, and my mother's anxiety over their direction filled my body. In the last of these memories I am looking out through the dark windshield of a truck, from my mother's lap, as we embark on the dangerous crossing of the last bridge open over the Red River. The truck's headlights shine on water, silky surging water and nothing else.

Possibly I remember these moments because they contained new, intense feelings of curiosity and excitement; but mostly I recall the shock—both exhilarating and overwhelming—at finding the well-known transformed. The immense stretch of water that floated the shacks and sheds and chicken and pigpens of the riverbank yards felt oddly familiar: yet when I looked at it I did not feel like myself: all sense of myself disappeared. When I stared into the narrow streams of light on water from the truck, I was gazing, in fact, at a lake first formed more than 10,000 years ago, and that had been waiting every moment of my short life to make its reappearance.

II

The Flood and its images and symbols and connections has appeared and reappeared in my poetry from my first pamphlet, *The Liberation of Newfoundland* (1973), to the present. The second poem in the collection, which is set beside a reproduction of the photograph of our islanded Seine Street house, is a re-statement of the elemental theory of the pre-Socratic philosopher, Thales, who lived in Miletus on the Ionian coast (now western Turkey) around 624 BC. The foundation of all things, and of change, is water, he said—an idea that, as we continue to explore the universe and its origins, remains significant. Water is key to all forms of life as we know it, so when there was confirmation from NASA's Phoenix Mission of water ice on the planet Mars, and discovery of geological features of river valleys and towering waterfalls that argued further for the presence of standing water on Mars for thousands of years, the idea of life having more than one home—a home on earth—gained sharpness and particularity. Our sense of the known inched forward; our perception of the unknown retreated a few centimetres and began to change the metaphorical picture. The planet, once red, hostile, cold, host of invading aliens, is beginning to offer promise as a place to begin afresh: to be a new world, allow a rebirth, a return to watery gestation for human civilization. The more recent poems about Mars that I've read are attempts not at fantasy or at contemplating the *other*, but to feel what it would be like to be human *there*.[1]

I do not know what Thales thought about Mars, but he was famous for predicting an eclipse in 585 BC. Although this ability may have appeared magical to those without his knowledge, it flowed from observation and study. His learning and discoveries were in the mixed fields of mathematics and philosophy and the sciences. There's a story about him that, as a poet, I particularly like. "For when they reproached him because of his poverty, as though philosophy were no use, it is said that, having observed through his study of the heavenly bodies that there would be a large olive-crop, he raised a little capital while it was still winter, and paid deposits on all the olive presses in Miletus and Chios, hiring them cheaply because no one bid against him." These days, we would call this investing in futures. The story continues: "When the appropriate time came there was a sudden rush of requests for the presses; he then hired them out on his own terms and so made a large profit, thus demonstrating that it is easy for philosophers to be rich, if they wish, but that it is not in this that they are interested."[2]

That is—if you'll allow me to press the point—Thales was ridiculed for wasting his time on intellectual and creative work: wasted, clearly, because he was poor. Does this sound familiar? His job, though—which he understood perfectly—wasn't to accumulate wealth but to make connections. To *under/stand*. To make evident the nature of the alliances at work within the ground—literally the earth and its place in the universe—on which humanity stands. One of his important tools was geometry, the mathematics of connected and interconnected forms, to express immediate and timely truths: how far is that ship from land; how high is that pyramid? The reason for needing to know such things isn't always instantly apparent: who cares how far away that ship is—unless it is heading our way carrying food which we need to survive, or people with weapons we'll have to face, or someone we love who has been absent too long.

The form and nature of poetry is to make connections. Each poet finds shapes and relationships that come to be heard and seen as her or his voice. Through use of the tool of metaphor, the poet connects the unfamiliar—what is not fully known—to the familiar, and this connection, this relationship, is expressed within a form—the poem—which can then be scrutinized: touched, listened to, sniffed at, exulted over, wept at: it makes a place within the body of the world. You, who are listening to me, may be drifting off as I speak partly because I am now using metaphorical language and we—perhaps even we poets—have lost some of our ability and willingness to keep actively in mind the spaces through which poetry travels: it is hard work when in ours, as in Thales's time, there is a societal context which dismisses its necessity. The challenge of the vast distances we may have to voyage in this way—by the metaphorical leap—to make valuable connections is represented for me in the space between the first and last Thalian principle as expressed in my little poem. I: The first principle and basic nature of all things is water; and V: All things are full of gods.

III

This spring, when I was thinking about the floods in Winnipeg and what I wanted to say about poetry, I was reading Kathleen Raine's book of essays, *Defending Ancient Springs*, from which I've adapted the title of this talk. In it, she considers the sources, the wellsprings of poetry in poets such as David Gascoyne, Edwin Muir, Shelley, Coleridge, Yeats, Blake and others: her work on symbol and the mythological is insightful and deeply thoughtful and she inspires in me a renewed sense of the value of poetry, its learning which is imaginative rather than rational, its reach towards expanded vision and consciousness. And yet I find myself, often, thinking of the other end of the metaphor's spectrum: the springboard of the literal and being curious as to how and why the poet finds or chooses or is drawn to his or her own starting places from which those leaps are made.

Andre Gide said, "The poet is he who sees."[3]

Gao Xingian said, "Language is the ultimate crystallisation of human civilisation. It is intricate, incisive and difficult to grasp and yet it is pervasive, penetrates human perceptions and links man, the perceiving subject, to his own understanding of the world."[4]

My cousin Sylvia, a pragmatist of the first order, said when she made her annual phone call on my birthday, "I've come to think, recently, that the world needs creativity."

My cousin and I shared a childhood in which the storytelling of our fathers and uncles and grandparents created a mythological world centred on Newfoundland and Winnipeg.

The uncles' stories were mostly of Winnipeg, where they'd grown up, but my father, the eldest and the only one born at Coley's Point, Newfoundland, where the family had settled in the early nineteenth century, had a stronger connection to the Homeland. When I visited there the first time, he sent me to his cousin, Muriel Wilson, who lived across the street in Clarke's Beach from where my great-uncle Ebenezer had had his ship-building yard. Muriel was virtually blind and had been so since girlhood, but she ordered her husband, George, to get the car out so they could take us around. As he drove, she would tell him where to stop. "Down there," she said, "just below the post office at the end of Gully's road is where your father was born." My grandfather, Benjamin, had built his house on land left to him by his brother James; and there was a poem, which Muriel would photocopy for me, written in James's memory by his father. As we drove and stopped and drove and stopped along Coley's Point South, Muriel described exactly where my great-great-grandfather (whose father was killed in the Napoleonic wars) had settled and how he and his friend, Benjamin Hayes, who arrived by ship with him, had divided Coley's Point between them, and then how it had gone to their various children—James, my great-great-grandfather, had had seven sons. It was an astonishing experience, that afternoon, to be guided through this landscape by Muriel. All the places of significance in the stories of my childhood were given to me stripped of the veils of modernity: the new houses and schools and lanes and roads were gone and in their stead the old houses, the extensive gardens, boat houses and the fishing stages, the paths down which my long dead relatives had walked were restored.

I had visited my great-aunt Ellen, who was then 101 years old, shortly before I'd come to Newfoundland. Muriel showed me the path to the beach—a beach of smooth stones, where Ellen had said you would step from one to the next—where it ran below where the causeway was now. Ellen had walked that way to school and to visit relatives in Mercer's Cove and down that path and along that beach she'd been followed by her little horse, Forest.

It was as if the entire area had been scraped clear—glaciated—of its accretions, anything at all that would mask the time of stories. I couldn't help but think, too, of the tradition of blind storytellers whose job it is to remember a time of meaning and connection and to pass it on.

After leaving Muriel, I returned to the shore and looked out over the waters of Conception Bay where my grandfather and one of his brothers had been fishing when their dory overturned in a storm. They called for help—they knew someone would come for them eventually—and they sang hymns to make themselves forget about the cold. I remembered sitting with my grandfather and listening to him tell the story. He had pleaded with his brother to hold on; but he couldn't and my grandfather had watched his brother's hands slip from the overturned hull only minutes before rescue came. I'd watched his face as he spoke, his eyes looking into the distance. *Yes*, he said, repeating the inevitable ending, *He couldn't hold on.* He nodded again and again, *Yes*.

In one of those very early poems in the book with Thales and the flood images the moment appears like this: "I escape / from the water / rise dreaming of sky, // reach for him in the waves; / his hands have stopped climbing below. // I was almost / asleep, he says / pulling me down."[5]

This kind of moment, of memory, is the experience Seamus Heaney describes when speaking of the trembling surface of the water in a bucket in the scullery when he was a boy: "Poetry," he said, "can make an order as true to the impact of external reality and as sensitive to the inner laws of the poet's being as the ripples that rippled in and rippled out across the water [of that bucket.]"[6]

Yeats got at the sensation of movement from the literal end of the metaphor this way when he was writing about Blake but he takes it to the limit of its extension so that we understand what the poet is facing: "The surface is perpetually as it were giving way before one, and revealing another surface below it, and that again, dissolves when we try to study it . . . [It] melts into the making of the earth, and that fades away into some allegory of the rising and setting of the sun. It is all like a great cloud full of stars and shapes through which the eye seeks a boundary in vain."[7]

There is no solid ground, instead there's the ripple making bigger and bigger circles, the view out a window at the endless flood waters, the present giving way to story giving way to the mythological, the geological; and if we don't find our ground we just keep on dissolving. Yeats says, "When we seem to have explored the remotest division some new spirit floats by muttering wisdom."[8]

Since we cannot live without boundaries, the other end of the metaphor has to acknowledge the concrete, too.

Kathleen Raine tells us that when Yeats had come to the end of what he'd been able to construct from "living in a society which has, on the whole, broken with tradition" and found "how impossible it is to build up from a series of intuitive flashes, that wholeness of context which great poetry requires"[9] he came up with *A Vision*, a book made from answers to questions he posed through the medium of his wife's automatic writing. The purpose of the "channelling" was to give him metaphors for poetry, he was told when he asked. Give him metaphors and symbols it did: the great wheel with its gyres and cones, the moon phases and incarnations, the great year; it was a structure that could encompass life and afterlife and reincarnation; that marginalized the subjective so that Yeats could have an objective and solid, if metaphorical, platform from which to write his great poems—*The Second Coming, A Prayer for my Daughter, Sailing to Byzantium, Byzantium, Under Ben Bulben* . . .

Yeats's solution isn't for everyone but it is similar to the strategy most poets develop: to make the metaphorical leap, the poet must have a sense of certainty; she doesn't have to have proof, but she does need an elemental positioning. Gwen McEwen found it in her affinity for the Middle East. Rosemary Sullivan says:

> What was called the "archaic" or even primitive imagination of ancient civilizations seemed to match her own and she turned to them in quest of the myth and symbols she needed for her poetic searches . . . . When asked if she had a "mythic imagination" she would reply: "Of course, what other kind is there?" 'Myth' is a word we use to describe a sort of bridge between the so-called 'real' world and the world of the psyche. And of course for the poet the two are one."[10]

Eirin Moure has done something similar by means of her adoption of Spanish, Galician and Portuguese poetic personalities. Her metaphors tend to be rooted in historical forms, language and literature encompassed by theory—a net—structure dependent on the notion of fragmentation but in effect not unlike Yeats's *A Vision*. The point being that the result for these poets is as Kathleen Raine says of Shelley: ". . . nor . . . is there any point at which we can draw a distinction between the physical and metaphysical objects of the poet's discourse. The metaphorical character of the whole lies in the perfect fusion of the two terms of the metaphor."[11] And the fusion depends on "the assimilation of object and apprehension."[12]

IV

In the vocabulary of metaphorical spaces, *feeling* is the engine of travel between the terms of the metaphor, between—in a perfect poem—the physical and metaphysical. In the poets I've mentioned the metaphors arc from the physical or natural or linguistic and through the historical, cultural, mythological, and often geological before they fuse. The resonance that engenders the *feeling* is formed, as Heaney said, by the impact of the external on the inner laws of the poet's being. When I am at Coley's Point with Muriel Wilson, I sense a resonance with the land and can follow this through family connections to the landscape of European settlement before 1682, but what I cannot do is continue in the same way to the deeper culture of those who have lived longer in this place with which my "inner being" finds harmony. I can do other things—examine the rocks, consider the climate—but in terms of imaginative wholeness I am in a bind. I can choose to re-locate or dis-locate, in a version of reverse immigration—an aspect Yeats sub-vented by the discoveries of *A Vision*—but I miss a step: the one that teaches me through the experiences and interpretations of those who have found ancient springs here and who have built culture from that resource. It is no accident that poets who sense resonance and affinity in familial or distant cultures, go *there*. Feet on the ground matter: instruction in culture, matters. It is likewise no accident that poets who tune in to the landscape of Canada find themselves drawn towards Aboriginal cultures—and confronted with difficulties that tend to gather under the term appropriation.

V

I first came across the work of Hermia Harris Fraser when I was at the University of New Brunswick in Fredericton and looking for anything-at-all to remind me of the west coast and (particularly) the Queen Charlotte Islands (Haida Gwaii) where I had been living and teaching. I found two Ryerson chapbooks by her, one published in 1945—*Songs of the Western Islands*—and the other, containing some of the same poems, *The Arrow-Maker's Daughter*, published in 1957; there was also a novel, *The Tall Brigade*, which she'd set on the Oregon coast. Eventually, when I returned to the west, I found her. She was a contemporary of Anne Marriott, and was in a Victoria writers' group with Marriott, Marjorie Pickthall, Floris McLaren, Doris Ferne and Laura Berton in the late 1930s and the 1940s. When I talked with her she kept returning to two things: one was the relationship possible in this country between a writer's work and Aboriginal myth; the other was the problems of struggle and neglect for our writers. I don't need to say more about the neglect: I doubt whether many—or even any—of you have heard of her.

What I liked about her poems were the words she used that placed the speaker in a relationship with the landscape—you must remember the time in which she was writing—these words were not then commonly found in Canadian poetry: *cedar bark, stone, clam mounds, raven, swansdown*. I was hard on her for her use of trochees and dactyls—rhythms which to my ear echoed *Hiawatha* but which, actually, are closer to the Sapphics my students now seem to be able to write so easily, trained as are their ears on the trochees of contemporary indie music and the cross-fertilizations of world music, unhooked from my own iambic chains. Hermia Harris Fraser had spent time on Haida Gwaii and in the Nass Valley and in Greece and this one verse (not dactylic) from her verse play, *The Arrow-Maker's Daughter*, catches, for me, some of my own land-feeling:

> The sun sends his light deep in the water,
> I am raising my hands to the sun
> I close them away from the sun
> How long rest the dead, knowing nothing,
> Like the sand and the tide, knowing nothing.[13]

VI

I've mentioned the pre-Socratic, Thales and family stories, and hinted at a synthesis of these and the experience I had as a child in the Winnipeg Flood when it came to engendering metaphors. But there is another layer. The first poem in what now seems to me to be a particularly unrealized little book, *The Liberation of Newfoundland*, emerged from the story of how my grandfather met my grandmother at her father's fishing camp in Labrador. But in the poem, all particularities of place, the woman and the narrator are both absent. She is "on the ice/ moving in silver/ bringing stars down."[14] There's a connection between the woman walking towards the narrator whose impulse is to hide from "this woman/ who crosses the ice/ like a girl/ becoming a bride" and "days when men drown."[15] The poem moves, as a poem is allowed to do, from the personal towards the archetypal. In the only other poem, one very near the end, that uses the image of the ice-floe, "ghost people/ paddle/ deep canoes."[16] The *ghost people* in their *ghost canoes*, who appear *daily*, are the Beothuk, hunted, harassed and displaced to extinction. They are a continuous and continually renewed presence underlying the other perceptions. The poem appears between two illustrations: one of ships and men engaged in the killing of seals on the ice, and another picture of our stranded Winnipeg house, this time lying deeper than ever in the water, sandwiched between lake and a distinctly lowering sky.

VII

It is a wet and windy February afternoon when I start the climb up from the village in which I'm living to the monastery on the mountain. I've been living on the island of Paros in Greece since the summer. While I've been away my little book has come out at home to thundering silence. Never mind. I'm here, although how I ended up in this sun-charred place is a little mysterious to me; I'd been heading for Spain, and if I'd had any sense I'd have gone to Miletus where Thales had lived. Nonetheless...

The sky is slick and grey; behind the mountain I'm climbing there are gathering black clouds. Above me, and looking down on the town, the monastery looms, appearing—with its big marble struts supporting it against the mountain—like a dam.

I'd been gazing at the monastery from my roof for months. In the morning it would be in full sun, dazzling against the barren cliff, and later, in shadow, it would soften, its sharp lines mellowing into the slope. No one lived there any longer. The monks had left one winter, taking the back path so that no one had known they'd gone until the woman who brought their milk returned the next morning to find it untouched and soured.

As always when I walk, I get lost. The paths leaving town are donkey tracks—earth with stone eruptions—and formed between heaped stone walls. One path led to the church, another to the cemetery and back by a gully to town; another ended at the generator; but at length I'd hit the right one. Up the hill over rock and dry earth between walls sheltering winter green fields where a few meadow birds hug the grass and feed on oats. Lizards scuttle and snakes slowly unwind as I pass. When the wind thins the cloud and turns so that it hisses in my other ear, the land lies clear and sharp and exposed to my eyes; then I take the wrong fork once again. It's starting to get dark, so I abandon thoughts of a path and scramble up, climbing where the October fire had turned the soil to ashes, every handhold crumbling away. When I reach one of the bracing marble struts, I rest, lean against the stone and look away from the hard mountain to the sea. A boat has just passed the point of Aghios Fokas and entered the harbour and I can see its path stretching all the way from the horizon. The sea seems as slow to close over the scar of the cutting keel as flesh over a wound. I'm on an edge, feeling like a swimmer who puts her feet down and finds no bottom, the tilt of my body just holding me to this open slice of earth.

Not far from that point with its church and lighthouse is another point; and below it, scoured deep into the steep wall of the coast, is the cave in which the poet Archilochus (who died about fifteen years before Thales was born) sat to compose his verses. When I'd gone there, walking across fields where I'd picked saffron and clambering down the jagged rocks until I came to the opening, I'd known little about him; but I'd been lonely and wanted to find some sense of kinship in this place so far from home.

I sat in the cave and watched the blue and green sea, rough with waves, and then as the local ferry, the Kyklades, left, watched a school of dolphins, showing large and dark, make big counter-waves against the wind. Later, when I had a copy of *The Penguin Book of Greek Verse*, I found Archilochus's famous poem which, now, reminds me also—because I'm looking for metaphors perhaps—of Thales and the eclipse he predicted, and his ideas about permanence and change.

"Nothing is unexpected or can be declared impossible on oath, or strange, since Zeus the father of the Olympians made night out of midday, hiding the light of the shining sun, and dreadful terror came upon the human race. Because of this men can believe and expect anything. Let no one be surprised if he sees the wild beasts take in exchange the salty pastures from the dolphins, and prefer the loud-sounding waves of the ocean to the land, and if they [the dolphins] find the mountains delightful."[17]

When I finally climb over the monastery wall, I find flower beds and trees; the cell doors have been left open. Inside the small church, above lit candles the icons peer through their masks of gold and silver. Before I leave, I find a tap and drink some water. Over my head is a line in the cloud, a great slit in the sky which is closing together, making a ridge at the meeting point.

VIII

I cannot leave you to close this exploration entirely on your own so let me draw together some of the threads I've been holding without, I trust, interfering too much with your own interweaving—which is what I hope this talk will provoke.

Hermia Harris Fraser and some others like her were not, in my opinion, wrong to cast their metaphorical lines across Aboriginal culture, but they were—like my mother, who because of the Flood lost the things that connected her to a world that couldn't be communicated without them—without the certainties that would allow (in Kathleen Raine's provisos for metaphor) the physical and metaphysical to be apprehended as one and the intuited world to make itself known. Something else goes on at this level of naming and vocabulary—the use of certain words that I mentioned—and it may be as simple and as important as acknowledgement of cultural presence and the existence of ancient springs. Acknowledgement says, "Message received," and then waits. It doesn't say "Now I know everything" or "This belongs to me" or even "This makes sense to me." As Archilochus tells us, the lesson of the universe is that nothing is impossible or strange, although it may seem strange if you don't get the references—if you don't know what causes eclipses, or if you don't, as happened to Archilochus after agreeing to trade away his cow one moonlit night to a group of wild women, know when you wake up with a lyre in your hand that you've just become a poet.

There's a robustness to the biology of culture, which makes me think that devising an abstract system like that of Yeats, or being linguistically inventive, aren't the only routes left for poets. Continuity matters: Thales said, "Water is the originating principle" more than 2,600 years ago, and a company named Thales developed the MARSIS instrument capable of detecting the presence of water on Mars to a depth of 5 km beneath the surface. It matters because the metaphors continue to unfold. In the case of the fragmentation of my mother's world and what this means to me, that keeps disclosing, too. Objects belonging to her mother have appeared from unsuspected storage, closed archives have, literally, opened; letters have arrived from strangers enclosing documents handed down within their families about my mother's family; stories and images kept within completely unsuspected lines of transmission have found their way to me.

It won't surprise you to know, too, that the unfurling of the buds within that first strange little book of poems of mine has not yet reached an end.

I think poets are given their metaphors: internal GPS co-ordinates, if you like, to the ancient springs they need. This happens, the Celts say, after strong emotion upturns the cauldrons of vocation and knowledge with which all of us are born, so that they can be filled.

> I was born by the Seine River:
> It rolled slowly, it spilled
> And soaked the grasses;
> Many birds traversed it.
> The river bank was forbidden
> Though aprons from the nearby houses
> Fluted the air like river gulls.
> The house was a living island;
> It wrenched loose on restless foundations,
> Edged close to the river bank and a final episode
> Of drowned children.
> *I was born by the Seine River.*
> *It rolled slowly, it spilled*
> *And soaked the grasses.*

The river was forbidden,
But many birds traversed its borders
And I loved them.

Notes

1. See *Martian Landscape Poems* by Richard L. Poss and *On Mars* by David Salisbury. Earlier poems such as Walter de la Mare's "Wanderers" and Robert Graves' "Star-Talk" or much further back to Sir John Davies's "Orchestra" layer human qualities *onto* the stars and planets.
2. Aristotle, *Politics* (1259a9-18) in *The Presocratic Philosophers*, ed. G.S. Kirk, J.E. Raven and M. Schofield (2nd edition, Cambridge University Press, 1983), 80–81.
3. Quoted in Hölderlin's *Madness* (Dent & Sons, 1938), 11.
4. From the 2000 Nobel Prize in Literature lecture.
5. Marilyn Bowering, *The Liberation of Newfoundland* (Fiddlehead Poetry Books, 1973), 17.
6. From the 1995 Nobel Prize in Literature lecture.
7. From "On the Necessity of Symbolism" by W.B. Yeats as quoted by Kathleen Raine, *Defending Ancient Springs* (Oxford University Press, 1967), 75.
8. Ibid.
9. Raine, 74.
10. Margaret Atwood and Barry Callaghan, eds. *The Poetry of Gwendolyn MacEwen: The Later Years*, Vol. Two (Toronto: Exile Editions, 1993), ix.
11. Raine, 146.
12. Ibid.
13. Hermia Harris Fraser, *The Arrow-Maker's Daughter* (Toronto: The Ryerson Press, 1957), 8.
14. *The Liberation of Newfoundland*, 3.
15. Ibid.
16. Ibid., 33.
17. *The Penguin Book of Greek Verse*, ed. Constantine A. Trypanis (Penguin Books, Great Britain, 1971), 130.

Poetry and Community

ANNE SIMPSON

Anne Szumigalski Lecture • Toronto, Ontario • June 12, 2010

> ... in Homer: two horses that refuse to budge ...
> Because they are in mourning for Patroclus
> Their charioteer, their shiny manes bedraggled
> Under the yoke pads on either side of the yoke.
> — Michael Longley[1]

THE SEEDS FOR THIS TALK WERE PLANTED LAST YEAR, DURING which time I was the writer-in-residence at the Saskatoon Public Library. There I met three poets: Mari-Lou Rowley, Katherine Lawrence and Lia Pas. We met on a regular basis throughout the year. Once, Katherine brought up the question of poetry's relevance: "How does the fact that we're poets play out in our lives, in our community?" In an attempt to answer her, I tried to write this talk. About the same time, I came across a poem by Michael Longley, about another poem, *The Iliad*, and I began thinking of our conversation, as poets, with other poets, and how this poetic conversation brings us into community.

Longley's poem, "The Horses," got me thinking about Patroclus, the beloved companion of Achilles.² Like a younger brother going to an older one, Patroclus cajoles Achilles into letting him go to battle wearing Achilles' armour. In other words, he goes to battle *as if* he were Achilles. For a while, he triumphs. But his ambition is over-weaning; he is caught in the grip of *até* as he pushes the Trojans back to the gates of Troy. To be overcome by *até*, which might be roughly translated as a kind of temporary insanity, is to be out of control. *Até* is also described as blindness: those who are afflicted with it can't see where they're going.³

Patroclus is not Achilles; to *resemble* Achilles—to appear to be what he is not—may be his first mistake. And to *act* as if he were Achilles may be his second mistake. But the idea of error is a contemporary way to look at it, since Patroclus is overtaken by *até*. He is not of sound mind. To succumb to *até*—that intoxication of the gods—is to be out of touch with oneself and with others. Patroclus is like a drunk who continues in his bloodlust beyond the bounds of convention: he forgets himself, he indulges himself. And he is checked, by the gods, and dies at the hands of Hektor.

Até is one kind of blindness, but at the other end of the scale we have another kind of blindness—*acedia*. I wanted to understand this idea in the context of *The Iliad*. *Acedia* might be understood as ennui, boredom, or tedium, but at a deeper level it can be seen as a kind of paralysis. When Achilles first hears of Patroclus's death, he is incapable of response. He avoids the rituals of mourning for days; Patroclus's body is left where it lies. He's afflicted by an inability to act, and this is interesting because he's a hero above all, one who is known for his action. And so he is alienated, alone.

Acedia is, I think, a condition that is worse than *até*. To be afflicted with it is to recognize the fear of never being able to escape it. It is consuming. And "at its Greek root, *acedia* means the absence of care."⁴ But Czesław Miłosz writes that "no one can call this ... simply laziness ... whatever it may once have been, nowadays it has returned to its original meaning: terror in the face of emptiness."⁵ I began with Achilles as an illustration of *acedia*, but I think that our own age has deepened our understanding of it. At its worst, it is neither boredom nor tedium, it is wakefulness, an insomnia combined with a sense of horror. The eyes can no longer close; the ears are full of noise.

Both *até* and *acedia* are excessive. As writers we recognize both *até* and *acedia* in terms of blocks to our craft: *até* might give us access to words—an abundance of them—while *acedia* might not allow us words at all because it seems futile to write anything. All of us recognize the symptoms. But to leave it here would be facile: there is more at stake. I wonder if *até* could be seen as a kind of self-indulgence that means the one afflicted with it disregards the relationship that could exist between self and other. And *acedia* might be seen as that condition in which the self is trapped by the self. There is no desire, let alone will, to acknowledge the other. We know things have come to a bad pass at this point. Paul Ricoeur explains that "as long as one remains within the circle of sameness-identity, the otherness of the other-than-self offers nothing original."[6]

But let's look at the opposite: getting out of the circle of sameness. Metaphor, for instance, tells us that sun equals spider, that earth equals drum. Jan Zwicky says that it allows for "seeing x as y—what is already present is seen as something else . . . ."[7] As a result, we hold two possibilities in our minds at once. While we can't hold on for long, since sun can't be spider and earth can't be drum, we have seen the way it could be. We have freed ourselves from merely seeing, to envisioning, and then when we return to seeing earth simply as earth, things have shifted. We have revised our thinking about earth: this is the re-visioning that happens with any imaginative endeavour.

Fundamentally, poetry is about relation—about one and the other, and the relation between one and the other—and so it moves between things: this is its dynamic. It travels. Whatever kind of poetry we make, it seeks, inevitably, to make a relation. As the poet Paul Celan says, "the poem intends another, needs this other, needs an opposite. It goes towards it."[8] Poetry needs another; it seeks the other out. Its trajectory is always towards the other. So we find ourselves looking at questions of existence, of identity—inevitably, poetry comes up against ontology.

If we surmise this is the case, we tend to turn to those philosophers who might help. Along comes Emmanuel Levinas. He argues that we have a sense of otherness that precedes all else. Self would not be self without the other. There's a sense of relief, when first encountering Levinas, that otherness is being taken into consideration. Thank God!—someone to get us out of the insistence on self that prevails throughout Western philosophy. Someone to get us away from the I-think-therefore-I-am way of thinking. Or the I-think-therefore-the-world-revolves-around-God-and-me-and-who-cares-about-you? way of thinking. Tim Lilburn says: "the ghost of Descartes hovers over the waste dump, the clear cut."[9] And he asks whether there's another way of knowing.

On first glance, it seems to be the way Levinas shows us. But there's more. Levinas argues that the relation between self and other is not a matter of desire; it is a matter of responsibility. *Because* we have a sense of the otherness within us, Levinas points out, we understand the significance of the other's call to us. In his words, there is "no self without another who summons it to responsibility."[10] But his demand on us is well-nigh impossible, since to be summoned is to be wholly obedient to the infinite, inscrutable, other. The other comes first. And so what is established, with the radical vision Levinas presents to us, is the predicament of the self in servitude to the masterful other.

But let's say that we respond to the other, not out of duty, not out of obedience, but out of a sense of solicitude, a sense of empathy—a different way from that shown by Levinas. If we accept that experiencing others is necessary to experiencing oneself, we also accept that some aspects of onseself *can* be shared (how to do the J-stroke while canoeing, or how to blow smoke rings), while some *can't* be shared (how it felt when you broke your ankle). No one can feel my pain; no one can die for me. I can't share either pain or death with anyone. But because I share other aspects of myself, I can share a sense of humanity. By way of solicitude, or care, or empathy, I can hope to participate in the life of someone else. I may fail in the attempt, but at least I can try. You are not greater than me; I am not greater than you. There is no asymmetry in this. And because there is freedom, not servitude, there is the potential for enlargement. I can experience something that has not happened to me *as if* it were my own experience.

Metaphor allows for this. It not only allows for it, it suggests the way of metaphor as a lived practice. I would say that seeing-as allows us to move towards being-as, or, more to the point, being-as-if-I-were-other. If we envision the other as if he or she were oneself, then metaphor is at work. It erases any sense of dominance or subservience. Metaphor, which has been called a mere decoration, a mere figure of language, becomes something powerful—not only a way of seeing, or seeing-as, but a way of being in the world.

I want to go back to *The Iliad* for a moment. Patroclus dies at the hands of Hektor; Hektor dies at the hands of Achilles. But before Hektor dies, he begs Achilles for an honourable burial. This is not granted. It may not be unusual to leave a body for the dogs and vultures, as Achilles says he will do with Hektor's body, but it seems wrong to us. Furthermore, Achilles slits the heels of Hektor's dead body, and lashes them, with strips of leather, to his chariot. For days, he drags Hektor's body around in the dust, circling the tomb of Patroclus. The gods protect Hektor's body from mutilation, but there is no stopping Achilles. Why such extreme rage? Does Achilles feel so much hatred towards Hektor because of the loss of Patroclus? Or does he feel so much hatred because, in Hektor, he sees himself?

Certainly Achilles reveals that *até* is the kind of excess that can result in atrocity. As Don McKay writes in "Fates Worse than Death," in *Apparatus*: "Achilles, the dumb fucker ... drags, / Up and down, and round and round the tomb / Of his beloved, the body of Hektor, / Tamer of horses ...."[11] It is almost as if the frenzy of Achilles going around and around is not so far from his earlier inability to act, as he circled around and around his thoughts. He's his own best enemy, his own worst enemy. In fact, I think the real argument of *The Iliad* is not so much between the Greeks and the Trojans, or between Achilles and Hektor, but between one Achilles and another Achilles, in which we also see the argument about what it is to be mortal (alongside the parallel argument of what it might be like to be immortal). It is as if he wages war on himself. Achilles kills Hektor, but he is also, in a sense, trying to kill himself, destroying the relation between the self and otherness within. Such is the condition of *até*, or that of *acedia*—the condition of no exit. Achilles needs to find a way out of himself.

So *The Iliad* asks us to imagine what it is to be Achilles—even in the midst of the events when he disturbs us most. Why should we care about such a dumb fucker? We care about Hektor, even though Hektor is gone, even as the significance of Hektor's death begins to dawn on us. And yet, before the end of the poem, it is possible for us to care about Achilles, because Priam shows us it is possible. The appeal of the father, for his dead son's body, is what humanizes Achilles. We see him as he has the potential to be, as a character who can give rather than withhold. This selflessness—in direct contrast to his self-interestedness—shows that he is capable of change. Poetry begins by concerning itself with what *is*, and what we may not want to see about what is, but it proceeds to reveal the world of the possible. It shows me this—myself as if I were Achilles, much as I might dislike him.

While I was writing this talk, I was working on a creative writing program at Sherbrooke Community Centre in Saskatoon. (I was the writer-in-residence this past year at the Saskatoon Public Library and this was a project I wanted to initiate within the community.) It came about because I heard the poet Sharon Olds interviewed by Hal Wake at the Vancouver Writers' Festival in 2008. She talked about a program she was instrumental in establishing: the workshop program at Goldwater Hospital, a long-term care facility for the disabled in New York. Through this program, her graduate students at NYU go into Goldwater Hospital and work on writing with residents.

When I started a program in Saskatoon, at the Sherbrooke Community Centre, it was nothing like the program at Goldwater. I had seen the NFB documentary, *A Year at Sherbrooke*, and it jumpstarted me into action. I had no idea that an art program could have such an effect on the lives of the residents, with various—and often quite severe—physical and mental challenges. The art program had its impetus with Thelma Pepper, a well-known Saskatchewan photographer, whose husband had to move to Sherbrooke when his dementia became incapacitating. Pepper's involvement with Sherbrooke led to a full-time art program in 2006 that was staffed by a young artist-in-residence, Jeff Nachtigall. After Jeff had worked with residents for about a year, he organized an exhibit—"The Insiders"—at the Mendel Art

Gallery in Saskatoon. At the end of the film, *A Year at Sherbrooke*, the residents, in formal attire, are shown about to enter the gallery for the 2007 opening. They are beaming.

One of the residents in the art program was a quadriplegic who had once been a professor at the University of Saskatchewan. He had been ready to go to Switzerland to commit suicide prior to his involvement in the program. It is a poignant moment in the film. But months after he began to paint pictures with a paintbrush held in his mouth, he moved away from the decision to end his life. At the opening of the exhibit at the Mendel Art Gallery, he is shown wearing a tuxedo and grinning from ear to ear. His life changed, radically, as a result of art: or, to put it quite literally, art had given him back his life.

When I walked in the door of Sherbrooke for the first time, I didn't know much about it except for the film I'd seen, and the fact that it was a long-term care facility, though not so much a facility as a community, one that treated each individual as a unique participant. I was warmly welcomed: Patricia Roe, one of the administrators, simply asked when I'd like to start writing with people. Within two months we had a writing program.

I had the help of an intern, a fourth-year English student at the University of Saskatchewan, and I also had the help of two local writers who had come to see me at the library about their own writing. And so we began. What we did was to sit by people's wheelchairs as they told us their stories. We wrote them down. It really was as simple as that. In so doing, Elise got to know Donald, Wes got to know Kelly, Ashley and I got to know Kathleen, I got to know Dennis, and so on. There were more people we worked with, but the thing was that they had stories to tell us about their lives, about their worlds. After a month or two, we had a huge Open Mike celebration, during which residents read their stories and poems. Above them were coloured pieces of paper with more stories and poems printed on them; these were pegged to a clothesline. So this program went on until the spring, a few weeks before I left Saskatoon. And I've been assured that things will continue with the help of other student interns from the university.

People asked me whether I'd write poems about that experience. Well, maybe so, but probably not. It wasn't a project. I didn't go into it with the intent of writing. But what is the link between what we *do* and what we *write*, to go back to Katherine Lawrence's question? I would say that it is the principle inherent in poetry: that we can be attentive. Poetry allows for this attention, as we know, and it doesn't conscript us into this work of attending—it simply makes a space for it. I would also say that *até*—whether we call it fury or folly—is the opposite of attention. *Até* and *acedia* are linked, if we see *acedia* as the complete exhaustion of *até*, the spirit's imprisonment. If the opposite of *até* is attention, the opposite of *acedia* is care. And care is a principle inherent in poetry. Attention leads to care.

I said before that seeing-as allows us to move towards being-as, or, more to the point, being-as-if-I-were-other. I also said that if we envision the other as if he or she were myself, then the principle of metaphor is at work, and that, when it is at work, it is not a relationship of dominance or subservience. I walked into Sherbrooke Community Centre as an able-bodied person, the one in authority, by virtue of my position. But as Jeff Nachtigall showed me, the residents are the ones who take the lead on any creative endeavour. The artist, or the writer, is the one who makes the space to allow it happen. In this particular instance, in a long-term care facility, where I was surrounded by disabilities of all kinds, I was less the teacher and more the listener. I was reminded of my own vulnerability. And whatever I gave, I received more than I could give in return.

If I esteem the other as myself, I have seen him or her as irreplaceable, just as I am irreplaceable. And this means, I think, that I see into the life of another. I have the capacity to imagine another life; if I did not have this capacity, I could condescend, undermine, violate the other without consideration for him or her. I would be closed off. In other words, I could not accommodate both sides of the relation: what it is to be me, what it is to be other. Poetry—all literature—is the work of seeing-as that points us towards being-as. But it stops short. I can't be you; you can't be me. You're irreplaceable and so am I. I can go so far and then I must return to myself. I relinquish; I let go. Yet the *as-if* is powerful—it shows me that we are in it together. I can't bear your pain, no, but I can stand with you. I can mourn with you; I can celebrate with you.

At the end of *The Iliad*, in Book 24, Priam goes to Achilles to ask him to return the body of Hektor. There is exceptional grace in this. He gets down on his knees and kisses the hand of the man who killed his son. The gift that Priam gives is, I think, far greater than the gift that Achilles gives to Priam, which is that he returns the body of Hektor to him. Achilles suffers because of the death of Patroclus, but Priam has suffered the death of his son. At this point in the poem, Achilles goes out and supervises the serving women in washing the body of Hektor, which Achilles himself lifts and puts on a bier in a wagon. For the first time, he shows respect to Hektor. He covers the body and returns inside, to Priam, to whom he offers food and drink. War will come between them again, but for now, they eat and drink together. The most arresting moment is when they look at each other. Priam looks at Achilles, "marvelling / now at the man's beauty, his magnificent build—/ . . . and Achilles gazed and marvelled at Dardan Priam, / beholding his noble looks, listening to his words." They are enemies, but they are free from hatred. They simply regard each other—they attend to each other not only with clarity, but with generosity and respect—and in doing so, they see into one another's lives.

Notes

1. Michael Longley, "The Horses," *Staying Alive: Real Poems for Unreal Times*, ed. Neil Astley (London: Bloodaxe Books, 2002), 228.
2. Throughout this talk, I refer to Robert Fagles's translation of *The Iliad* by Homer (New York: Penguin, 1990).
3. E.R. Dodds, "Agamemnon's Apology," *The Greeks and the Irrational* (Berkeley: University of California Press, 1966) 1–27.
4. Kathleen Norris, *Acedia & Me: A Marriage, Monks, and A Writer's Life* (New York: Riverhead, 2008), 3.
5. Czesław Miłosz, "Garden of Knowledge," cited by Kathleen Norris in *Acedia & Me*, 312.
6. Paul Ricoeur, *Oneself as Another*, trans. Kathleen Blamey (Chicago: The University of Chicago Press, 1992), 3.
7. Jan Zwicky, *Wisdom & Metaphor* (Kentville, NS: Gaspereau Press, 2003), Left 25.
8. Paul Celan in Gerald L. Bruns, Maurice Blanchot, *The Refusal of Philosophy* (Baltimore: The Johns Hopkins University Press, 1997), 96.

9   Tim Lilburn, "Preface," *Poetry & Knowing*, ed. Tim Lilburn (Kingston, ON: Quarry Press, 1995), 8.
10 Emmanuel Levinas cited by Paul Ricoeur, *Oneself as Another*, 187.
11 Don McKay, "Fates Worse than Death" in "Matériel," originally published in *Apparatus* and selected for *Camber: Selected Poems, 1983-2000* (Toronto: McClelland & Stewart, 2004), 135.

Pristine and Startled
Ways of Seeing
GLEN SORESTAD

Anne Szumigalski Lecture • Toronto, Ontario • June 11, 2011

LET ME FIRST SAY THAT I HESITATE TO CALL WHAT I AM about to offer you a lecture. A lecture, to me, conjures up images of academia—tedium, copious notes and final exams—things that, for the most part, I no longer care to remember and, thankfully, do not expect to face again. I'm not even sure Anne Szumigalski would have liked the descriptor, *lecture*, in this context and, in fact, I can well imagine Anne, in that erudite manner with which she could persuade by the force of her passionate arguments and precise diction, arguing for the use of some other, more listener-friendly term. What I would like to offer on this occasion are a few random thoughts, call them musings, if you like, drawn from a relatively lengthy life in poetry, and I can think of no better starting point for such reflections than with the remarkable woman and poet in whose name this annual presentation is given.

When I arrived in Saskatoon from the much smaller city of Yorkton in 1967 with my life partner, Sonia, our three small children and the fourth on the way, it did not take me long to discover that Anne Szumigalski was a well-known writer in the city. By contrast, I had written nothing more than a smattering of creative prose pieces in high school and in university. Szumigalski has said that at the age of four she knew she was going to be a poet, or perhaps that she knew she was a poet even then. At the age of four I had no such convictions or notions. If I had any four-year-old thoughts at all about what I would be, it probably was a fireman or policeman, or perhaps a shipyard worker like my father, since we were in the midst of the Second World War. By age ten those child-of-four dreams had dissipated and had been replaced by more illustrious and grandiose ones. I was convinced that my budding athletic prowess destined me to become either an NHL hockey star or an ace baseball pitcher bound for the major leagues. Nowhere in my childhood was there even the remotest thought that I would become a poet. Yet, just as Anne Szumigalski's childhood in England undoubtedly did much to shape her future as a poet-to-be, I have no doubt that my own childhood in two different parts of this country—Vancouver and rural Saskatchewan—accomplished the same thing, in my case by sowing seeds that would lie ungerminated in the soil for many years. But I want to say more about childhood and its influences a little further on.

When I arrived in Saskatoon to teach school, I was thirty years old, a young married man with four children, the family paycheque-earner. Despite being preoccupied with what Zorba the Greek called *the whole catastrophe*, I became increasingly aware of an existing writing community in the city and in the province and I began to meet people who were interested in writing, all of this coming as a decided novelty to me because I had known no writers until then. What I suspect now was that within me there lay a smouldering but dormant interest in writing, even if I was not entirely aware of it. This unexpected literary interest was kindled by several local writers, one a high school English teacher whose poems had been published in *Queen's Quarterly* and *Tamarack Review*, the other a freelance writer of everything and anything for which he could get paid. Whenever we happened to get together, the other two talked about what they were writing or had recently written and I quickly realized that if I were to become a meaningful part of our conversations, I'd best have some writing to talk about. That, in a nutshell, was how I came to launch a career in writing in Saskatoon in 1968.

My first encounter with Anne Szumigalski was at a meeting of writers—late in 1968 or early 1969—called to discuss the formation of the organization that was to become the Saskatchewan Writers Guild (SWG). I remember Anne as a forceful and articulate person who passionately argued that such an organization must be *for professional writers only*—and I believe in her view that meant only published writers of poetry and fiction. She was formidable and fiery in her views and absolutely impassioned when she spoke about poetry. After that initial meeting with Szumigalski, and after the formation of the SWG, I began to see her more often at various literary events, though I was never a member of any of her ongoing poetry groups in the city. In fact, I never belonged to any writing group in my entire writing career, though I was certainly aware of their potential as positive motivators for writers. I didn't need the motivation; I needed the time to write. So my decision to abstain from regular writing groups was partly by choice and partly because my teaching life was so time-demanding that I couldn't imagine trying to work a writing group into the full-ahead, breakneck momentum my high school English position demanded or, perhaps more accurately, that I demanded of myself.

My favourite memory of Anne was of driving from the Qu'Appelle Valley to Saskatoon after a writing conference. She and Joe Rosenblatt were passengers. Talk about a lively conversation, almost non-stop for the entire trip, with Anne's voice always rising as she clinched another point with Rosenblatt. At one point in the conversation I recall Anne saying, with absolute conviction, "When I write, I become a child again." Those words are like a Post-it note that has stuck to my fridge ever since. At first, I thought it a rather strange statement for a woman of Anne's age to make—she was fifteen years my senior—and I was ready to dismiss it as a moment of exuberant hyperbole. But the more I read her work or heard her read and speak and the more I came to know her, the more I realized that this was quite true of Anne; this *was the way she wrote*, something fundamental to her own distinctive process of writing, her own unique way of seeing and sharing her world. I would love to be able to tell you that as a result of hearing this,

I became a better writer because I found myself capable of the same thing, becoming a child again. I can't say this because I couldn't become a child again in the manner Anne could. What I discovered was that the way Szumigalski wrote was unique to her and that the way I write is different. It has nothing to do with right or wrong. It has to do with human differences. The way we unlock the words and tap into the flow of language, into the rhythms coursing through us, into the images that flash into the mind, is unique to each of us. We all go back to our childhoods from time to time to sift through the treasure chest of memory, but we enter that distant realm, grown dim with time, in our own inimitable manner and with our own particular and personal discoveries. And that is how it should be.

Sometimes childhood memories creep or flash into your life in unexpected places and times, as this one did for me in Cuba in February of last year. There, in a resort area outside Santiago de Cuba, along came a poem I called "Suspension of Belief":

Cables, ropes and wooden slats
create a seemingly fragile
sagging arc high above
the crash and dash
of Capilano Canyon.
I am five.

In my eyes this is not
a bridge—but rather,
some adult deceit
designed to instill fear
in a small boy.

Father takes my hand,
envelops it in warmth,
strength and security
a child comes to accept
as truth. "Come on,"
he says.

I step forward.
Beneath my feet
my faith and my trust
teeter and sway
side to side,
nothing beneath me
but a void
my fear has filled.

"No," I say.

What we remember of our childhoods, that is to say, what we believe we actually remember, may not conform in every respect with actuality. But it is truth, as our memories disclose it, and with each unfolded memory note I am closer to knowing who I am and closer to accepting that knowledge. That strikes me as being one of the best reasons for writing anything.

So, how did I embark on this forty-plus-year poetry journey, this meandering, labyrinthine trip I am still very much travelling? I began my first serious attempts at poetry in 1968 in Saskatoon and by the end of that year I had begun to be published. I now realize that I was extremely fortunate to have received from different magazine editors considerable positive encouragement to those early, awkward poetic efforts. Once I began writing stories and poems, I became increasingly aware of, and began connecting with, the flourishing writing community in Saskatchewan. I met more writers and became even more excited and seized by a feeling, which later became a belief, that I had become part of something tremendously exciting that was happening not only in my home province but across the entire country, a desire of Canadians to create their own literature, to tell their own stories. I began attending every poetry and prose reading I could. I ransacked used bookstores for books of poetry and began reading voraciously and randomly, but with an underlying purpose: I wanted to see what other poets across the country and elsewhere were writing, what they were saying and how they were saying it. I tried to read as many different poets in English and in translation as I could find. I was embarked on a mission of self-education in the poet's craft, though I may not have thought of it in those terms at the time. My unspoken goal was to discover everything I could about poetry and how it is written.

At this point, I'd like to take off on a slight tangent to say that I did not at that time and generally still do not read books of poetic theory. I read poetry itself. I have always believed that poetry and how it is written is largely self-taught. So I was delighted to discover, several years ago now, Ted Kooser's down-to-earth book on writing poetry called *The Poetry Home Repair Manual,* because that is precisely what Kooser, a former Poet Laureate of the United States, also believes. What I have learned about the writing of poetry has come almost entirely from my reading of other poets and, most especially, the poets I admire and return to again and again because their words and their lines never lose their lustre for me. They serve to restore my faith in poetry on those occasions when I happen to pick up a literary magazine or a volume of poetry and read poems that fill me with a sense of despair because of their obtuseness or their stubborn refusal to let me, as reader, into the poem for at least some fleeting glimpse of warm, breathing humanness. What I am confessing here might qualify as heresy in academic circles and in a country where creative writing schools are busily turning out new generations of writers whose heads are filled with the writing theories of the day. But if I am uttering heresy, I don't much care. You see, I have now reached an age where I can say whatever I damn well want because I can easily be sloughed off or dismissed as prematurely senile.

When I started writing poems I was little more than a dozen years removed from my high school days and one of my recollections that is germane to these musings was the moment of startling revelation, or even epiphany, that happened for me when, at age seventeen, I read for the first time a particular Canadian poem in our literature text called *The Book of Good Poems*—and isn't that anthology title worthy of a "lecture" all by itself? The poem in question was Anne Marriott's "The Wind Our Enemy." It delivered an unexpected, sharp punch to my solar plexus, took my breath away, and changed the world of poetry for me in an instant. Until that time in my life, though I enjoyed reading poems, I had always thought of poetry as the artfully archaic works of English or American poets, mostly men, mostly dead, who wrote about people and places far removed in subject and sentiment from my own humdrum and bucolic life growing up on a small Saskatchewan farm and attending high school in a dusty prairie town. Marriott's poem overwhelmed and amazed me. Here was a poet, a woman, writing about a place and time and people and situations that I could fully appreciate and understand—no castles or knights in shining armour, or highway rogues galloping in the silvery moonlight over the English moors. Here instead were wind, barbed wire, wheat kernels, looming thunderstorms and ordinary farming folk. And what's more, this poet was still very much alive—and a Canadian, too. I had no idea, at that moment, just how profound an impact the Marriott poem would have on me. But I do know that my first two books, *Wind Songs* and *Prairie Pub Poems*, published about twenty-one and twenty-two years later, grew from that single poem that I had read and reread with the ecstatic wonder of discovery. Marriott's poem was one of my earliest models. Sometime after those two books were published, I wrote to Marriott and told her how important her poem had been in my life; in fact, I think I sent her copies of both books. In another side-track, I didn't know at the time that I was following one of the common practices of poets-to-be—modelling poems on those of our predecessors—until I read Dylan Thomas's collection of radio broadcasts in which he talked about his Robert Service poems and other poems he modelled on different poets he enjoyed, long before he found his own distinctive voice and poetic structure. I also recall hearing Al Purdy say that he had written two or three Black Mountain poems and then moved on.

In 1979 I joined The League of Canadian Poets. I remember being at my first annual meeting, feeling uncomfortable, out of my element and, as newcomers so often feel, rather like an impostor, when a woman came up to me and said, "You're Glen Sorestad, aren't you?" It was Anne Marriott. She had recognized me, she said, from the author photo on my books. I was flabbergasted—that a poet whom I almost worshipped for the writing of a single poem that had changed the direction of my life, should be so generous and kind as to introduce herself to a new and mostly unknown poet. I have never forgotten that moment, and bless you, Anne, I have tried my best to replicate that act of kindness and generosity by following your example whenever I could and by making myself available to younger writers who sought me out. From that early Marriott moment, I did not need further convincing about the value of the League and its drawing together of poets from across this country. Over the thirty-plus years that I have been a member of this organization, I have made a great many friends who have enriched my life. I could sense a family spirit among members that made me feel especially good about belonging.

I also discovered early in my years with the League that, almost without exception, members are accessible and unhesitant in sharing their ideas. It may have been at the same meeting when, walking to one of the session rooms, I noticed Michael Ondaatje sitting by himself in a lobby area. I had never met Michael before but I, too, recognized him from photos on the many books of his I owned. So I introduced myself, and before long we were ranging over random topics. Ondaatje's openness to an unknown from Saskatchewan made me feel that perhaps I wasn't, after all, an impostor among all the legitimate and much published poets of the League.

I must also pay proper homage to the late John Newlove, who was very much a mentor of mine with his amazing poems, especially "Ride Off Any Horizon." I still love that poem and I keep returning to it and rereading it as a way of replenishing the spirit and restoring the enormous importance and impact of the incredible music that can be found in the simplest and most precise expression of our language. One of the reasons I was initially drawn to Newlove and his poetry was that we were of the same generation and had, in fact, spent our boyhoods in east-central Saskatchewan within thirty or forty miles of one another without ever knowing this until much later in our adult lives. So we clearly had shared many common experiences of young boys growing up in this parkland area of the northern plains. Sonia and I visited Newlove and his wife Susan in Toronto in 1979 or 1980. Newlove was, like Marriott and Ondaatje, welcoming, open and generous with his time, though he knew little about us when we arrived on his doorstep. I was full of questions about poetry and although Newlove was essentially a shy man and a loner, not much inclined to talk about his art, he nevertheless took us in and showed great patience with both my ignorance and my clumsy attempts to probe his art.

Reading Newlove is, for me, to receive a lesson in the economy, precision and musicality of our language. When my book *Leaving Holds Me Here* was to appear in 2001, the editor-in-chief of Thistledown Press, Patrick O'Rourke, managed to persuade John Newlove to take on the selecting and editing of this collection of selected and new poems covering the twenty-five years to 2000. I couldn't have been more delighted because it seemed so fortuitous and, in a sense, so appropriate, considering Newlove's influence on much of my poetry. As it happened, this book was apparently the last that Newlove edited before his health went into serious decline leading to his death in 2003. Though Newlove was known to some people for his sometimes erratic, anti-social behaviour, I saw another side of him. Several months after the book finally appeared on the scene, I received a package from Newlove in the mail. Inside was a stuffed cushion, shaped like a trout, with a little note attached in John's tiny, wavering scrawl that read, "For Sorestad, the troller for trout and truth." Sound-conscious always, Newlove could also show great generosity of spirit. With this gift he was recognizing the new book, my love of fishing and my poetic responsibility all at the same time.

How do you grow a poet? The esteemed late Robert Kroetsch asked this now well-known question many years ago in his wonderful book, *Seed Catalogue*. *So, Sorestad, if you didn't know at four, or even at seventeen, that you wanted to be a poet, what led you to become a poet anyway?* I hear Kroetsch—and others of you—asking. I used the image earlier of dormancy, of seeds that lie in the earth for years before they germinate. I cannot speak with any certainty about the sowing of the seeds, but I do have a feeling it all begins in childhood with the sounds of nursery rhymes and stories and poems. Somewhere in the deepest recesses of memory there's a voice I recognize as my father's intoning, "Wee Willie Winkie runs through the town/ Upstairs, downstairs in his nightgown." Did this really happen? I can't be one hundred per cent sure, but I suspect it did. I have to trust the voices I hear, the voices that intrude on the consciousness from wherever they may loll or linger in the distant silence. I love what Timothy Findley had to say about voices: *Writers do not steal voices—they hear them. And what I hear, I will write. This is my job.* Amen, I say.

For isn't it the voices we hear, or even imagine we hear, the echoes that manage to make their way down the long hallway from the past, that shape us and, eventually, what we write? For as long as I can remember, I loved story, song, rhyme, rhythms, and especially the power of language to stir and drive the emotions, to set the hair a-tingle, or to send cold shivers vibrating deliciously down the spine, to tantalize the ear and set the tympanic membranes thrumming. This love of language and sound, fostered in earliest childhood, never left me, nor I suspect does it leave any of us who were fortunate enough to have grown up among books and stories and songs and loving parents or grandparents who believed it important to make these things part of our earliest experiences. Both of my parents were readers who placed a premium on books and on the ability and the time to read and enjoy them. Though we were far from wealthy, our family always managed to find books to read and enjoy.

The next phase of my life that could provide some answers to Kroetsch's question unfolds in a one-roomed country schoolhouse in east-central Saskatchewan in the early 1950s. I attended this school from age ten to fifteen. There were roughly eighteen students from grade one to ten, so the teacher spent most of his or her time with the grade ones and twos, leaving everyone else either to learn how to work independently or to fail. I loved the independence and thrived on it. I especially loved reading the poems in our literary texts of the day, poems like Tennyson's "The Lady of Shallot," Alfred Noyes's "The Highwayman," and "Kew in Lilac Time," Walter de la Mare's "Silver" and "All That's Past" (I think of this latter poem every time I walk through the woods—"very old are the woods/ and the buds that break/ out of the brier's bough/ when March winds wake"). I memorized entire poems, sometimes huge chunks of others, or just a stanza that really appealed. I didn't have to do it, although there was, as I recall, a minimal amount of memorization required in our courses. I did it because I loved the sound of the language, the rhythms, the rhyme schemes. Sometimes it was the story that appealed, as in "The Bannerman of the Dandenong," an Australian poem by Alice Werner about a brush fire and a lone rider's heroic sacrifice. Even today, I can recite passages of poetry that I memorized sixty years ago and I still love the feel of those words rolling on my tongue. Were these lines of poetry absorbed into my being in a kind of linguistic osmosis? Are these the seeds of the future poet? Is this intense love of language the necessary essence, the sprouting seedling of the poet-to-be? If you are twelve or fourteen and you are carrying around a head full of poems and poetry fragments, perhaps it should not be unexpected that at some future date this might manifest itself somehow in the life of the adult. In my case, it took two decades before this occurred.

Incidentally, that rural Saskatchewan school, which is no more, was named Wergeland School. In the five or six years I attended it I had no idea what the school's name signified, nor did any of the teachers ever tell us, if indeed they knew, unless I have forgotten any mention of it. Much later, I learned that the school was named by the early Norwegian homesteaders to the community, among whom were my own maternal grandparents, after Norway's famous poet and playwright Henrik Wergeland. None of his poetry was part of our studies. Now fast-forward to Norway in 1998. Exactly fifty years later, my friend and colleague, Norwegian poet Arne Ruste, took me to see a huge statue of the famous poet and we had our photo taken together at the foot of it. I wonder what Kroetsch would make of all this, if he were to hear this unfolding of a life in poetry?

I think of the irony involved in how as a young country lad I memorized poems about knights and castles, Sir Launfal and Sir Lancelot, and the wretched, solitary Lady of Shallot—those exotic, faraway, mythic figures and places—never imagining for even the most indulgent moment, that one day in 2002 I would find myself standing on a stage in the famous Ljubljana castle, perched on the heights above that Slovenian capital, reading my poems to an international audience of several hundred that included the president of the country and the mayor of Ljubljana. When I stepped onto the stage that evening, in the flickering lights of simulated torches that cast dancing shadows across the walls, I actually flashed back to that younger me in Wergeland School reciting, "She left the web, she left the loom/She made three paces through the room" and I thought about how fortunate I was to have accepted the challenge to follow the poetic Muse. "Two roads diverged in a wood and I —/ I took the road less travelled by/ And that has made all the difference."

You'll note that now Robert Frost has slipped into these remarks and I'll confess that this is by no means accidental or inappropriate, because when I consider the poets from whom I have learned what I have come to know about the writing and crafting of poetry, Robert Frost is certainly one of my early mentors—and an important one at that. One of the many things I learned from Frost was to be highly attuned and attentive to the natural world, for it is a never-ending source of imagery and symbol and metaphor. Consider the uses poets have made through the ages of words like *river, moon, the sea, a grain of sand, a red rose, birds (like the dove, lark, raven or owl), the snake, any tree, clouds, mountains.* Wallace Stevens once called poetry "a pheasant disappearing in the brush," as if to suggest that poetry can best be seen in terms of the world of nature. Mary Oliver called the natural world "the old river that runs through everything." The natural world played a hugely significant role in shaping my life. It forged in me a deep love and respect for the flora and fauna around me. I spent my formative years learning firsthand and through books everything I could about that world, so it is not surprising that much of my poetry, despite my having lived in an urban environment now for more than fifty years, still explores that natural world and its images, often through memory, that has shaped my views and beliefs about the world and about life. In my poem "Beginnings," which I wrote more than thirty years ago, I speak of the poem as "the impaled wing/the sole reminder/of a sharp-tailed grouse/that flaps now on the wire," the kind of image that formed a key part of the distinctive world of the prairies in which I grew up.

The natural world calls to me all the time, and happiness can be as simple as a walk through the falling aspen leaves of autumn, along the Meewasin Trail in Saskatoon or through my own community-serving Lakewood Park. Nature gives me great pleasure and provides moments of incredible beauty, moments of intense joy and, especially important to a writer, a stimulating of the curiosity that so often leads me to want to write about what has taken hold of my emotions or my intellect. But the natural world can also be harsh, unforgiving, brutal, and totally indifferent to us. Perhaps it is this duplicity in the natural world that provokes our curiosity, piques our interest, and makes us want to seek out and recognize its images and use them as a way of seeing our own lives, or of simply trying to make sense of our world. Has anyone ever captured this two-sided natural world better than John Newlove did in "The Double-headed Snake"?

All writing is a way of *saying,* and it was Newlove who said in his poem "When I Heard of the Friend's Death," *There is always so much more to be said than can be said.* Like the early balladeers and minstrels and like Chaucer, that first great English poet, I am a storyteller at heart and my poetry, whether it begins with an image or a few lines or an intense emotion, always has some narrative element and much of the time is driven by the desire to say something. Often I am uncertain as to what a poem wants to say, or what it may eventually end up saying. I suppose, when you strip everything away and get down to the bare bones of poetry, what it adds up to is that as poets we are all telling our own stories—the stories (which may ultimately become one saga) of who we are, possibly where we believe we may be sited in this unfolding of a life and perhaps where we think we may be heading. We are, all of us poets, on a journey, and we are compelled to say things about this journey and what we are experiencing along the way. We struggle to make sense of it all and to give utterance to the anxieties and the confusions of the obstacles and impediments that thwart and frustrate us. But we also want to celebrate those moments of insight and epiphany and sheer joy that, happily, we experience as well.

So why do I write poetry? Alden Nowlan, early in his career, was asked this question. His response was something like, "What else would I do?" I don't suppose it even occurred to Nowlan that he could be doing something else. Again, I come back to John Newlove because of the brilliance of his craft and because of one of the cogent observations he made in his Caroline Heath Lecture in Regina in 1988: that there are two kinds of people who write, *those who would and those who must.* Newlove and Nowlan definitely belonged to the latter of Newlove's categories. Poetry may have been a choice for me at thirty-one, but it is no longer a choice. You could say I seized the opportunity, but more likely, with the passage of time I was seized by poetry and there was never a thought of turning back from the road that diverged in the yellow wood. I write poetry because it is what I do, it is my way of interacting with the world, my way of what Wallace Stevens called "getting the world right." Poetry for me is also, to steal an image from Arthur Miller, my way of leaving my thumbprint on a block of ice on a hot July day. My poetry is what I have to show for the journey I've made, for what I have seen and felt and thought about and wrestled with, emotionally and spiritually and intellectually, as a caring human being.

So what *keeps* me writing then? Obviously beyond the need that desires fulfillment there must be some satisfaction—and probably that should be pluralized. One of those, for me, is, and always has been, *the element of surprise*, that the unexpected is never far away, once the first few words are committed to the page. Sometimes it is a genuine surprise that the poems still come at all, up from that mysterious well of remembered images, voices, tales, impressions. It's the unexpected word or phrase that leaps onto the page and catches me off-guard, the suddenly remembered image, the phrase that resurfaces from a childhood game, anything that appears as if by some mysterious and unheard calling, something unbidden that offers itself to the poem and finds its way into the flow of the lines. *Surprise keeps me writing.* If the day should come when I am no longer surprised by things I write, I expect that will be the signal to stop writing. To cease writing would be to cease caring. How can we live and not care? When I write something new, I want and expect to be surprised. I anticipate it and I'm disappointed if it doesn't happen.

I feel the same way about the poetry I read. I want to be surprised and delighted by the unexpected turn of phrase, the perfectly placed word choice, the abrupt reversal of expectation. An Arkansas poet named Jo McDougall, whom I met at a reading I gave in Little Rock a few years ago, has a unique talent of being able to catch me by surprise. I've read every book she's written and while I've learned much about both conciseness and preciseness from her, I doubt I shall ever be able to achieve her ability to blindside the reader with brilliant word choices, as she does in this excerpt from "What Happens When We Leave":

Leaving a room, we remember arriving,
the first turning of the key,
the room, pristine and startled,
opening to take us in.

Now, who would have thought of a familiar room, upon returning to it, as either *pristine* or *startled*? Can you think of a less likely pair of candidates for describing a room as you walk through the doorway? In fact, *startled* is, to my ear, startling, a most surprising choice, as is *pristine*. This ongoing wonderment with language, the element of surprise and delight at the unexpected juxtapositions poets come up with, is surely one of the best reasons we read poetry and it is certainly one of my personal motivations for writing as well. I just love it when, out of somewhere, call it the blue if you choose, a word leaps out of the grassy ditch and onto the page, a single word that, because of its placement, makes all the difference in the world. To the poem, to me, to the reader. Whether it's a matter of being attuned to the voices, listening attentively to the silences or, as I said in my poem "We Need These Silences," *the knowing/ that this silence, too,/ is a gift*. We write for as many different reasons as we are unique human beings, but language and the silences between words and lines is what we work with as we move towards that perfect expression, that perfect poem.

I don't know whether I found poetry or poetry found me or whether it was a bit of both. But does it really matter? I do know this: poetry has made of my life something that I could not have imagined, has taken me places I would not have gone, and has set me among some of the world's most remarkable human beings. For that, I am truly thankful.

Coming (back) to Poetry

ROBERT CURRIE

Anne Szumigalski Lecture • Saskatoon, Saskatchewan • June 16, 2012

GOOD AFTERNOON, LADIES AND GENTLEMEN. I'D LIKE TO dedicate this talk to the memory of Andy Suknaski, who died on May 3rd, 2012, in Moose Jaw. Andy was a talented visual artist as well as an exceptional poet, and in his prime he was a kind of wandering one-man publishing house, churning out chapbooks from Wood Mountain or Deer Lodge or wherever else he happened to be. What an inspiration he was for the rest of us.

Now let me begin by sharing my fascination with the way poets see poetry, with the way they define it and describe it, with how poetic their prose on that particular topic is. For example, Patrick Friesen says that poetry is "a way of thinking, a way of being. It's life-blood. Jugular music."[1] Stephen Dobyns believes that "a poem is a window that hangs between two or more human beings who otherwise live in darkened rooms."[2] According to Irving Layton, "A poem when you are done with it, must be able to get off the page, turn the doorhandle, and walk directly into the lives of people."[3] Lorri Neilsen Glenn says that "poetry remains the erotic hearth we are drawn to ... it is a sacred sort of space, a state of being and of heart, tender, raw, and often exhilarating .... And," she adds, "poetry is the grace we can find in the everyday."[4] Molly Peacock takes only a slightly different approach. "Poetry," she says, "is the art that responds to the anxiety of living."[5] Rosemary Griebel notes that "each of us comes to a poem listening / for perceptive words that will crack open / the meaning of this world."[6] I think you'll agree that poets often have fascinating ideas about this art that means so much to us. Yes, but it's equally fascinating to learn how they come to poetry, these artists who so often go on to dedicate their lives to their art.

It's no surprise to learn that some young men turn to poetry for the same reason that others begin playing rock and roll. They hope that it will provide them with a way to impress the girls, or, better yet, to win the girls. Let me give you two examples that may surprise you, both examples from poets whose work you probably know. The older of the two had this to say: "I began poetry as a substitute for sex—I was a shy teenager with buck teeth and a repressed desire to emulate Jefferey Farnol's heroes in my relations with women...."[7] Now Jefferey Farnol isn't much known today, but a century ago he was one of the best-selling authors in the world, famous for his swashbuckling romances featuring honourable, handsome heroes, innocent heroines and, of course, the most villainous of villains. Who can blame a young poet for wanting to be the kind of hero who might win a beautiful heroine? The second young writer said this about his beginnings: "When I started falling in love with girls, all of whom were older and more mature than I was, I began to imitate various forms of writing, in the hope of bluffing my way into their hearts."[8] The first quotation is from Fred Cogswell, who for fifteen years served as an editor for *The Fiddlehead* and later as the sole editor and publisher of Fiddlehead Poetry Books; at one time or another Fred probably published the work of more than a few in this audience. The other quotation comes from Gary Geddes, well-known for his own poetry and for various versions of *Fifteen Canadian Poets*, from which many of us learned our early CanLit lessons. How good it was for all of us that their desire to charm the ladies brought these two men to a lifelong love of poetry.

Others come to poetry in vastly different ways. Some lucky ones have composed poetry as long as they can remember. I think of one child who had begun to consider poetry her life work even before she was old enough to read and write. She had—as she was quick to emphasize—"the great good luck to be born into a family whose chief amusements were language games."[9] One of those games was, in fact, "the poetry game," which required players to write poems based on folded papers handed them, papers which contained a word they must use and a question they must answer in a poem. It's no wonder that this child began to glory in her play with the multitude of words floating in her head. She was soon finding ways to make them sing and dance, turning them into poems that never saw the page, keeping them in her memory until she had the chance to recite them to her aunts. Later, when she learned to read and write, she found she could no longer memorize her own poems, and writing new poems was a struggle involving false starts, crumpled pages and many tears. Luckily for her, something which later came to be called "wit-walking" was an art practised in her family for generations. This involved the method of so-called modern freefall workshops, letting ideas run freely and take her where they would, and later looking for the subjects, themes and characters that might inspire a full-fledged work of art. She soon learned that even when no complete poem results, "there is still the exercise itself to rejoice in: words tumbling from the mind and seeding themselves higgledy-piggledy on the paper like plants in a wild-flower garden."[10] In her case, of course, many wonderful poems did result, and this child grew up to be that remarkable poet who is memorialized in this lecture series.

When Anne Szumigalski moved from England to the Big Muddy Badlands of southern Saskatchewan, it was not that enormous non-English landscape that disappointed her, but the fact that she had come to a land that didn't know its own poets. That would begin to change at least in part thanks to Anne—because of her poems, her teaching, her mentorship—in short, her inspiration and example, for she was perhaps the most influential poet in the history of this province. It's interesting to note that Anne said, "it is the sense of community that I found in Saskatchewan rather than the sense of space and isolation that has most influenced my work."[11]

Not every writer takes such a direct route to poetry. I think now of a boy whose beginnings as a writer go back to age ten when he was the proprietor, journalist *and* delivery boy of the *Home Street Clarion*, each issue of which he wrote by hand and personally delivered to his Home Street neighbours. When issue number three caused a neighbourhood scandal by revealing that a couple down the street belonged to a nudist colony, his mother brought his journalism career to an abrupt end.

Shortly after that, luck played a part in turning his attention to poetry. He won a prize from a fish pond at a church bazaar, and that prize was a copy of an old poetry text. If I remember rightly it was the text with that most deadly of ambiguous titles, *Enduring Poetry*. At any rate, it was a faulty copy with many blank pages. One night this young lad started to read a poem in the book, but instead of an ending there was just another blank page. That's when he began writing his own endings for the poems. Before long, he was filling other blank pages with complete poems of his own, and he was hooked; after all, there were his poems side by side with those of Wordsworth, Browning and Tennyson.

In high school, chance played a further part in his journey to poetry when he noticed that his social studies text picked Dante's *The Divine Comedy* as one of the best books of all time; he figured with that title it had to be funny; imagine his shock when he saw that what he was borrowing from the library was a monumental epic poem from the fourteenth century. But he liked the "snazzy lingo" and—as he put it—"sailed through that whopper of a book / in I'd say only about two or three months."[12]

I think perhaps that reading Dante helped make Gary Hyland the remarkable poet he became, the author of eight books, including *Love of Mirrors*, which cleaned up at the 2008 Saskatchewan Books Awards, winning not only the Poetry Award but also the Book of the Year Award. As you may know, Gary was the man who created the Saskatchewan Festival of Words, and was a founder of Coteau Books and the Sage Hill Writing Experience. He was one of the most influential arts activists Saskatchewan has ever known, but despite his endless hours of volunteer work he always found time to write his poems. Even when he was bed-ridden with Lou Gehrig's disease and could only respond by blinking, he was using an alphabet board and still working with a friend on revising a final suite of poems.

Let me cite another example of the part chance can play in bringing people to poetry. This is the case of a married teenager earning a bare-bones living doing deliveries for a pharmacist. Once, while delivering a prescription to an elderly man, this young fellow was invited into the house while the old gent went searching for his chequebook. Looking around the living room, the young guy noticed there were books everywhere, not just in a personal library carefully arranged in a wall of shelves, but on the coffee table, the end tables, even on the floor. Checking more closely, he discovered a little magazine called *Poetry* and a book called *The Little Review Anthology*, both of them full of poems. He was astounded by his discovery and immediately began to wish they were both his own. More astounding was the fact that the old gentleman noticed his interest and gave him the magazine and the book, telling him that maybe he'd write something himself some day, and he'd need to know where to send it. Well, Raymond Carver did write some things himself. Eventually, he did send his work to *Poetry*, and the editors agreed to publish six of his poems. Of course, one can argue that Carver would have become a writer even if he'd never met that generous book-lover, but here's what he said about that encounter: "I was just a pup then, but nothing can explain, or explain away, such a moment: the moment when the very thing I needed most in my life—call it a polestar—was casually, generously given to me. Nothing remotely approaching that moment has happened since."[13]

How many children, one wonders, write little poems about their pets or about playing in the snow and then as adults never write again? How many high school cheer-leaders write poems that the cheer-leading squad can chant in support of their school's football or basketball teams, and then give up writing as soon as they graduate? In both cases, a good many, I suspect. Lorna Crozier was a kid who did that kind of writing. Was it chance that made her different—or something else? One can make an argument for chance because, in her first full-time job, teaching in Glaslyn, Saskatchewan, she was lucky enough to have a principal who wrote poems. Lorna valued that relationship, for now at noon hours and recesses she had someone with whom to discuss poetry, each serving as audience, critic and fan of the other's work. Two people keeping poetry alive.

Nor was that the end of the role of luck in Lorna Crozier's early poetry career. When she was twenty-three, she met her first live writer, Ken Mitchell, who had come to Swift Current to conduct a creative writing session organized by the high school English department where Lorna now taught. Everyone attending had to submit a piece of creative writing ahead of time, and everyone felt trepidation about doing that. The fear was groundless, for Ken offered gentle criticism to everyone—everyone but Lorna. He said he was sure he'd never seen a poem from her. She was disappointed, of course, but she lied and told him it didn't matter. A month later she was surprised to receive an airmail letter from Greece. It was from Ken Mitchell with the news that he'd found her poem. "It's good," he wrote, and added, "Have you ever sent any poetry out? Why don't you send this and some of your more polished pieces to *Grain*?"[14] In truth, Lorna had no "more polished pieces," but she sat down and wrote one, and in due time Caroline Heath accepted both poems for *Grain*. All this because Ken Mitchell chanced to find her missing poem under some papers on his desk.

Is it possible that, if he hadn't made that lucky find, Lorna Crozier would never have become the poet she is today? I don't think so. Though Lorna grew up in a working-class family that didn't keep books around the house, she somehow—and very early—developed a love of reading and writing. Years later she would say, "It was just some itch that I was born with, to put words down on paper. I can't think of any other way to describe it."[15] Lorna also recalled an incident from grade one when she wrote a poem about a dying dog and her teacher tacked it up on the bulletin board for everyone to read. After that, it seemed that people expected her to do something with words. Or maybe—and this is what I believe—she expected it of herself.

At this point, perhaps, a few words about my own beginnings with poetry might be appropriate. I was the kind of a kid who'd been writing little stories as long as he could remember, but who'd never even considered trying to write a poem—except once, when forced to for a class assignment in grade eight or nine. However, at university I was lucky enough to take a CanLit class, and that prompted a change. Here's a poem about what happened next:

Contact

In the U. of S. bookstore, pricing texts for intersession,
I'm drawn to a wire rack, a rugged face, slashes of red
and gold across a thoughtful visage. I seize
the book, the price so low I know for sure
there's been a grave mistake, I rush
to the till, fling down my cash before
some harried clerk can raise the price.
On the first bench outside I begin
A Red Carpet for the Sun.

Wandering in the stacks where I once lost
all my powers of concentration, finding
Desmond Pacey's *Creative Writing in Canada*
bookmarked with what seemed to be a snapshot
of the German actress, Maria Schell, her smile
enough to melt ice from January windshields,
today I spot a pamphlet, yellowed pages
bound by staples, *When We Are Young.*

Tonight I jot down an image, play
with words, try to give them shape.
There's been no official diagnosis,
but already I know I'm afflicted
with a fever that I pray will
rage through all my days.[16]

Well, I'd have to say that fever is still raging, and I thank Irving Layton and Raymond Souster for their fine examples that set the fever off.

If chance played its part in the way I and these other writers first came to poetry, I have to think that they would have made that trip at other times, in other ways. Each of them had a burning desire to write.

More than a desire, perhaps. Isn't a need to write a common factor here? Perhaps the question I should be asking isn't how writers come to poetry, but this: what keeps them coming back again and again?

Certainly, there's the excitement of reading in a little magazine for the first time the poem that you have written. There it is, in print, with your name upon it, ready to be read by people you'll never know, validated somehow by that process. And that is nothing compared to the thrill of holding your first book in your hands, staring at the well-designed cover—there's your title, your name in that space where the author's name belongs, yes, it really is *your* book—then the thrill of riffling through the pages, every one containing a poem of yours, perhaps even your photo looking out at you from the book's final page. It has a heft to it, a certain bookish smell, this book of yours; it is, in fact, quite wonderful.

Better still, perhaps, is that feeling of being accepted into the community of poets, for the comradeship of poets is special. Meeting them at readings and workshops, joining them in poetry groups, befriending kindred souls who value just as much as you the magic of language, its music, its rhythms and its subtleties. I personally have been blessed to belong to a poetry group that began in 1975 as the Moose Jaw Movement. That name was partly a joke: we figured if George Bowering and those west coast poets could get their shit together and call it TISH, the least we could do was have a Moose Jaw Movement. But the name was also serious: our way of saying you didn't have to live in Vancouver, Toronto or Montreal to be a poet. Over the years the group, which is now called The Poets Combine, has evolved in extraordinary ways, but it's always kept me coming back to poetry. In fact, it's been a touchstone of my life. I suspect that some of you belong to poetry groups that matter just as much to you. Where else can we find conversation so concerned with diction, with imagery and metaphor, that it constantly fires our imaginations?

There's something else that matters to a lot of poets, and that's the hope of writing something that will last. The best poetry, after all, is timeless. When I began writing poems, I never thought about such lofty ambitions, but then one day I read a story by a writer I'd never heard of before, the Hungarian novelist Lajos Zilahy. He told a powerful tale which I'll attempt to summarize. Its protagonist is John Kovacs, a journeyman carpenter, who falls ill and dies suddenly, in October of 1874. A man who left behind neither wife, nor child, only a distant cousin. Five years after Kovacs's death, the old carpenter for whom he worked died, and nine years later so did the old woman in whose shed he lived. Fourteen years after the death of John Kovacs, his cousin—his only living relative—died too. Then in 1895 a group of drunken men in a pub got to reminiscing about their military service and how they'd once forced a new recruit to stick his head in the oven and while he was down on all fours they'd paddled his behind. After much raucous laughter—and some difficulty—one of them remembered the name of that recruit. John Kovacs. And that was the last time ever his name was spoken aloud. Four years later an old woman lay terrified in a lonely hospital room because she knew she was dying. Looking back upon her life, she remembered briefly a gentle young man who once romanced her on a summer's night, and that was the last time anyone on this earth thought of John Kovacs. The next year a fire destroyed the rectory that held the records of his birth and death. In the hard winter of 1901 a ragged man who feared that he would freeze to death stole two crosses from the village cemetery to build a fire. One of them marked the grave of John Kovacs. Years later, in 1920, a lawyer made an inventory of his father's estate, checking every scrap of paper in every drawer. One paper he threw out was an old receipt of payment for two chairs, signed by John Kovacs. That crumpled receipt ended up on the ground in a pouring rain, the rain gradually washing away the signature—except for the letter v, where John Kovacs had pressed hard with his pen.

> Then the rain washed that away too.
> And in that instant—forty-nine years after his death—the life of the journeyman carpenter ceased to exist and forever disappeared from this earth . . . But for this . . .[17]

Well, I don't know how that story affects you, but it made me think of the possibility of writing something that might just possibly outlast its author. A poem that might endure, one whose music might come ringing down the ages like a bell tolling somewhere far across the snow on a clear winter's night. A romantic idea, no doubt, but one that has a certain appeal for many a poet—though we all recognize how slim our chances are.

Now let's turn to something else that keeps us coming back to poetry: the physical reality of sitting down with a piece of paper or a computer and writing a poem. Struggling with that attempt to create something from nothing, and then settling in for the long run of revision, returning to the poem again and again in the hope that we can make it something that others will want to read, the hope—dare I say it?—that we can create a lasting record of something which would otherwise disappear. Time and again we face the challenge of shaping an experience in such a way that others will not just read about it, but fully share that experience. We try our best to create images they will see, emotions they will feel, ideas they can share, always with the hope our language will take their breath away. No one grows rich by writing poetry, but that wonderful struggle to write the poem does enrich our lives.

It's the joy of working on the poem that brings us back to poety. If you don't believe me, listen to what Ted Kooser says about working on a poem: "Revision, and I mean extensive revision, is the key to transforming a mediocre poem into a work that can touch and even alter a reader's heart. It's the biggest part of the poet's job description... You can learn to love tinkering with drafts of poems till a warm hand from somewhere above you reaches down, unscrews the top of your head, and drops in a solution that blows your ears off."[18] Yes, poetry offers surprising pleasures, but the greatest thrill comes while we're writing, doing the actual work of wrestling with the poem. Then we're transported beyond ourselves, the boring world burned away as we stoke the fires of creation, straining for that magic flame that might transform our words to art. There's the work that matters—and the joy that returns again and again.

Let me make a statement that is true for most of us: poetry is a spiritual and emotional necessity. I believe that just as we are graced by loving friends, we are graced by poetry. Mary Oliver makes that point with lyrical dexterity. "Poetry," she says, "is a life-cherishing force... For poems are not words, after all, but fires for the cold, ropes let down to the lost, something as necessary as bread in the pockets of the hungry."[19]

When I think of the necessity of poetry, I tend to think again of Raymond Carver. Here was a man whose short stories were often compared to those of Chekhov, a major American writer who changed the way the world thought about short fiction, a man who chose to write poetry although his fans argued that his reputation came from fiction and that that was where he should spend his time. Carver, however, wrote what he had to write. As you no doubt know, Raymond Carver was someone who had conquered his alcoholism, only to have his life cut short by cancer. In his last year he received intense treatment first for lung cancer, then for a brain tumour and, after a brief respite, had tumours reappear in his lungs. In the final months before he died on August 2nd, 1988, he found himself giving more and more of his time to poetry. Writing poetry had always been much more than a change of pace from writing fiction. It was essential. Tess Gallagher was Carver's loving partner during his last ten years, and here's how she describes the importance of poetry in his life: "as his companion in that life, I'm glad to have helped him keep his poetry alive for the journey, for the comfort and soul-making he drew from it so crucially in his too-early going."[20] Poetry—a necessity indeed.

And now I'd like to return for a few moments to the more mundane idea that it's contact with other poets that keeps so many of us coming back to poetry, meeting poets we admire, reading their work, learning that they accept us into the valued community of poetry. Let me back up that belief with a story from the summer of 1974. There was a poetry reading at Fort San, the former T.B. sanatorium that was once the home of the Saskatchewan Summer School of the Arts. The site of the reading was to be the little one-room schoolhouse where some of the creative writing classes took place, but it was a muggy evening in July and the heat drove everyone outside onto a patch of grass encircled by trees and caraganas. There were perhaps three dozen people, old and young, staff and students, clustered around the fire that someone started to drive away mosquitoes. There, for an hour, Anne Szumigalski and an emerging writer read their poems. What struck that emerging writer was the fact that, with Anne reading, the heat and bugs were soon forgotten. But not the poems. Here, he thought, was a poet who made all the wild and poetic definitions of poetry ring true. Her poems worked at the gut level—you really did read them with your nerves and you'd be crazy to try to translate them into prose. And what's more, *he* was reading with her, and she was treating him like an equal. Over the years he would read with her again, introduce her on a number of occasions, even appear with her on a panel. They would become friends, in fact, though not close friends, for he regarded her with too much awe for that to happen. He was a great admirer, not only of her poetry, but also of her leadership, the way she inspired so many other poets, and not just those who met with her in the Saskatoon poetry group or studied in her workshops. Sometimes, when you admire someone's poetry, there's one poem that takes on special significance, and Anne's poem, "Nettles," did that for him. Anne knew how much he loved the poem, and he thought it must have pleased her, for in his copy of *Instar* she wrote the inscription "love in a field of nettles." As a matter of fact, Anne used to kid him that he should read the poem at her funeral. He told her he'd be happy to do so if she'd only wait at least twenty years for that event.

Sadly, she couldn't wait, and in 1999, when she was far too young, she died. The writer of whom I'm speaking drove to Saskatoon for her funeral, wondering all the while, What if she wasn't kidding? He was too shy to bring it up, of course, but folded inside the pocket of his jacket was a copy of "Nettles," just in case. The funeral was a fine testament to a wonderful person, and there was no call for him to read her poem.

A few years later, he was going through another book of Anne's and came across an inscription his memory had somehow managed to repress. There, on August 7th, 1994 Anne had written, "To Bob—who has promised to read a poem at my funeral." Yes, I was that Bob, and I'll never know whether she was still kidding me—though I seem to remember an impish grin and think perhaps she was. Still, I felt terrible because I may have let her down. A few weeks after reading that inscription I took a trip up to Saskatoon and drove out to Block 70a of Saskatoon's Woodlawn Cemetery and found the grave that says, "Poet, Pioneer, Prairie Woman." The sun was shining brightly that afternoon, a prairie wind blowing from the west, flowing down the slope from the house where Anne once lived, where so many friends and relatives had met to reminisce about her after the funeral. For a long time I stood silently beside her grave, the sunlight stinging my eyes. I read the poem for her then, and I'd like to read it for you now.

Nettles

When I am old
I will totter along broken pavements
the strings of my boots undone
smelling a bit strong like any
fat old woman who has forgotten
which day is Tuesday
(my bath night if you like)

stiff my clothes from old dirt
not sweat at my age mumbling
the cracked enamel mug

eleven cats playing
in my weedy yard drinking
my little ration of milk
with me   and withy withy
the cats circle around my house
at night singly filing
in and sleeping on the
saggy stained bed and the chair
and the crumby tabletop

One day they will find me dead
O dead dead
A stinking old bundle of
                dead

and in my hand
a peeled wand
and in my ear a cricket sitting
telling me stories and predictions

and the time of night [21]

Reading that poem by her grave, I wasn't at all sure I'd paid off my debt to Anne, but I did feel very much a part of that community which gives its allegiance to poetry, the one art we come back to again and again because we value it so highly.

May that art long bind us all together.

Notes

1. Patrick Friesen, "Jugular Music," *Freelance* (November/December 1998): 7.
2. Steven Dobyns, *Best Words, Best Order* (New York: St. Martin's Press, 1996), xii.
3. Irving Layton, Foreword to *The Tightrope Walker* (Toronto: McClelland & Stewart, 1978), 9.
4. Lorri Neilsen Glenn, *Threading Light: Explorations in Loss and Poetry* (Regina: Hagios Press, 2011), 117.
5. Molly Peacock, Prologue to *The Best Canadian Poetry in English, 2010*, ed. Lorna Crozier (Toronto: Tightrope Books, 2010), vii.
6. Rosemary Griebel, "Silence Broken," *Yes* (Calgary: Frontenac House, 2011), 55.
7. Fred Cogswell, "Happy Poet," *Salt* #10 (Winter 1973–74): 2.
8. Gary Geddes, "Letter from the West Coast," *Salt* #11 (Summer-Fall 1974): 2.
9. Anne Szumigalski, *The Word, The Voice, The Text* (Saskatoon: Fifth House Publishers, 1990), 33.
10. Ibid., 58.
11. Anne Szumigalski, "Beginnings," *A Woman Clothed in Words*, ed. Mark Abley (Regina: Coteau Books, 2012), 22.
12. Gary Hyland, "Deke and Dante," *Love of Mirrors* (Regina: Coteau Books, 2008), 33.
13. Raymond Carver, "Some Prose on Poetry," *A New Path to the Waterfall* (New York: The Atlantic Monthly Press, 1989), 71.
14. Lorna Uher (Crozier), "Beginnings," *Salt* #15 (Fall 1976): 4.
15. Lorna Crozier, "Against the Grain," *Books in Canada*, date unknown, 14.
16. Robert Currie, "Contact," *Running in Darkness* (Regina: Coteau Books, 2006), 37.
17. Lajos Zilahy, "But For This," *The Writer's Craft*, ed. Frederic A. Birmingham (New York: Hawthorn Books, Inc., 1966), 248–251.
18. Ted Kooser, *The Poetry Home Repair Manual* (Lincoln: University of Nebraska Press, 2005), 16–17.
19. Mary Oliver, *A Poetry Handbook* (New York: Harcourt, Inc., 1994), 122.
20. Tess Gallagher, Introduction to *A New Path to the Waterfall*, Raymond Carver (New York: The Atlantic Monthly Press, 1988), xxx–xxxi.
21. Anne Szumigalski, "Nettles," *Woman Reading in Bath* (Toronto: Doubleday Canada Ltd., 1974), 82.

A Garden Is Not a Place[1]
Poetry and Beauty

A. F. MORITZ

Anne Szumigalski Lecture • Toronto, Ontario • June 8, 2013

SINCE THIS IS THEIR MOMENT, I'M GOING TO TALK ABOUT gardening, and beauty. It's the season of gardening, spring, when nature puts forth its sexual splendor in the young, urging them on to their function. In fact, it makes everything and everyone a part of youth, for the putting forth of beauty surrounds and penetrates all, even those that it no longer seems to inhabit. "Among the bones of the dead," says Juan Ramón Jiménez, speaking of the spring blossoming,

> Among the bones of the dead
> God opens his yellow hands.[2]

The cemetery has always in modern times been a garden spot, and in it exists a totality that includes the harmonizing labor and results of gardening, the beauty of plants and flowering, and the ugliness, or at least the non-beauty, of the dissolution to which every earthly thing is committed. And of course our own presence, as we come alone or together, to venerate, reflect, enjoy, talk, mourn, be disconsolate or horrified.

The beauty of Jiménez's lines owes little to their allusion to golden blossoming flowers. It is a human beauty, part of a human garden, one that we carry within and manifest in poems. "There are no more gardens than those we carry within," say Octavio Paz.[3] This garden of course is a garden tradition, a series of gardens, or series of attempts at the garden. It is compacted of natural growth and renewal, architectural beauty of the cemetery manifesting human genius, decay, simple pleasure in the spring, sadness and horror and despair at death, longing and struggle. It is hard to define, in fact, as beauty. It seems to lead toward a definition of beauty almost as tragedy, almost as frustration and defeat and annihilation. And yet, unremitting responsiveness to these is its comprehensive and particular element.

One remarkable fact about it is this: it manifests how the human confrontation with death automatically involves the co-presence in us of the natural and artificial, what is given and what we must reason out, plan and perform. The poem itself, like the garden or cemetery, only more expressively, is an intellectual governing of the irresistible upspringing in us of liveliness, of emotion and thought, arising out of sensitivity to our surroundings, out of pure vivacity, and, as well, out of what in us is frightening and frightened, discouraging and discouraged, dead.

The beauty of Jiménez's lines belongs, then, fractionally to the image of the flowers, and mostly to thought and vocal statement, the making practical in language of a human response to the total situation of the human being. In the poem's words and rhythm we glimpse a person experiencing a recognition, an idea, that a triumphant power moves toward continuance and pleasure among the dead without obliterating them or pretending to reduce them to an illusion. The poem's voice conveys someone recognizing that flowers are hands, and that thus, equally, hands must be something in addition to themselves. All we see, without ceasing to be simply itself, joins another activity. Flowers, hands, our actions including our attempts to reconcile ourselves to death are more than we generally understand. Because the poem is built frankly and fully upon what it struggles with, it makes us simultaneously love this glimpse of hope, and doubt it as fantasy and wish fulfillment.

Even beyond this, the poem expresses the pathos of the reader recognizing himself or herself as that sort of being who perpetually hopes to survive, or at least to achieve meaning and reconciliation, who sees garden possibilities and experiences garden moments, and then doubts, mocks, loses the sight, is driven out, first into inert discouragement and then, it seems inevitably, into taking up the quest yet again. In the poem we contemplate ourselves simultaneously expanding our view of existence in confidence, and pitying ourselves for the nostalgic futility of this feeling, and rejecting this tragic illusion that finds in the vision of hope only nostalgia ... and so on, in a seemingly never-satisfied tail-swallowing. This activity, which is simultaneously a stasis, a stunned, horrified, marvelling and admiring contemplation, seems at the heart of being human.

This activity, given in language, is poetic beauty.

How can I maintain this? What are we talking about when we say "beauty," a word with so many meanings? Most broadly, it is an honorific, merely a plus sign; anything that pleases is "beautiful," just as it is "great" or "awesome." Then, it means the attractive, what we are drawn to, a person, object, a room or dwelling for its design and setting, and so forth. The attractive relates beauty to the desirable, in many objects but especially in persons: it means attractiveness that arouses sexual desire. This I think is the central meaning of beauty, and the most complex, problematic one. It brings out that we primarily take beauty as a visual category: the beauty of the desired person, who therefore becomes, in the famous phrase, the object of love.

The object of love: a phrase expressing something truly horrible. Beauty becomes the stasis of a person made an object, and all action that might be associated with beauty now is taken away and given to the desirer; action and beauty are divided. We have beauty, and the beast. As we have seen, this is the opposite of anything that can be gathered about "beauty" if it were defined in terms of poetic beauty, the beauty of Jiménez's lines. That beauty is all activity. Even the single objective component, the image of the flowers, is presented as the act of opening, which in our physical looking at flowers cannot be seen. Beauty in Jiménez's poem is completely a matter of the action of the human heart and mind engaging the world, as experience, yes, but also as knowledge. In this way, in the poem the time and process of experience are extended to the ends of the universe. The poem comprehends the dead who have lived and now moulder, the future unfolding before us, the mortal situation that surrounds us as far as we can see, and our constant movement in this universal milieu.

Another meaning of beauty is the philosophical sense it has had since Plato as one of the three prime aspects of being, which are invisible but inhere in visible things: truth, beauty, goodness—though this trio was not fully defined until Aquinas and Bonaventure in the Middle Ages. Later these three "transcendentals" became qualities for some thinkers, moral ideals for others. They were involved in the argument over the reality or unreality of universal ideas: are they existing things, or just abstractions we make and sometimes take for real? For us today, they are remotely present in our questioning of the so-called "reality status" of the concepts we develop of things and of human purposes.

We can see, though, that these meanings of beauty are not simply unrelated. Beauty as a transcendental or universal involved the separation of the contemplated fact from the activity of the contemplator, though at least in this line of thinking, active aspiration to beauty did remain the centerpiece. We might say that the philosophical tradition, with its tendency to abstraction, helped result in the harmful separation of beauty from action that exists in the practical, socio-cultural ideas and behaviors around beauty as an erotic object. In linguistic terms, this has weakened the older sense of the word "lust" as synonymous with gusto, élan, brio, a comprehensive active enjoyment of life based on constant fluid interchange between person and world. Even in the weakest sense of the word "beauty," the honorific, the same tendency exists to realize that action is the essence. Often what is beautiful is a goal, an insult, a move. The onlooker recognizes that the athlete, the wit, the chess master has suddenly delivered a stroke that takes the whole of the pre-existing situation, diffuse or at best merely tense, and suddenly reveals its potential and shows its previously hidden structure.

Then is beauty the action that reveals the structure in completing it? This would make beauty ultimately stasis, object, the resulting conclusion of the explosive act. Or is beauty the action that does this revealing and completing? Both, I think. One ever feeding back into a new instance of the other. While philosophers have tried to abstract or define the essence, poetry has seen beauty as comprehensive. It is a unity, and one deeper than a "fusion" of elements. It is the apprehension of the identity of intimate and specific personal experiences with the realities we call the transient and the permanent, and with our recognition that the permanent is hard to achieve or conceive and may not exist, and with our consequent recognition of our desire for permanence as our deepest and most self-contradictory hunger, and with our ever-renewed determination to go on in quest of the possible-impossible discovery that this self-contradiction is not ultimate.

Here we come to the question of adventure versus security. I've always felt that adventure-versus-security is the deepest, most powerful of all the various polarities. Poles are the extremities of a single thing. A polarity, then, is a unity which encompasses divergent, even contradictory or seemingly contradictory aspects which appear to have their own reality, like east and west, top and bottom, positive and negative. The poles can seem—can *be*—so real in themselves that their unity is hard for us to fathom or achieve. It might seem that the primary polarity must be the wish for life and the wish for death, but I believe that adventure-versus-security encompasses life-versus-death, and not the other way around.

With regard to the image of the garden, adventure-versus-security makes us recall that the garden implies, necessitates, and pairs with the road. The image of the gardener or garden dweller pairs with the image of humanity the traveller, the pilgrim. It makes us wonder if the basic human image is not the garden but the wanderer, though once in a while he may stop in a pleasant spot. Often, as in Wordsworth and Beckett, he does not have even that: no pause, no shelter, solely and utterly driven out on the road. The garden is only a longing, or still less, an absence. This image of the wanderer past gardens appears again and again in modern literature. For instance, this from Friedrich Hölderlin:

> ... the soul withers in that mortal
> Who wanders with the daylight, a penniless
> No one, across the holy Earth.
>
> Too powerfully, you ever-changing ones,
>   You drag me towards the heights of the heavens:
>   You storms in the bright day, tearing my heart
>   With your godly, wayward power.
>
> But today let me quietly walk the long-known
>   Path to the little woods, its tree crowns now
>   Golden with dying leaves, and touch
>   My mind too with belovèd memories!
>
> And so that my mortal heart can stay here and be
>   A peaceful retreat like the hearts of the others,
>   And so that my soul does not leap beyond
>   Our life here and be homeless forever,
>
> You, song, be my loving refuge: bringer of joy,
>   Be cultivated now with loving care, you garden
>   Where I, walking under your budding
>   Flowers, perpetually young,
>
> Live in a strange innocence, while beyond me
>   With all its waves, the every-changing one,
>   Almighty Time, roars far away...[4]

Along the road the speaker of the poem passes the gardens, farms, homes of others, and he experiences his own restless travelling as a destructive aspiration or a demand for the more-than-human. It goes too far and may cause him to "leap beyond our life here" and be "homeless forever." The garden, thus, is home, and home is, basically, a measure of contentment with this life. In order to combine a human measure of security with his venturing, to combine content with aspiration, form with perpetual change, stability with newness, timelessness with time, Hölderlin's speaker conceives of making song his home, the garden for his spirit.

Above I quoted Octavio Paz from "A Tale of Two Gardens": "There are no more gardens than those we carry within." This is a related perception, and Paz often develops it in one way or another, for instance in "Epitaph for No Stone." This poem speaks of his natal village, not a garden, but in his poetry the village is often presented in terms of the garden in his grandfather's home there:

Epitaph for No Stone

Mixcoac was my village: three nocturnal syllables,
a half-mask of shadow across a face of sun.
Our Lady, Mother Dustcloud, came,
came and ate it. I went out in the world.
My words were my house, air my tomb.[5]

These poems I've quoted bespeak the modern poet's desire to combine advance and stillness, adventure and security, in the stress of the perceived beauty and necessity of continual motion, poised against the equal beauty and need of repose, stable and even eternal form, which is hard anymore to believe in. But the poets glimpse that motion itself, in the form of song, of poetry, might be that garden: "You, song, be my loving refuge: bringer of joy,/ ... you garden/ Where I, walking under your budding/Flowers, perpetually young,//Live in a strange innocence, while beyond me//Almighty Time, roars far away."[6]

Song—the garden which is the wanderer and his or her wandering through all that he lusts and fears to encounter, the unknown, the beyond, the wholly other, the wild, and which mysteriously at the same time is the body, stability, a place to be, a home. That is, the beauty of the garden is not the static form of its appearance, but this *plus* the action to make it, the knowledge that it grows and decays and must be renewed in concert with nature, and the realization that even within it there are paths we must wander and will sometimes be lost on, seeking. This wholeness of the garden is expressed often by Octavio Paz, strikingly in "A Tale of Two Gardens," in which he speaks of the garden of his family's decaying house:

> That one in Mixcoac, abandoned,
> covered with scars,
>   was a body
> at the point of collapse.
>   I was a boy,
> and the garden for me was like a grandfather.
> I clambered up its leafy knees,
> not knowing it was doomed.
> The garden knew it:
>   it awaited its destruction
> as a condemned man awaits the axe.[7]

Inside the garden there were wars with his childhood friends in imitation of the horrors of history read in books, in which boys take delight, as Paz records in his *Pasado en claro* [*Final Draft*, 1974]. And there were features such as the great fig tree, a goddess, the Mother, humming with "irascible insects":

> The cleft in the trunk:
>   the world half-opened.
> I thought I had seen death:
>   I saw
> the other face of being,
>   the feminine void,
> the fixed featureless splendor.[8]

These rich lines add still more components to our account of the garden. I'll only mention that at the end of this passage Paz comes back to the idea of stasis, in the word "fixed," *fijo*. But what is fixed, a stable form, is the splendor beyond forms that, rather than death, is felt to be the other face of being. This is discovered in the garden, because of the garden, the garden's own inherent movement in beauty, which takes in decay and adventure into the void.

    I said that poetic beauty is action that is the unity of our concrete personal experiences, our sensitive responsiveness, with transience and permanence, despair and hope, doubt and confidence, and the constant self-transcending contemplation of ourselves as all this. I called it a unity deeper than any fusion. But we inevitably think of fusion, rather than unity or identity, because we are so often faced with putting back together, or healing, what has been broken, or wounded. Let me give an example from Walt Whitman.

Reconciliation

Word over all, beautiful as the sky,
Beautiful that war and all its deeds of carnage
    must in time be utterly lost,
That the hands of the sisters Death and Night incessantly softly
    wash again, and ever again, this soil'd world;
For my enemy is dead, a man divine as myself is dead,
I look where he lies white-faced and still in the coffin
    —I draw near,
Bend down and touch lightly with my lips
    the white face in the coffin.[9]

Here the poem is the word, reconciliation. This poem-word is over all: over all words and all things. It is beautiful as the sky, which is over all things earthly, but the sky turns out to be representative of something else: death and night, which are sisters, human, and perform a humble, beneficent service continually forever. This is what the sky more particularly is, this eternity of humane yet a-human or ultra-human peacefulness. This is what death and night are: reconciliation: the re-establishment of close and harmonious contact, through a meeting, *concilium*, a talking together: a garden and people in the garden. But a garden built by people in response to the glimpsed nature of the vastness of given existence within and around us: repeated reproduction and cherishing of the human being, to and beyond time's end, into all that may be meant by "night." "Reconciliation" comes very close to Jiménez's "Yellow Springtime": no yellow flowers among bones in a children's cemetery, but the budding of the kiss, living lips on dead. Through Jiménez we see that flowers are also hands and hands are also the divine; through Whitman we find that flowers are lips, are the kiss, and the kiss is reconciliation, eternal word.

The poetic imagery of the garden involves the fact that all human roads begin from the garden in the form of the first exile. It involves the fact that roads go past gardens, and that within gardens themselves there are roads, paths. It involves the constant thinking and labor to create the garden, maintain it against decay, and reconceive it in ways that combine shelter with venture, that preserve it from becoming static and stifling, that maintain its status as a dwelling that reflects reality and our changing sense of it:

> Not wholly in the busy world, nor quite
> Beyond it, blooms the garden that I love.[10]

The garden is continually penetrated by time, just as Hölderlin's singer wishes his walking along and his singing, aspects themselves of continual change and homelessness, to be his garden.

> News from the humming city comes to it
> In sound of funeral or of marriage bells;
> And, sitting muffled in dark leaves, you hear
> The windy clanging of the minster clock; . . .[11]

The garden always has to contemplate the ruined cottage, the forsaken garden, which it is in prospect and one day must become. And the garden receives one of its threats from other gardens: the city, which humans build as a house and garden and where they constantly contend and manifest brutal change. It must attend to news: everything that human beings think and do that fills an individual person with the sense of threatening speed, by promoting developments that trouble us, and by affirming change and only change.

In a way that at first seems the very opposite of "Reconciliation," Whitman often comes championing change, urging change itself as beauty, as in "To a Locomotive in Winter":

> Fierce-throated beauty!
> Roll through my chant with all thy lawless music...
> Law of thyself complete, thine own track firmly holding...
> Launched o'er the prairies wide, across the lakes
> To the free skies unpent and glad and strong.[12]

"Fierce-throated beauty": Whitman is defining here his own traveller's song. Compared to Hölderlin's images, Whitman's images emphasize not the security of the traveller's song but its movement, which Whitman wishes to be fierce, lawless, a law unto itself, fast, firm and strong, happy, unbound and unbounded: "Type of the modern—emblem of motion and power."[13] But it is impossible not to see that the locomotive is an attempt to assert a change that will include the unchanging, that will allow the change that afflicts each human being to be carried through time in a form that is permanent reconciliation with time. Forever will Whitman's locomotive be barreling gladly through vastness with its triumphant form: its panoply, measur'd dual throbbing, black cylindrical body, metrical pant and roar, its knitted frame.

If we sometimes are filled with verve by change that sweeps all away, seeing in it our garden, and other times find the prospect fearful, so it is. Pär Lagerkvist took up the image about fifty years after Whitman, in "Father and I." The father and child are walking home along the tracks through the woods at night:

> ...we suddenly heard a huge thundering behind us! We woke out of our thoughts terrified. Father pulled me down the embankment, down into the abyss, held me there. Then the train careered past. A black train, lights out in all the carriages, it was going at a furious speed. What sort of train was that... The fire glared in the huge engine where they were shovelling coal, the sparks

poured wildly out into the night.... The driver stood there, pale, motionless, his features as if paralysed, lit up by the fire....

Overwrought, panting with anguish, I stood and watched the wild sight. It was swallowed up by the night. Father took me up to the track again, we hurried homewards.

"That was strange," he said, "what train was that?"...

But I was trembling over my whole body. It was all for me, for my sake. I suspected what it meant, it was the anguish to come, all the unknown, what Father knew nothing of, what he wouldn't be able to protect me from. For this world, this life, would not be for me as it was for Father. Where everything was secure and known. It was no real world, no real life. It was only careering, burning, into the total darkness which had no end.[14]

In fact, stability and form are identified by us, inevitably, with reality, and speed with loss of reality, disregard of reality, disrespectful and harmful conduct toward reality, even devouring and ruining conduct.

The Imagist revolution in early twentieth-century poetry, somewhat different from the simultaneous revolutions of Jiménez and Ungaretti, was aimed at removing the busy, self-regarding ego from verse and turning the poem into an instance of contemplation, in which the self was annihilated in pure absorption and the moment became still, a garden in perception. This responds to Schopenhauer's thought, formed against the nineteenth century's prideful utilitarian cannibalization of all things. For him, truth is opposition to what is utilitarian and swift, and consists in an eternal unity of a total moment of self and world, "the quiet contemplation of the natural object actually present." He says: "... in as much as [the human being] loses himself in this object ... and only continues to exist as ... the clear mirror of the object, so that it is as if the object alone were there, without anyone to perceive it ... he ... is no longer individual ... but he is *pure* ...."[15] Thing and person pass out of individuality and are merged in the Idea; both achieve eternal reality and are rescued from speed, and man in addition from his egotistical espousal of it. This might seem the ultimate meaning of the garden.

It is moving, useful, as a response to the all-corrosive doctrine of speed. But it does not satisfy me. The garden, the poem, is a total that includes ultimates such as the eternal moment, and what we are, do and experience every day. Whitman is righter. The Idea, the all and nothing and the unthinkable that encompasses them, *samsara* and *nirvana* and their interchangeability, are all components of the human being who exists and lives in the body now. So too they are components of the house, the garden, the cat and the ripening peach in the sun, or the garden being destroyed by the storm, or lying abandoned, ageing and faltering. These things have not just their importance, but their only reality in the particular things that exist. We know ourselves really to live, really to be, when we live the moment fascinatedly, willingly, pleasurably. This experience always transcends mere self even when it is not self-forgetful; in fact, it most transcends the self when it includes the self too in its selfless embrace. *This* experience is the garden that time drives us out of, into dreariness, disaster and pain; a part of it is that we know it will end, is ending. When we are in it, we feel time most deeply, time passing in the heart of the eternal: "the real present / conquered by the hour," to quote Paz again.[16] As Czesław Miłosz says in exhorting lovers to cherish their garden moment:

> . . . two faces in a mirror
> Are only forever once, even if unremembered,
> So that you watch what is, as it fades away,
> And are grateful every moment for your being.[17]

Schopenhauer's eternal moment, joined with eternal activity and with the change we cannot diminish, is what Juan Ramón Jiménez sought throughout his career, to incarnate it in his work. Like Hölderlin, he looks for an eternal garden-refuge of song while knowing that, as word, history, content of education and culture, his poetry will first be misunderstood, then minimized, then forgotten, and ultimately obliterated. The passionate vibration between achieved eternity and re-experienced casting out into time defines the turbulent beauty of his work, its mixture of realistic fear and strange assurance, as in this poem from his 1923 book *Belleza* (*Beauty*):

> I know that my work is like
> a painting on the air;
> the winds of the ages
> will erase it entirely, as if
> it were perfume or music;
> all that will remain of it,
> a ruined yes among the noes,
> in the great solar silence, will be
> the ignorance of the moon.
>   No. No. One day, erased,
> it will be a vast existence,
> a revelatory power,
> like the early sun it will be
> the impossible norm of beauty:
> endlessness of anguished longing,
> deep mine of highest secrets...
> Mortal flower my immortal
> queen of the air of this day.[18]

The work, achieved, erased by time, will remain as "the impossible norm of beauty," which is the "endlessness of anguished longing." It is beauty because it is perfected form, but the material of this form is the ceaseless action of change and of the quest driven by anguished longing: from this derives its intensity, constant renewal and surprise, other basics of beauty.

Miłosz gives another light on this in a brief prose poem:

> To find my home in one sentence, concise, as if hammered in metal. Not to enchant anybody. Not to earn a lasting name in posterity. An unnamed need for order, for rhythm, for form, which three words are opposed to chaos and nothingness.[19]

This sentence—Jiménez's poem, Miłosz's aphorism—is the finding of one's home in one's work: "My words were my house, air my tomb."[20] Song is one's garden refuge while walking through the world in the aftermath of the sweeping away of other homes by the dust storm, by the deeds of carnage, by the busy world and the humming city and the windy clanging of the clock, by mighty Time, the changeable. It encompasses the most powerful action driven by the deepest, strongest, unnameable need, can be fierce-throated as well as tender, and can subdue, use, and thus even take the form of the technological.

Blake, an early prophet against the evils of the rationalist approach to reality, engages this aspect of garden-making or home-making profoundly. In one of his poems he gives the following picture of poetry and art as they are being produced in the workshop of Los, his figure for the creative and constructive imagination:

Some Sons of Los surround the Passions with porches of iron & silver
Creating form & beauty around the dark regions of sorrow
Giving to airy nothing a name and a habitation
Delightful: with bounds to the Infinite putting off the Indefinite
Into most holy forms of Thought (such is the power of inspiration)
They labour incessant, with many tears and afflictions:
Creating the beautiful House for the piteous sufferer.[21]

This poet, for whom "Energy is Eternal Delight,"[22] places supreme importance on construction, on a home, on forms of Thought that can give us shelter from the vast indefinite, a dark region of sorrow, as glimpsed by Lagerkvist up ahead of the train of the modern submission to change. Blake, who said "Energy is Eternal Delight," also said that "He who sees the Infinite in all things sees God."[23] We tend to place all the emphasis on "sees the Infinite," but the passage about "Creating the beautiful House" shows that Blake himself put equal emphasis upon 'in things'.

Let me gather together some of the signs that have appeared in this essay in terms of their equivalence, one coming forward after another to stand for and give a different emphasis to all the rest: what Paz calls "signs in rotation." We see this at work in Blake's passage, in which house, poem, labor, creativity enabling labor, the forms of Thought, the present society of the workers, the future society for all, are equivalent terms. No one of them is the subject, and the others only metaphors or metonymies. Signs that have rotated thus through this essay are garden, garden-dweller, endless road, traveller, garden path, house, city, train (i.e., technological construction), thing, body, song. More briefly: garden, house, body, song. From the other direction: road, path in the garden, the traveller, song, the garden itself.

Most of these signs are inherent in the poem-word, garden. Its basis, the syllable "gard," means an enclosure, implying a wall. It is related to girth, gird, girdle, garth. Another form of it, yard, means the grounds around or amidst a building or buildings; this includes the house within a garden, or even a small familial community, as in "farmyard." In one language, Russian, garden is cognate with the word for a town, "górod." Once we move from considering the word lexically to considering it culturally, we remember that God "planted a garden eastward in Eden." Eden is a Hebrew word, 'ēdhen, that is translated "delight": God planted a garden in the east of delight: in the particular region of delight signifying its repeated renewal, its dawning. This is reaffirmed in a great affirmation of poetic beauty as action, Pablo Neruda's second "Ode to the Book" from his *Odas elementales* (*Elemental Odes*):

> Book,
> beautiful
> book,
> small forest,
> leaf upon
> leaf the scent
> of the elements
> breathes
> from your pages...[24]

Here the book itself is the house or garden, but is also the forest in which they are set, against which they are usually seen as a refuge. As the poem continues, the book contains "roads and roads" that allow for the encounter with "fraternity," "communal actions" and the "stone by stone" construction of "the human castle." The book is song, and also is travel, the meeting with men and women, the building of the house, and observing it and praising it. Neruda calls on this "book of poetry / of the dawn" to give us ever again "the fountain in the woods."

This fountain is like the garden planted in the east of the wilderness of delight. Our garden, song, which is also house, city, society, is planted ever again in the midst of Eden, wilderness of otherness, energy which is eternal delight, energy of the existence given around and within us: nature, the unfathomable, the forest, the abyss, which is we ourselves, for we are made up of it.

Visionary poems see this wilderness as delight. Do we know it to be so? Or do we only hope? Do we trick ourselves by imagining delight as the pith of given existence and thus as a possible future, a destiny if we can only make it? Blake sees the act of giving to "airy nothing / A local habitation and a name,"[25] formulated ironically by Shakespeare's Duke Theseus, as labor which is a basic part of existence, and the essential human part. He sees Shakespeare as making his mocking Duke say truer than he knows.

My final point is to agree with Blake. Desire is knowledge, and poetry is desire. Poetry is a form of knowledge. Since it is simultaneously desire, it is the essential form of knowledge, which is the vision of things to come. This vision, which often seems the latest, the most constructed and rational, the most merely human, is mysteriously also the deepest, most original, most identical to energy and material and pattern as given in and around us. It is the earth, dawn, and night, the house and garden and the creating of them. Poetry as knowledge is that

> ... desire, like all strongest hopes,
> By its own energy fulfill'd itself,
> Merged in completion ...[26]

Blake's passage already is the house, and at the same time it is the prophecy of the fully achieved house and society, Wordsworth's "image of a better time."[27] Tennyson speaks of a perfected "type / Appearing ere the times were ripe,"[28] and there is a great truth in this but it is equally true that the times are always ripe—"Behold, now is the acceptable time; behold, now is the day of salvation"[29]—and that the poem itself is already a full realization of what it calls for.

One further, necessary emphasis. What is desired must be critically desired, not left to wish and fantasy. This point is inherent in what we have seen about the garden as song, as requiring full inclusion of change, of all that is seemingly at odds with the garden and yet is its substance. A valid, critical desires comes to exist; it exists between existence and the non-existence of not yet. Jiménez gets this perfectly:

> How close already to our soul,
> what still remains so immensely
> far from our hands...[30]

Life, he says, "creates itself / inside us with the indestructible / light of a day of delight / that is shining somewhere else." It is a day fully and intimately with us, and yet at the same time it is shining only elsewhere. And he concludes, "how sweet, how sweet, the truth / that is not yet real—how sweet."[31] This working of poetic desire is seen brilliantly by Czesław Miłosz in his poem "The World," in one section of which a mother asks her children "to learn to look at yourself / The way one looks at distant things / For you are only one thing among many." If the person achieves this, she continues,

> A bird and a tree say to him, Friend.
>
> Then he wants to use himself and others
> So that they stand in the glow of ripeness.[32]

There is the definition of the garden in a few phrases. Tree and man free equals. Hold yourself only equal to the bird, the tree, the rock, the soil, all "the things of earth" that are the wild and also the material of gardening, and they speak to you and call you friend. We tend to object to this: isn't the rock still stubborn and indifferent? And of course, the Sons of Los know that human beings are equally stubborn and indifferent, many of them. But this is a cooperative effort, and part of it is to attract into the building of the garden all people and things, so that no one is merely imposed upon, no one is excluded, but all "stand in the glow of ripeness."

Poetry is the form of critical desire, desire always examining itself to find if the joy it comprehends is real, and if all are invited to the education, the construction, of desire. Poetry as critical desire is the essential form of knowledge. What is this knowledge? Says Duke Theseus, "imagination bodies forth / The forms of things unknown."[33] Says Octavio Paz, "time hungers for incarnation."[34] What is seemingly the basic form of existence, time itself, quite apart from any human desire, desires to be body, to be garden. This is one source of the desire in us, and the perpetual resurrection of the hope that universe and man can realize "That all, as in some work of art, / Is toil cöoperant to an end."[35]

Can we believe in this? What does "believe in" mean? We labor to find and to make, guided by desire. Visionary poems glimpse that this is a total finding and making, not just ours. The form of this making is an adequate body, that is, a glorious body, a garden. Time itself hungers for this. The body, house and garden, their achieved beautiful form, are not made so much out of skin and limbs, boards and bricks, trees and flowers and layouts, as out of time, motion, restlessness itself. Says Paz,

>   A house, a garden,
>   are not places:
>   they spin, they come and go.
>   Their apparitions open
>   another space
>   in space,
>   another time in time.
>   Their eclipses
>   are not abdications:
>   the vivacity of one of those moments
>   would burn us
>   if it lasted a moment more . . . .
>
>
>   A garden is not a place.
>   Down a path of reddish sand,
>   we enter a drop of water,
>   drink green clarities from its center,
>   we climb

>   the spiral of hours
> to the tip of the day,
>   descend
> to the last burning of its ember.
> Mumbling river,
>   the garden flows through the night.[36]

How right Paz is to compare the garden, which we usually take as an image of peace and even too much peace, too much quiet—to compare the garden to Rilke's famous angel, who would consume us "with its more potent being," because the angel is beauty and beauty is "nothing / but the beginning of terror" which, while we stand admiring, "disdains / to destroy us."[37] With this, I emphasize once more that modern poetic beauty, and immemorial poetic beauty, is the greatest and most difficult energy, namely, balance, not an extreme but the inclusion of all real extremes. It is the quest for the permanent reality of the body. It mirrors the balance of forces in the body and thus forecasts the achieved house, garden, society. It is the form that, composed of change, gives an assurance of the body's eternity.

Can we believe in this? I've insisted here that the tension of this quest for belief is in itself the form of beauty today. This critical awareness is searingly incarnated in the couplet with which Czesław Miłosz ends *From the Rising of the Sun*:

> And the form of every single grain will be restored in glory.
> I was judged for my despair because I was unable to understand this.[38]

Notes

1. Octavio Paz, "A Tale of Two Gardens," *The Collected Poems of Octavio Paz, 1957–1987*, Eliot Weinberger, ed. and trans. (New York: New Directions Books, 1987), 293.
2. Juan Ramón Jiménez, "Primavera amarilla," *Poemas májicos y dolientes* (Madrid: Librería de Fernando Fe, 1909), lines 17–18. Trans. AFM.
3. Paz, "A Tale of Two Gardens," 305.
4. Friedrich Hölderlin, "Mein Eigentum" ("My Possessions"), *Sämtliche Werke*, Stuttgart, 1951, lines 26–47. Trans. AFM.

5   Octavio Paz, "Epitaph for No Stone," *The Collected Poems of Octavio Paz, 1957–1987*, Eliot Weinberger, ed. and trans. (New York: New Directions Books, 1987), 551.
6   Hölderlin, "Mein Eigentum."
7   Paz, "A Tale of Two Gardens," 293.
8   Paz, "A Tale of Two Gardens," 293–294.
9   Walt Whitman, "Drum Taps — Reconciliation," *Leaves of Grass* (1891–92) in *Complete Poetry and Collected Prose / Walt Whitman* (New York: Viking Press, 1982), 453.
10 Alfred Tennyson, "The Gardener's Daughter; or, the Pictures," lines 31–32.
11 Tennyson, "The Gardener's Daughter, lines 33–38.
12 Walt Whitman, "To a Locomotive in Winter," *Leaves of Grass* (1891–92), lines 18–19, 21, 24–25.
13 Ibid., line 13.
14 Pär Lagerkvist, *Guest of Reality*, trans. R. Fulton (London, New York: Quartet Books, 1989), 101–102.
15 Cited in Czesław Miłosz, *New and Collected Poems 1931–2001* (New York: HarperCollins Publishers, Inc., 2001), 372.
16 Paz, "The Balcony," *The Collected Poems of Octavio Paz, 1957–1987*, Eliot Weinberger, ed. and trans. (New York: New Directions Books, 1987), 167.
17 Miłosz, "After Paradise," *New and Collected Poems*, 407.
18 Juan Ramón Jiménez, untitled initial poem, *Belleza (en verso) 1917-1923*: text from Belleza (Madrid: Editorial Taurus, Edición del centenario, 1981), 47. Trans. AFM.
19 Miłosz, untitled poem, *New and Collected Poems*, 452.
20 Paz, "Epitaph for No Stone."
21 William Blake, "Milton a Poem," Plate 28.
22 Blake, "The Marriage of Heaven and Hell." Plate 4.
23 Blake, "There Is No Natural Religion."
24 Pablo Neruda, "Oda al libro (II)," *Odas elementales* (Buenos Aires: Losada, 1954), 113–115. Trans. AFM.
25 William Shakespeare, *A Midsummer Night's Dream*, V.i., lines 16–17.
26 Tennyson, "The Gardener's Daughter," lines 232–34.
27 William Wordsworth, *The Recluse*, line 856.
28 Tennyson, *In Memoriam*, Epilogue, lines 138–9.
29 2 Corinthians 6:2, Douay-Rheims Bible.
30 Juan Ramón Jiménez, untitled poem I, *Diario de un poeta reciéncasado*, 1916; text from *Diary of a Newlywed Poet: A Bilingual Edition*; intro. and ed. of Spanish text Michael P. Predmore, trans. Hugh A. Harter (Cranbury, NJ: Associated University Presses, 2004), 90. Trans. AFM.
31 Ibid.
32 Miłosz, "The World," *New and Collected Poems 1931–2001*, 30.
33 Shakespeare, *A Midsummer Night's Dream*, V.i., lines 14–15.

34 Paz, "The Balcony," 171.
35 Tennyson, *In Memoriam* CXXVIII 23–4.
36 Paz, "A Tale of Two Gardens," 291–293.
37 Rainer Maria Rilke, "First Duino elegy," *The Poetry of Rilke*, trans. Edward Snow (New York: North Point Press, a Division of Farrar, Straus and Giroux, 2009), 283.
38 Miłosz, "From the Rising of the Sun," *New and Collected Poems 1931–2001*, 331.

Black Voice
Context and Subtext

LILLIAN ALLEN

Anne Szumigalski Lecture • Toronto, Ontario • June 7, 2014

LET ME ENGAGE IN RITUAL BY MOVING OFF THE PAGE, MOVING beyond language to create with you a moment of magic—of the poetic, in *ssssound*—an engagement in a collective sound poetry experience.

We as Stories

Language dances motion meaning
A word dimension beauty feeling
Sound as sight images as sound
Language is our skin, like a blanket we live in
our talk our bark like the Baobab,
the Baobab tree grows so righteously
Tongue and pen a dance poetic
romancing the idea of wordsong

wordsong

Passion sings the spirit
liberation as ritual and art
Meaning and message
To free ourselves
From the (ad)dress of the Imperial pen
how we free up wi-self from European song
the rabble, reggae resistance of voice
jazz's sublime circuitry
and the African drum
                          drum
                                drum

At home on our tongues, moist of words
Stories assembled   actions poetic
poetry as conversation   dialogic
we revel in specificity   cultural
West Indianism in the brew becoming Caribbean
Africa rebranded in the new

Symbols allusions   code referencing
Whose sounds shall chant   chant a new vision
Seizing everydayness of voice talk
Sculpt and stylize our beating heart
Finding language forms and an art to our talk
Riddim words alight against a politics of alienation
Bringing inclusion to all things we love as humans

Curvature wordsound
culture jamming and resistance
A complete energy-beat
rhythms of freedom so sweet
Resolution insight imagination
repetition   word   wordplay
Riddimwize, we are announced with the beat

bu dup bu dup   heartbeat
And then it goes back   and then it goes back
to the sound that no one hears
and then it goes back, and then it goes back
to the silence   the mother of all sounds
back b ac k ba ck b ack bac k b a c k back
leaving behind the dub
only a dub
; our story
our lives as stories
We stories

In her 2011 acceptance speech at the National Book Awards for Poetry for *Head Off & Split*, Black American poet Nikky Finney began by referring to the 1739 slave codes of South Carolina: "A fine of $100 and six months in prison will be imposed for anyone found teaching a slave to read or write. And death is the penalty for circulating any incendiary literature. . . ." Finney goes on, "The ones who longed to read and write but were forbidden, who lost hands and feet, were killed by laws written by men who believed they owned other men . . . words devoted to quelling freedom, insurgency, imagination, all hope—what about the possibility of one day making a poem?"[1]

Let's begin by understanding that dub poetry was never intended to compete with traditional European-derived poetry, just as reggae music was never intended to compete with European classical music. The truth is that dub poets love all poetry, and especially the best of the poets we were raised on—Yeats, Chaucer, Wordsworth, Tennyson, etc. We responded to the alienation that this poetry engendered when it was taught, and generally accepted that these creations came from a "universal" author. This work was propagated in a way not to emphasize that these were creations of individuals who worked out of a specific cultural context, in the throes of particular historical times and rooted in particular landscapes.

Dub poetry did what good poetry should do, and that is reach for and reflect its own space and vernacular, the concerns of the personal, social, spiritual and political, in its own time.

Dub poetry emerged, or rather crystallized, in the early to mid-seventies, when cultural contestations were being waged by disenfranchised and racialized peoples, in places like Kingston (Jamaica), London, Soweto, New York City, Seattle, Vancouver, Ottawa, Montreal, Peterborough and Toronto. It has since spread mostly on the wings of popular culture around the world to godmother rap and hip hop, and has given birth to and helped the spoken word form take root. Some will argue about the influence of the Beat poets on the birth of dub poetry, and indeed some spoken word poets can point to the Beat poets as their specific connection, but I can assure you that the first wave of spoken word artists were not looking to Beat culture for guidance or inspiration. And, as funky as Walt Whitman was, the dub poets' reach went way beyond him. It is well documented that Langston Hughes and Walt Whitman had a very fruitful poetic relationship, a relationship initiated by Langston. They were connected by poetics and by their marginalization: Langston Hughes by his race and his same-love sexuality, and Whitman for his same-sex love. And who could forget Langston's memorable poem, "I, Too, Sing America," in its delicious response to and conscious entanglement with Whitman's anthem, "I Hear America Singing"?

The African oral tradition has been one of the oldest and strongest artistic threads in human history, and in fact has served to influence music and literary movements in the West. Indeed, most contemporary Black American writers, especially the poets, will point to the Harlem Renaissance and its influence.

The Harlem Renaissance was an African-American arts movement developed around 1918 in response to the pervasive notion in America that Black people had no culture and could not make or appreciate art. The people who followed the slave codes by banning reading and writing for their slaves didn't seem to notice the culture growing right under their noses. Organized by a "remarkable concentration of intellectual and creative minds," the movement was fuelled by creative artists from the literary, theatrical, musical and visual arts, and by academics, curators, critics, publishers, patrons and venue owners. The aim was to present alternative conceptions to the white stereotypes of "the Negro" and to present a view to American society countering the dehumanizing and racist conceptions entrenched in American beliefs about Black people. It also set out to articulate that Black people had a long history and rich culture that should serve to redefine Black presence in America, beyond enslavement.

It was through a tied and twisted history and interconnections with the Caribbean peoples, who had similar concerns, that writers and poets in the Caribbean saw this artistic blossoming of the Harlem Renaissance as a cultural, intellectual and psychic homecoming. The effects of this movement triumphantly resonated throughout the grassroots in the everyday lives of black people in America and in the Caribbean.

Poets like Claude McKay, who came from the Caribbean, Langston Hughes and Countee Cullen; later, poets of the Black Power movement like Maya Angelou, Ntozake Shange and Nikki Giovanni; Jamaica's Louise Bennett and the fierce young Bob Marley were the kinds of writers dub poets wanted to emulate.

Kwame Dawes contends that dub poetry owes much of its spiritual sensuality to reggae music by a "stillness, with the hint of undulation . . . a place where the rhythm is in complete control." He describes it as "a place of sweetness, a spot in a groove that is perfectly comfortable, perfectly right . . . . shaped by the music. A poem, a poem. This is the taste of reggae—it emerges in the way people move to it." I couldn't agree more with Dawes's inference that dub poetry "cannot stand in the place of the reggae song . . . . Instead, the poem must try to capture the spirit of reggae in its own terms as poetry, using all the resources of poetry."[2]

Maria Caridad Casas, in her PhD thesis "Orality & the Body in the Poetry of Lillian Allen and Dionne Brand: Towards an Embodied Social Semiotics" (2002), which she later expanded and developed into a book, *Multimodality in Canadian Black Feminist Writing: Orality and the Body in the Work of Harris, Philip, Allen and Brand*, applied literary and linguistic theory to dub poetry and concluded that dub is a new modality. Dub poetry, she reasons, cannot be fully explained from either or both of the tool kits of literary and linguistic theories, as most other kinds of poetry can.[3]

So, you may ask, what are some of the distinctive features of dub? How does it work as a piece of art or poetry? The poetics of dub will seem quite ordinary in these times, especially with the proliferation of rap, hip hop, the very vocal spoken word movement and writers from all walks who are reading their work to public audiences.

But if you for a moment contemplate the fact that dub poetry broke out of the gates and rushed the barricades in the early to mid-seventies, before we even heard of Public Enemy, and before the widespread emergence of rap, you perhaps will discern the effect of the trailblazing that dub poetry provided. It was with great pride that the late, great American poet June Jordan claimed dub poet as one of her many titles.

Reggae music paved the way for the international, cross-cultural popularity of dub poetry. Bob Marley's rise to global stardom enabled his uncompromising message of freedom, peace, and love to be more widely encountered and embraced. His appeal crossed cultural and racial lines and seemed to lend validation to the lives of many and awaken aspirations of fighting back. For once, there was a deeper esthetic need awakening in the grassroots audience, who so far had been mostly served popular, commercial music. The poetics of reggae combined music and message, with lines like "my fear is my only courage ..." and the poetic comfort of recurrence, repetition and insistence: "Get up stand up. Stand up for your rights, get up stand up, don't give up the fight," "Cold ground was my bed last night and rock was my pillow," and "No woman nuh cry ... I remember when we use to."[4] Who of the grassroots was not moved to recall and add at least one such tender moment of longing in a life of hardship? Bob Marley's life-imitating metaphors spoke to dub poet Klyde Broox's notion of the need for "reloading the can(n)on with homemade ammunition."[5]

In addition to the regular and traditional attributes of "poetry"— recognizable image, evocative language, metaphor, simile, assonance, etc.—dub brings a host of other elements while prioritizing and playing with different aspects of "sounding" for effect, grounding emotional centres in language phrases and working with transmutation of energy, all of which are culturally coded and so essential to creating, awakening, and validating shared and visionary ideas and experience: necessary ingredients for creating community.

This community-acknowledging approach of dub poetry has expanded and invigorated the idea of poetry such that more people are reading and creating poetry than at any other time in human history. Today any scholar would be hard pressed to discuss poetry in the twenty-first century without thinking about the impact and importance of dub poetry, hip hop, and spoken word.

What the early critics of dub poetry did not readily get was that they and all poets, including dub poets, shared a common ground: a passion to submit one's life to the apprenticeship of words, a strange and complicated love affair with language. A line of a poem can evoke the same beautiful shivery feeling as a tender expression of love can, or an irking frustration when we as poets tackle words and phrases that will not do exactly what we have in our imagination or can feel in our body.

Dub poets enter language to explore the complexities of marginalization from literature and from dominant culture. We also enter it as a place of sheer pleasure and resistance and a place of insistencies. Poetry is ritual for us—the way we commune, as service to the world of texture, image, sound, rhythms and possibility, we bring to our audience/community. In the communities that dub poets, hip hop poets and spoken word artists are closest to, poetry does not equate to "book."

The first project of dub is to recreate ourselves in language, to assert our right to exist! Dub is a poetry of possibility, a possibility that Nikki Finney knows too well. The same question asked differently might be, "What about the possibility of changing the claustrophobic narrative of being poor, marginalized, and oppressed?"

Dub is concerned with emerging: the individual voice is rooted in the context of collective culture because dub calls simultaneously for justice, equality, redress, unity, aesthetic satisfaction, and accountability.

Dub poetry's loudest scream is that voices need to come from specificity, and that if there's a cultural table or a cultural stage, all voices need to be there. (Instead of those with opportunities thinking they have to give up space, imagine how we can collectively create more space, open our hearts and minds, and influence and connect with each other.) Dub poetry philosophy will argue that connecting with an open heart to other human beings, especially the "other," must be as worthy and beautiful as a good poem.

We ask, When did the project of poetry turn into an idolatry of "excellence"? Appreciating and striving for excellence is one thing; worshipping excellence is just a misguided excuse for elitism and some other kinds of isms. What is urgently needed in our culture is for us to be stewards of excellence, and not gatekeepers. We know all too well that "excellence" takes time, opportunities, persistence, nurturing, and good effort in whatever context it is situated. We must remind ourselves that any poetry that is "great" today was not great when the poet started out.

The project of poetry is for us to enter the realm of new experience and ideas through language and, by feeling the magic and power of language, to be more fully human. We are different and diverse because our job on this earth is to discover and rediscover the other, and discover the other in us, and ourselves in the other. There is no pursuit more fulfilling than to enter the realm of what we never thought possible or whose possibility we never knew existed.

The great Uruguayan writer Eduardo Galeano, in his 1978 seminal essay "In Defense of the Word,"[6] tells us that the best way to colonize consciousness is to suppress it. Let us consider that we are hearing from youth, marginalized, and a range of diverse cultures only because they/we have stormed the barricades, trampled the "no entry" signs. Did these voices not exist before? I ask you to consider the ideological agenda in claiming poetry for one section of society. Shouldn't all lovers of poetry be asking Finney's question of all those voices they have not heard from in our society?

Thinking about Annie Dillard's construct of fiction, poetry could then be seen as "an aesthetic or epistemological probe by means of which the artist [poet] analyses [explores] the universe—the world of things [in] encounters with ideas, wresting language from its familiar contexts."[7] Poems are always in relation to ideas and things, because that's what we have in the world: ideas and things. It is no accident, then, that the meshing of ideas and things in our new and evocative use of language has the deepest resonance beneath the skin. Poetry is not only the pathway to your inner voice, it is also a pathway from the inner voice. William Wordsworth contends that poetry gives access to "the breath and finer spirit of all knowledge,"[8] concurring with

Jamaican dub poet Mutabaruka that the poem "is to be continued in your mind... in your mind."[9]

Luckily for us, marginalized people have always resisted the silencing and have employed any means available in the articulation of their experiences, vision, and creativity. The word has always been crucial to various groups of the oppressed, the dispossessed, and the ignored. Sometimes the word was the only thing they possessed, their word their only fight against absurdity and injustice. This challenging of normative, everyday contradictions has contributed much to literature and literary expression, and has been as much on the level of ideas, content, and consciousness as on the level of form ... spoken word, dub poetry, rap, hip hop ... hybrid explorations. Form is perhaps the most revolutionary of those four categories.

New form creates spaces and beings and processes where none existed before. New forms are especially powerful as they remind and assert for us that there are new possibilities. If dub didn't exist, there would not be this new brand/genre of English literature and this particular cross-cultural wave of community interaction. If rap/hip hop didn't exist, we would not have heard from that slice of America and young people around the world rapping about what they think is important in the world. Yes, that section of the population exists. What they hold as worth rapping about is nothing less than a comment on the body politic of the human condition.

What are we up against as a culture? Is it the distinctive poetic expression—perfect or imperfect—of the "other" as a threat to the institution of poetry? If gatekeepers of "good poetry" could step out of their niches, they would see that the real threat to excellence in a contemporary world is a lack of diversity and the commodification of our value to each other as community. A real threat is a global mass media machinery that is hyper-focused on training and manipulating our desires in an insidious move to greater conformity; a goal that is pursued with impunity by insatiable profit-driven capital, as Galeano asserts, "for the purpose of hampering and betraying communication."[10] And what would you suggest is the answer? A *Revolution* of thought, some would say. But for us who have taken up the pen, poets everywhere, it is so obvious—poetry! More poetry, more and more poetry—create it, multiply it, nurture it, support it, grow it, water it everywhere you see the seeds, and yes, plant seeds in the most unlikely ground, water buds from the most unlikely places.

Kwame Dawes argues that street poetry—that is, dub and spoken word—"is in fact one of the mainstays of poetic expressions in our society today." It has reminded scribal/book poets of "the value of voice" and "the SOUND of a poem," introducing to, or rekindling for, Western society "an ancient tradition of oral poesy."[11]

In the same essay Dawes discusses the dilemmas of aesthetic and social class in the world of poetry, noting that this dilemma of "highbrow" and "lowbrow" supports an idea that creativity is not a universal phenomenon but is unique to only some communities and cultures. I invite you to consider that dub and spoken word poetry is largely identified with African-derived cultures and radicalized and marginalized groups including First Nations, Indigenous peoples, working classes, the uneducated, and youth. Much of the energy for the evolution of Eurocentric poetry came from the sound of folk language and oral culture—the great Irish epic, the early Greco-Roman bards—yet today, certain pejorative connotations are reserved only for the poetry of the racialized and the marginalized. If we agree with Gabriele Rico's view that "the essence of intelligence lies in our mind's flexibility,"[12] one way to judge how intelligent we are is by a willingness to exercise that most compassionate and generative aspect of human consciousness—a flexible mind, which is a creative mind.

Dub poets acted on a postmodern, decolonizing impulse to create a multimedia, multi-sensorial and slightly mashed-up activist poetry, but dub poetry can also be quite modernist in its awareness of criticism, and is not at all unconcerned about the claims it makes for itself. However, I'd like to list some of the more important claims of contributions of dub poetry to our society:

- Community mobilization—building audience and excitement
- Disrupting established discourse in order to insert its own agenda
- The expansion and democratization of categories of both poet and audience

- Highlighting the inherent link between poet and audience that was greatly diminished through surrendering the work to elitist arbiters of culture
- Engendering working class solidarity (gotta love George Elliott Clarke, who declares: "from the working class I have come, to the working class I shall return"[13])
- Through the feminine voice and concerns, dub infused what is largely a masculine field of reggae culture with feminist views, and strengthened feminist voices across cultures
- Opening up the space for ideas and discourse has been one of dub's most successful and most powerful endeavours: ideas cannot be ignored once brought forward, especially when backed up by the lived experience of a group; dub speaks across generations and the wider consciousness
- Dub can be seen as a remedy for ongoing fragmentation in our daily lives; it is an integration of media and senses: music, musicality, sound, voice, words, images, self, ideas, message, audience, community, poet and responsibility
- Actualizing dialogue through artistic practice, infusing ideas and knowledge in the everyday realm to help "school" the people, in a way that provides for recognition, participation and validation
- Stylizing everyday speech and elevating vernacular language to art
- Providing a weapon against being rendered invisible
- Asserting and opening up new possibilities for expression
- Offering a mechanism, vehicle and processes for coming to voice (where would all those spoken word artists be if we had not created this space of possibility—the possibility of one day making a poem?)
- Poetry is a timeless mode of knowing, an alternate epistemology; it is knowledge itself, and through poetry we have come to know so much about the world, and the other; dub poetry has allowed many to enter and explore their unknowns, opening their eyes and hearts to the othered

- Addressing the cellular search for breath and beauty, that deep aesthetic need we have for the rhythmic beauty of ideas—a breath to lift us out of the everyday. This cannot and should not be fulfilled by any one ideal; the enjoyment and engagement of art should never be the sole domain of any one group of people, especially those in control
- Creating nodes of interconnections for the experience of marginalization
- One of dub poetry's higher callings is creating psychic sites of human connectivity
- Dub poetry is a call to action and, along with spoken word, integral to connecting with the so-called "illiterates" and the great masses of the "unwashed"—don't they, too, deserve poetry? What of their possibility of one day making a poem?

Bringing the gifts that my ancestors gave,
I am the dream and the hope of the slave.[14]
("Still I Rise" by Maya Angelou)

This movement of people, young and old, educated and not, who are taking up the WORD is unstoppable. For dub poetry itself, we have now spawned at least three, possibly four, generations of wordsmiths with wide-reaching influence, from the first-generation activist poets (myself included), to the second generation of cultural workers. These are poets who are mostly drawn to the form by cultural, social, personal, and artistic ideas and concerns, and by a desire to connect to community. Examples would be D'bi Young, Klyde Broox, Naila Keleta-Mae, Anthony Bansfield, Kaie Kellough, Dwayne Morgan, Motion and Andrea Thompson, to name a few; these straddle the generations and move easily between spoken word and dub and experimental poetics. We see yet a third generation, who are attracted to the community of creative performance and writing, and they are mostly the spoken word artists working with the influences of their own generation. And yet there is a fourth identifiable generation—not by age but by influence—who are attracted to the style as voice and artistic expression with little concern for politics or social issues, and who have found a vehicle to chart their own voice in a way that builds and connects to community. Along a spectrum allowing and acknowledging each generation as they speak to different core audiences, audiences become interchangeable at the edges, and together we are building a community of interactive listeners, readers, emerging critics and supporters of the arts.

Almost forty years ago, three upstarts (Clifton Joseph, Devon Haughton and myself) called ourselves "de dub poets." We took the Canadian poetry establishment by storm with our fiery voices. Dozens, sometimes hundreds, of people came out to see us read/perform our poetry—this at a time when the most well-known Canadian poets could attract only a handful to their readings. We read/performed at folk festivals, in bars, on street corners, in community centres, night clubs, schools, churches, universities ... Young people in the Black community learned our poetry by heart. The political, feminist and cultural communities enthusiastically embraced us. The poetry establishment was bitterly divided on what to make of us and our new kind of poetry. In an interview with *Fuse* magazine's Clive Robertson, I vowed never to stop until our kind of poetry—dub poetry—became part of Canadian culture. (Now you know why Lillian Allen is smiling!)

We didn't know Nikky Finney then, but, like her, we were confident in our history; and knowing that Black voice can't hide, we wondered for the generations to come: Where will they find their possibility of one day making a poem?

I will end with my tribute to all the young folks who have taken up the word.

Black Voice Can't Hide[15]

What does a voice become when it stands for something

A voice signifies the real, relational
                                    spirit thought quest
model dependent breath

A shadow's feel, noh soh real
apparition imagination digital
Virtual & reality and virtual reality
Physics' dualities
Beyond conventions to reinventions

What does a voice become when it stands
                         when it stands for something

Questioning and voicing to feel
                         a sense of the real
Poets turning routine into rituals
Resounding sound symbols of language
                         into language play

un-ravels embroidered geometry of the uni-lateral real(ity)
intricate layers of who, when, where and how to feel
The what shall speak for itself, the poet says
                         the poet says
The what shall be what the poet sees
what the poet sizeses

Voice threading stance and eyes and light
pulled through cracks in things that let the light in
(Mr Leonard Cohen)

An order against disorder and randomness expressed
in the poet's sound   voice sounding, sounding,
re-sounding sounding in the poet's sound

So to young poets who stand up
                         voice crafted vision
sight-ups inna lines set alight the energy in words
image shapes colour vibes
Say what you have to say so you don't burst-up

BLACK VOICE: CONTEXT AND SUBTEXT

Say to self-define, so yu don't walk blind

To you word chatterers goes the glory
                                     a play forward link in our
                                      ancestors' story
word sound powa connectivity stations
spiritual underground railroad vibrations
                               self determination navigation
Charting your own book of life   vital ital alive with
pride   a movement worldwide

Spoken word dub poetry vibe/ hip hop hip hop

Black Voice can't hide
Black voice can't hide
What does a voice becomes
A voice becomes when it stands
When it stands for something

Notes

1. http://entertainment.time.com/2011/11/25/galley-girl-poet-nikky-finney-rocks-the-national-book-awards/
2. Kwame Dawes, *Wheel and Come Again—An Anthology of Reggae Poetry* (Fredericton, NB: Goose Lane Editions, 1998), 16.
3. Maria Caridad Casas, *Multimodality in Canadian Black Feminist Writing: Orality and the Body in the Work of Harris, Philip, Allen and Brand* (Amsterdam and New York: Editions Rodopi B.V., 2009).
4. All quoted lyrics are by Bob Marley.
5. Klyde Broox, "Reloading the Can(n)on" in *My Best Friend Is White* (Toronto: McGilligan Books, 2005), 17.
6. Eduardo Galeano, "In Defense of the Word," in *The Graywolf Annual Five: Multi-Cultural Literacy*, ed. Rick Simonson and Scott Walker (St. Paul: Graywolf Press, 1988), 114–118.
7. Annie Dillard, *Living by Fiction* (New York: HarperPerennial, Harper & Row, 1982), 106–7.
8. William Wordsworth, "Preface to the Lyrical Ballads."
9. "Dis Poem": https://www.youtube.com/watch?v=Pn-f8PgLVjU.
10. Galeano, 124.

11 Kwame Dawes, "Dichotomies of reading 'street poetry' and 'book poetry'," *Critical Quarterly* 38 no. 4: 10–11.
12 Gabriele Rico, *Writing The Natural Way* (New York: Jeremy Tarcher/Putnam, 2000), 215.
13 This is from Clarke's toast following my keynote lecture at the Weatherhead Center for International Affairs Canada Program Seminar, Harvard University, October 28, 2013.
14 Maya Angelou, "Still I Rise," in *The Complete Collected Poems of Maya Angelou* (Random House, 1994).
15 A slightly different version of this poem appears in *The Great Black North: Contemporary African Canadian Poetry*, eds. Valerie Mason-John and Kevin Anthony Cameron (Calgary: Frontenac House Poetry, 2013), 108–9.

Conversation with the Poet/
Who didn't know my aunty
GREGORY SCOFIELD

Anne Szumigalski Lecture • Winnipeg, Manitoba • May 28, 2015

THIS STORY IS TOLD IN ORAL TRADITION IN A VOICE MUCH older than mine, a voice whose thought process and first language is Cree. The story, though written in English, is a translation. I've heard old people speak in both Cree and English many times and I am immediately drawn into their rhythms, the poetry of their voices.

> a few years ago   at a reading
> of erotic poetry
> a poet read a poem
> by another poet
> about a toothless Eskimo woman
> in a bar
> looking for someone, anyone
> to buy her a drink   and

what she did, what
that Eskimo woman did for a drink

Long ago when my aunty was no longer Mean Man's wife—
Punching Bag Woman she was called—she had met a moniyâw, a
white man. He was the one who called her Good Cooking Day
Woman, or Good Laundry Day Woman, or sometimes, Good With
The Money Day Woman.

Now, my aunty had TB in her lungs—which took her from Edmonton
down to a hospital in Vancouver. I used to hear about it at that time; it
must have been hard for her.

She had three sons, my aunty did. But two of her boys got sick and
died in Wabasca. Her other boy, John Houle he was called, was killed
in a car accident coming home for Christmas. I used to hear
her talk about it sometimes. She'd say to me, *One night back home I
was sitting having tea and I looked out at the clothesline and sure enough
there were three owls sitting there, just sitting there hooting away on my
clothesline. It's true*, she told me. *And those owls, those owls started
making somersaults, spinning around and around like this*, she told me.

a few years ago   at a reading
of erotic poetry
a poet read a poem
by another poet
about a toothless Eskimo woman

who could be:

ni-châpan, Hunting To Feed The Family Woman   *my great-great-
                                                grandmother*

who could be:

CONVERSATION WITH THE POET / WHO DIDN'T KNOW MY AUNTY

    ni-mâmâ, Holding Up The Walls Woman   *my mother*

    who could be:

    a kaskitewiyas-iskwew,   *a black woman*

    sekipatwâw-iskwew,   *a Chinese woman*

    moniyâw-iskwew   *a white woman*

    running from a white man,
    any man
    into the arms of a poet

    in a bar
    looking for someone, anyone
    to buy her a drink

My aunty, as I was saying here before, lost her boys early on. That is how I came to be her son: "nikosis, now you take the place of my John," she used to say. And I treated her as my mother: ni-mâmâsis, my little mother, I used to call her. My own mother —Dorothy was her name—did not mind this arrangement, for it was good for me to have two mothers.

It was these women who raised me by themselves. They were poor, my mothers, but it did not seem to matter—there were many things to keep a young boy occupied: books, music, stories and beadwork. I recall one time watching my aunty sew some moccasins. So interested was I that I kept moving closer and closer to her work. She did not seem to mind this ... Now, my little mother used to sew with very long threads and her needle would move very quickly. But this time I did not pay attention, so engrossed with the moccasins was I. She must have known this, for she took her sâponikan, that needle, and poked me right on the nose. *awas, ma-kôt!* she said. *Go on, big nose!* That is what she told me.

a few years ago   at a reading
of erotic poetry
a poet read a poem
by another poet
about a toothless Eskimo woman

she was fat, a seal
for the taking

she was dirty, a bag
of muskox bones
crawling with lice

she was dumb, her language
click, click
made people laugh

she was looking
for someone, anyone
to buy her a drink

I will not say my mothers did not have trouble with drinking or they did not lose days keeping the house in order. It is true: they had weaknesses here and there, just like other people.

And as far as my little mother goes, though she loved me a great deal, she did not get over losing her boys. I guess that is why today I speak so proudly of her, for she taught me many good things.

CONVERSATION WITH THE POET / WHO DIDN'T KNOW MY AUNTY

a few years ago   at a reading
of erotic poetry
a poet read a poem
by another poet
about a toothless Eskimo woman

and what she did   that woman
did for a drink.

It was in a bar:

it could be
the one from my childhood,

a room of white faces, a poetry hall
of uproarious mouths,

a room of unbound limbs
laughing
deep in their bones

or it could be
my aunty's rape bed, the man
who took her like a monument,
step after violent step

or it could be
her deathbed, all sixty-nine years
of her
lost in the translation
of a policeman's report

it could be, yes
the bed

where she told me stories

â-ha, the bed
where I lay dreaming

❦

This is as much as I am able to tell about my aunty. But there is another thing, one more thing you should know: I loved her very much and I still think of her whenever I am lonesome. ekosi, I am done.

Back then I was new to the world of Canadian literature and poetry, barely comfortable touting my third collection of poems, *Love Medicine and One Song*, in a room filled with some of Canada's most celebrated poets. What I remember most about that evening, however, was the sudden shift of my perceived belonging turning into something dishearteningly familiar. I'd wanted so much to belong to this exclusive circle, to be the young Metis kid who'd found a place among these brilliant word painters. But instead, I felt like the dumb Metis kid with his pitiful collection of Indian love poems suddenly looking from the outside in, helplessly watching the Eskimo woman in the middle of the room being jabbed by their sticks of laughter, stripped naked by the long-ago verse of some self-important poet whose name is left to speculation and likely to the anonymity of colonial voyeurism. What was most disappointing about that evening was that I'd gone from being a poet to being invisibly present at an ethnological exposition, a human zoo where the Inuit woman was treated no differently than Saartjie Baartman, the Khoisan woman named the Hottentot Venus, who was displayed in London in the early nineteenth century and whose vagina, brain and skeleton continued to be displayed as specimens of wonder long after her death.

My aunty is one of almost 1,200 missing or murdered Indigenous women in Canada whose death in 1997 remains unsolved. She is one of almost 1,200 missing or murdered Indigenous women in Canada whose life and history is forgotten somewhere in a case file, left in a box on a shelf or housed in a storage room where the fluorescent bulbs are occasionally turned on and off. My aunty is one of almost 1,200 missing or murdered Indigenous women in Canada who carried a name. Her name was her bundle.

The story goes something like this: when she was a little girl, living up there in Wabasca, Alberta, she got lost in the bush one day. No matter what she did, she couldn't find her way home. It was all just bush and trees and the blue, blue sky. Not even the birds were singing. There was nothing, no sound. Nothing. Only silence and her own crying and the blue, blue sky. Then she felt something pick her up by the shoulders. And suddenly she was standing on the path that led to home. From then on the old people, the kêhtê-ayâk, called her sîpwêypiyow: The One Who Flies.

My aunty carried both of her names, sîpwêypiyow and her Christian name, Georgina, in the bundle of her skin that was tied together by the tendons and muscles that were housed in a lodge made holy by her bones. I could say we all carry our names in the bundles of our skin, tied together by the tendons and muscles that are housed in the lodges made holy by our bones. I could say this and much more. But for now I will continue telling you about my aunty.

My aunty Georgie, my Little Mother, as I called her, is one of almost 1,200 missing and murdered Indigenous women in Canada whose death in 1997 remains unsolved. My cousin Virginia and I were never told why the coroner held her body or why we weren't consulted by the RCMP or why we had to muddle through the terrible silence surrounding her death. Instead, we were told they'd found a glass of wine beside her bed. So, in other words, we were told she was responsible for her own death. In other words, it could be said, we were told she was a drunken Indian woman. Now to put this in today's terms, we were being told that Indigenous women in Canada are 3.5 times more likely to experience violence or death than non-Indigenous women. We were never told, however, who was to blame or where the road to justice began or ended. Therefore, I suppose it could be said their words or lack thereof cut out our tongues and in turn we were given a feast of silence shared by the families of almost 1,200 missing and murdered Indigenous women in Canada.

Being in my early twenties at the time, I didn't think about the feast of silence we were being made to swallow. I didn't question the lack of utensils we were given or the fact we were told to eat blindfolded. My only thought was about my aunty's favourite scarf, the one she used to sweep up her hair before Bingo. And I thought about the clothes Virgie and I needed to buy her from Zellers, the ones in which to bury her. Back then I didn't feel the nub of my tongue or the pain of this new silence. I thought only about the crucifix that hung above her bed, the Little Gold Jesus she'd been given from residential school. The root of my seven-year-old tongue lived in that memory:

"Aunty, how come Jesus is all taped to that cross?"
"wâcistakâc, my boy! Cuz he was tryin' to wiggle off from dere!"
"mah! ki-môhco! You're crazy!"
"tapwe! He dold me he's damn tired of hanging on dere!"

The truth was Little Gold Jesus had been packed and unpacked so many times his tiny wrists and ankles were broken. But his crucifix looked as new as the day He'd dragged it up the wall above her bed. The root of my tongue lived in her dreaming room, this memory:

"Aunty, how come you cry in here sometimes?"
"I miss John, my boy!"
"But Aunty, I don't want you to cry no more."
"It's okay to cry."
"I don't like to cry."
"nikôsis, God gives us tears to let out dah sadness. It's okay to cry."

The truth is if I were to count the number of times I heard my aunty cry for John, it'd be more than 1,200. But numbers, I suppose, are fleeting and easily forgotten. They fluctuate. They change and become obsolete unless, of course, we're talking about money.

My aunty didn't have money. Nor did my mother. Nor did my great-grandmother. Nor did my great-great-grandmother, who was born in 1863, a short distance from where I now stand. She was born close to the banks of the Red River, the same river that cuts through the ribs of this city. She was born with the river in her blood because it flowed in her mother's blood and so on. Because of this, the river also flows in my blood. But I am getting ahead of myself. I was talking about numbers.

Last summer, in August 2014, the body of fifteen-year-old Tina Fontaine, a young Indigenous girl, was pulled from the Red River. Her body was discovered wrapped in a bag. Police ruled her death a homicide, but did not reveal how she died. No charges have ever been laid. Eleven years earlier, in 2003, the arm and leg of sixteen-year-old Felicia Solomon Osborne was pulled from the same river and from the same spot where Tina's body was found. Felicia's killer has never been caught. Neither has Tina's.
Neither has my aunty's.

When my aunty was a little girl, maybe five or six, there was an old lady named Iskocês, Little Fire, who every year set up her tipi in the yard for the entire summer. For some reason the old lady was particularly fond of my aunty, finding any excuse to make her visit. Every morning, without fail, Iskocês would be waiting with her bear grease and sharp-toothed comb, ready to smooth and pull my aunty's curly auburn hair into two neatly divided braids. As a child, I imagined the old lady to be more like a witch; a magical old woman who, like her name, could make fire with her fingers, who had medicines and brightly coloured ribbons that hung from the poles inside her tipi and who, like my aunty, could fly without wings.
I think about this story now and how stories, which could be poems, have the ability to make you think about other stories that are related like relatives, who have the same features and colouring, and who might also share the statistical probability of an increased 3.5 percent likelihood of experiencing violence or death in relation to an unrelated story, which might be in a poem about an Eskimo woman in a bar, looking for someone, anyone, to buy her a drink.
And I think about Tina Fontaine's great-aunty, the woman she called "Momma," who raised Tina as her own. I think about Tina's father, who was beaten to death on Sagkeeng First Nation in 2011; I think

about her mother, who was unable to care for her; again I think about the numbers; I think about Portage Avenue and the many roads in this city that lead down to the river, the same river that flows in my blood. And when I think about blood, I'm reminded of Iskocês, the old lady, who could fly without wings. I imagine her hands thick with grease dancing over my aunty's head, smoothing and pulling at the newness of her brain. I think about a young girl's ceremony and the transfer of an old lady's knowledge, and I wonder if Tina or Felicia ever had an old lady comb their hair.

But this, of course, was before the government schools and Little Gold Jesus. And this, of course, was before Tina's little body was pulled from the river and before Prime Minister Stephen Harper, in regard to a national inquiry into missing and murdered Indigenous women, was quoted as saying, "Um, it, it isn't really high on our radar, to be honest... Our ministers will continue to dialogue with those who are concerned about this."[1]

Thinking back to that long-ago evening of erotic poetry, what strikes me as odd is that no one appeared to be offended, no one seemed the least bit concerned. It is true that great poetry, poems that seep into our skin, can make us see the most trivial of things, those seemingly inconsequential happenings we all take for granted. It's true, I believe, that great poetry has an ability to become a part of our marrow. It can, without physical coercion, take us from being apathetic to being aware. And it's true that great poetry, no matter the constructs of the poet, can lead us deeper into the graves of ourselves, those very places we believe are beyond exhumation. In short, great poetry gives our unearthed bones new movement; it gives us reason to dance. It gives us reason to dialogue. It should give us reason to be concerned.

Last year Rinelle Harper, who was sixteen at the time, was left for dead during a violent assault that took place on the banks of the Assiniboine River here in Winnipeg. A twenty-year-old man and a seventeen-year-old boy have since been charged with attempted murder. A month after her assault, Rinelle addressed more than 3,000 chiefs and delegates at the Assembly of First Nations gathering, who'd come together to elect a new national chief. She said:

> I wish to continue on with my life and I am thankful I will be able to go back to school to see my friends and be with my family. Some people who have visited me have shared stories of healing. I ask that everyone here remember a few simple words: love, kindness, respect and forgiveness. As a survivor, I respectfully challenge all of you to call for a national inquiry into missing and murdered Indigenous women.[2]

And so, as Prime Minister Harper promised, his ministers continued to dialogue with those who were concerned about this. For example, in response to Rinelle's call for an inquiry, Minister Valcourt was quoted as saying, "Listen, Rinelle, I have a lot of sympathy for your situation. And I guess that victims . . . have different views and we respect them."[3]

Earlier I mentioned the feast of silence my cousin Virginia and I were made to swallow. I spoke about the lack of utensils we were given and the fact we were told to eat blindfolded. I spoke about the root of my tongue and how it lived in my memories. But I didn't speak about the ceremony of calling names. I didn't speak about the violence that mutes us close to home. I didn't speak about the generations of powerless men who take the food from their sons' plates and who leave them starving. I didn't speak about the generations of powerless men who take the utensils from their sons' hands and who then blame the women for their destructive actions. I didn't speak about the ceremony of calling names, such as those who left Rinelle Harper on the banks of the Assiniboine River, or those who steal the lives of our women, because this is not a ceremony yet welcomed in our communities.

Conversation with My Stepfather

Now that I've bundled my mother's bones,
Sung them home

On the backs of four aging horses,
I can tell you, old man,
It'll take more than the wrecking ball
Of your fist, the hoe of your heel

To rattle this house, undo
The frame of my timbers

That held up each death-marching year
You'd buried me over

And over in the yard
Or the pedophile down the street

You'd prayed to do you some kindness,
Some small, traceless bone act.

But here, see old man,
I've laid out my mother's bundle;

Put your eyes upon her jawbone
What voice will you give it?

Put your eyes upon her cheekbone
What prayer will you speak it?

Put your eyes upon her collarbone
What song will you sing it?

Put your eyes upon her wristbone
What offering will you bring it?

Put your eyes upon her shinbone
What root will you heal it?

Put your eyes upon her backbone
What bag of shame

What medicine bag of words
Will you give her?

Old man, because of you
I've traveled four lives

On the backs
Of four aging horses. But see

Now I am painted
And I've built my house

From the last of your marrow,
From the last of your bones.

Like my mother, my aunty lived with violence throughout her life. And like my mother, she also lived with health and addictions issues. It's important, however, that you don't see them as victims but as survivors. By virtue of their love and devotion, I am the embodiment of their dreams and hopes, their beliefs and convictions, their strengths and weaknesses, as well as their struggles and the ability to persevere. I am the repository of all these things, a storage room of files that have yet to be opened.

My aunty is one of almost 1,200 missing or murdered Indigenous women in Canada whose death in 1997 remains unsolved. The man who I believe murdered her, or who had knowledge of her death, was allowed to slip into obscurity, his final days spent in an old folks' home not even a mile from the rental house and the concrete steps where she reportedly fell in a drunken stupor. He was permitted the grace of leaving his own bones. And he took with him the truth; he was the one who called her Good Cooking Day Woman, or Good Laundry Day Woman, or sometimes, Good With The Money Day Woman. But I knew him as Uncle Harry.

But truths such as these aren't really gone. They live in the lines of poetry, occasionally exposing their broken teeth and the shadowed fists that kept them hidden. They live in the strokes of paint made visible on surfaces we believe are unable to hold them. They live in the notes of music that can penetrate the cracks of apathy. They live in the dancer's bones, 206 free-flowing truths that I suppose could be counted among the 994 names of the 1,200 missing and murdered Indigenous women in this country.

But they also continue to live in the lines of a poem written by an anonymous poet in the early twentieth century, a poem that was read by another poet a century later, and whose recitation of colonial brutality was a fist in my aunty's face; a fist in my mother's face; a fist in my own face and the face of my great-great-grandmother, who was born in 1863. Her name was Mary Henderson, and she was born close to the banks of the Red River, the same river that cuts through the ribs of this city. She was born with the river in her blood because it flowed in her mother's blood and so on. Because of this, the river also flows in my blood. And because the river flows in my blood, I'm related to Tina and Felicia, whose bodies were pulled from the river. And because I'm related to these little sisters, I am responsible to share my aunty's story.

The beginning of her story, as I said, came before the government schools and Little Gold Jesus. It was about an old lady who was particularly fond of her. It was about an old lady who had medicines and brightly coloured ribbons that hung from the poles inside her tipi. It was about an old lady who could fly without wings, the same gift that was given to my aunty.

But this was before the rental house and the concrete steps and the feast of silence and the clothes Virgie and I bought her from Zellers. This was before the root of my tongue lived in this story. And this was before I had a conversation with the poet, who didn't know my aunty.

    Once   at a reading
of erotic poetry
a poet read a poem
by another poet

CONVERSATION WITH THE POET / WHO DIDN'T KNOW MY AUNTY

about a toothless Eskimo woman
in a bar
looking for someone, anyone
to buy her a drink   and
what she did, what
that Eskimo did for a drink.

She could be:

ni-châpan, Hunting To Feed The Family Woman

who could be:

ni-mâmâ, Holding Up The Walls Woman

who could be:

a black woman

a Chinese woman

a white woman

running from a man,
any man
into the arms of a poet.

I was born with the river in my blood. Sometimes when I'm quiet and I allow the wind to take the ugliness from my being, I can hear the Old Ones whose stories are made of mud and clay. Sometimes I'm fortunate enough to be given a name that becomes a line that becomes a stanza that becomes a poem. I like to believe the root of my tongue once lived in their stories, although it's more likely the roots of their tongues live in *my* stories. Either way, when I'm quiet and I allow the wind to take the ugliness from my being, sometimes I'm given a song that connects me to the river and to my own broken but healing bones.

Prayer Song for the Returning of Names and Sons

YA-HEY-YA-HO
YA-HEY-YA-HEY
YA-HEYA
YA-HEY-HEY-YO

HIYA-HEY
HEY-HI-YA-HEY
YA-HEYA
YA-HEY-HEY-YO

HIYA-HEY
YA-HEY-YA-HEYA
YA-HEY-HEY-YO

HEY-HI-YA-HEY
HEY-HI-YA-HO
 —prayer song taught to me by my adopted brother
  Dale Awasis from Thunderchild First Nation, Saskatchewan

â-haw, ni-châpanak Charlotte, Sarah, Mary ekwa Christiana.	*an invocation, my ancestral grandmothers*
â-haw,	
kayâs ochi nikâwîmahk	*my mothers of long ago*
natohta my song, nikamowin	*listen the song*
âw, this song I am singing	

CONVERSATION WITH THE POET / WHO DIDN'T KNOW MY AUNTY

to give you back the
polished swan bones,

the sewing awl, the birchbark bundle
holding the whetstone

the drawing stone, the pounding
chokecherry stone, âw

the spirit of your iskwew   *woman*
names, the ones

not birthed from the belly
of their ships, not taken

from their manitowimasinahikan,   *bible*
âw, their great naming book

ni-châpanak Charlotte,   *my ancestral grandmothers*
Sarah, Mary

ekwa Christ-i-ana,   *and*
these are the names

I've thrown back across the water,
I've given back

to their God
who has two hearts, two tongues

to speak with.
âw, natohta   *listen*

my song, nikamowin   *the song*
the renaming song

I am singing
five generations later,

natohta   *listen*
my prayer song

so you will be called,
sung as:

Tattooed From The Lip To The Chin Woman,
êy-hey! Sung as:

She Paints Her Face With Red Ochre,
êy-hey! Sung as:

Charm Woman Who Is Good To Make A Nation
Woman, êy-hey!

I give you back
ni-châpanak   *my ancestral grandmothers*

the names to name
the names of bones, oskana   *the bones*

you laid down
to build them a house, âw

the blood, mihko   *blood*
and warm skin

earth, askîy   *earth*
that built them an empire.

natohta   *listen*
my song, nikamowin   *the song*

CONVERSATION WITH THE POET / WHO DIDN'T KNOW MY AUNTY

the prayer song
I am singing

to bring back
your stolen sons

whose sons and sons
and their missing bones

are unsung geese
lost in a country

across the water
ni-châpanak   *my ancestral grandmothers*

I've thrown back
your names;

nâmoya kîyawaw   *you are not*
Charlotte, Sarah, Mary

ekwa Christiana.   *and*
nâmoya kîyawaw môniyaskwewak.   *you are not white women*

â-haw, ni-châpanak   *an invocation, my ancestral*
kayâs ochi nikâwîmahk   *grandmothers*
                                         my mothers of long ago

natohta   *listen*
my song, nikamowin   *the song*
this prayer song
I am singing.

êy-hey!

NOTE: My châpanak of five generations past and my mothers of long ago came to find me while I was researching my maternal genealogy. The meticulous records that the Hudson's Bay Company kept on their employees, now available in their archives, serve as an invaluable source of information for many Metis and half-breed people, especially those who originate from western Canada. My grandfathers of that era, many of whom came from the Orkneys and London, arrived in Canada in the mid- to late 1700s. Some of them, such as James Peter Whitford, landed at York Factory, one of the Company's principal posts. Records state his full name, the parish he belonged to in London, the date he entered service, his various appointments and positions, the dates of his postings and his death on May 5, 1818, at Red River Settlement. Below this information, it simply states: *Wife: Sarah, an Indian woman. Married pre-1795 at Severn (?) Buried 27 Apr. 1845, 70 years old, at Upper Church.* I am certain my châpan Sarah, my kayâs ochi nikâwî—who eventually gave birth to eight children—came to my ancestor/grandfather carrying a name too sacred for him to pronounce. During my research I began to talk to her in a language that caused her bones to shift beneath the earth. I asked her to help me, her little ni-châpanis, to find and sing the proper names, even though the old names are forever lost. The women of my blood, my other châpanak, came to listen. I was grateful to have made this connection, to be a part of a ceremony that cannot be recorded.

Notes

1. Quoted in Tanya Kappo, "Stephen Harper's comments on missing, murdered aboriginal women show 'lack of respect'," CBC News online, December 19, 2014.
2. Quoted in "Rinelle Harper Calls for National Inquiry into Missing, Murdered Women," Red Power Media, https://redpowermedia.wordpress.com/tag/assembly-of-first-nations/page/2/.
3. Quoted in Mark Kennedy, "Valcourt urges First Nations, provinces to take action on murdered aboriginal women," *Ottawa Citizen*, December 12, 2014.

Contributors

MARK ABLEY grew up in western Canada and has lived in the Montreal area for many years. As a student in Saskatoon, he was mentored by Anne Szumigalski and she became a lifelong friend. His books of non-fiction include *Spoken Here: Travels Among Threatened Languages* and *Conversations with a Dead Man: The Legacy of Duncan Campbell Scott*. In 2015 Coteau Books published his new and selected poems.

LILLIAN ALLEN is an internationally renowned dub poet, writer and multi-dimensional artist, and a professor of creative writing at the Ontario College of Art & Design University. Named a "Fore Mother" of Canadian poetry, her work is studied across the entire educational spectrum. Her publications include *Psychic Unrest, Women Do This Everyday, Why Me,* and *Nothing But a Hero*. Her recordings *Revolutionary Tea Party* and *Conditions Critical* both won Juno awards. Her latest CD entitled *ANXIETY* was released in 2012. Allen's work seamlessly combines art, social critique, community engagement and transformation.

MARGARET ATWOOD, whose work has been published in thirty-five countries, is the author of more than forty books of fiction, poetry, and critical essays. In addition to *The Handmaid's Tale,* her novels include

Cat's Eye, short-listed for the Booker Prize; *Alias Grace*, which won the Giller Prize in Canada and the Premio Mondello in Italy; *The Blind Assassin*, winner of the 2000 Booker Prize; *Oryx and Crake*, short-listed for the 2003 Man Booker Prize; and *The Year of the Flood*. She is the recipient of the *Los Angeles Times* Innovator's Award, and lives in Toronto with writer Graeme Gibson.

MARILYN BOWERING is a poet and novelist who lives in British Columbia. Her most recent works are *Soul Mouth* (poetry), *What It Takes To Be Human* (novel), and the libretto for *Marilyn Forever* (Gavin Bryars, composer). She has been short-listed for the world-wide Orange Prize, twice nominated for the Governor General's Prize, and received awards including the Dorothy Livesay, Gwendolyn MacEwen, Ethel Wilson and Pat Lowther Prizes as well as several National Magazine awards. She was a 2008 Fulbright Scholar. www.marilynbowering.com.

ANNE CARSON was born in Canada and teaches ancient Greek for a living.

GEORGE ELLIOTT CLARKE is revered for his poetry, including the prized volumes *Whylah Falls* (1990, 2000, 2010; issued in Chinese, 2006), *Execution Poems* (2000, 2001, 2009), and *Blues and Bliss* (2008). His selected poems outed in Romanian (2005) and Italian (2012). He has also published verse drama (see *Beatrice Chancy*, 1999, 2008) and opera libretti (see *Quebecite*, 2003). Currently at work on an epic, "The Canticles," his newest book is *Traverse* (2014), an autobiographical poem. He was the Poet Laureate of Toronto, 2012–15.

ROBERT CURRIE is a poet and fiction writer who lives in Moose Jaw, where he taught for thirty years at Central Collegiate, winning the Joseph Duffy Memorial Award for excellence in teaching language arts. He is the author of ten books, most recently the novel *Living with the Hawk*. His next poetry collection will be *The Days Run Away*. Currie was Saskatchewan's third Poet Laureate. In 2009 he received the Lieutenant Governor's Award for Lifetime Achievement in the Arts.

TIM LILBURN has published nine books of poetry, including *Killsite, Orphic Politics* and *Assiniboia*. His work has received the Governor General's Award, among other prizes. A selection of his poetry is collected in *Desire Never Leaves,* edited by Alison Calder. Lilburn has produced two books of essays, *Living in the World as if It Were Home* and *Going Home*. He also has edited and contributed to two influential essay anthologies on poetics, *Poetry and Knowing* and *Thinking and Singing: Poetry and the Practice of Philosophy*. He currently teaches at the University of Victoria.

DON MCKAY has published a dozen books of poetry and three books of essays, some of which have been recognized with nominations and awards such as the Governor General's Award and the Griffin Poetry Prize. He is a fool for birds and rocks, and other aspects of natural history, including the current extinction event. He lives in St. John's, Newfoundland.

A.F. MORITZ has published eighteen books of poems, and his poetry has received various recognitions: the Griffin Poetry Prize, a Guggenheim Fellowship, the Raymond Souster Award of the League of Canadian Poets, the Award in Literature of the American Academy of Arts and Letters, selection to the Princeton Series of Contemporary Poets, the ReLit Award, an Ingram Merrill Fellowship, the Bess Hokin Award of *Poetry* magazine, three selections as a finalist for the Governor General's Award, and others.

GREGORY SCOFIELD is one of Canada's leading Indigenous writers whose seven collections of poetry have earned him both a national and international audience. He is known for his unique and dynamic reading style that blends oral storytelling, song, spoken word and the Cree language. His maternal ancestry can be traced back to the fur trade and to the Métis community of Kinosota, Manitoba, which was established in 1828 by the Hudson's Bay Company. His poetry and memoir, *Thunder Through My Veins* (HarperCollins,1999), is taught at numerous universities and colleges throughout Canada and the U.S., and his work has appeared in many anthologies. He has served as writer-in-residence at the University of Manitoba, University of Winnipeg, and Memorial University of Newfoundland. His collection *Kipocihkân: Poems New & Selected* (Nightwood Editions) and the re-publication of *I Knew Two Métis Women*, along with the Companion CD (Gabriel Dumont Institute) was released in Spring 2010. His most recent collection of poetry, *Louis: The Heretic Poems*, was released in 2011 (Nightwood Editions/Gabriel Dumont Institute). He is assistant professor of English at Laurentian University, where he teaches Creative Writing. His eighth collection of poetry, *Witness, I am*, is due for publication in 2016.

ANNE SIMPSON writes fiction, poetry and non-fiction. She has won a number of awards for her writing, among them the Griffin Poetry Prize for *Loop*. As well as her four books of poetry, she has written two novels, *Falling*, long-listed for the International IMPAC Dublin Literary Award, and *Canterbury Beach*. Her book of essays, *The Marram Grass: Poetry and Otherness*, delves into issues of poetry, art, and empathy. She has been a writer-in-residence at libraries and universities across Canada.

GLEN SORESTAD is a well-known poet from Saskatoon who has had nearly twenty-five volumes of poems published, has been included in over sixty anthologies and textbooks, has been translated into seven languages and has given close to 500 readings of his work throughout North America and in Europe. He is a Member of the Order of Canada.

PERMISSIONS & ACKNOWLEDGEMENTS

Excerpts from "The Angel of the Woods" by Anne Szumigalski are reprinted with the permission of the Estate of Anne Szumigalski.

"Nettles" and excerpts from "Theirs Is the Song," "Our Sullen Art," and "A House with a Tower" by Anne Szumigalski are from *A Peeled Wand: Selected Poems of Anne Szumigalski*, published by Signature Editions, 2010. Reprinted with permission of the publisher.

The excerpt from "Kill-site" is from *Kill-site* by Tim Lilburn, published by McClelland & Stewart Ltd., 2003. Copyright © Tim Lilburn.

"Insomnia" and the excerpt from "The Man-Moth" from *The Complete Poems: 1927–1979* by Elizabeth Bishop. Copyright © 1979, 1983 by Alice Helen Methfessel. Reprinted by permission of Farrar, Straus and Giroux, LLC.

Excerpts from the works of Frederick Ward are reproduced with the permission of Frederick Ward.

The excerpt from "Montreal" by A.M. Klein is from *Complete Poems*, edited by Zailig Pollock © University of Toronto Press, 1990. Reprinted with the permission of University of Toronto Press.

The excerpt from "In Memory of W. B. Yeats," copyright © 1940 and renewed 1968 by W. H. Auden is from *W. H. Auden Collected Poems* by W.H. Auden. Used by per-

PERMISSIONS & ACKNOWLEDGEMENTS

mission of Random House, an imprint and division of Penguin Random House LLC. All rights reserved. Any third party use of this material, outside of this publication, is prohibited. Interested parties must apply directly to Penguin Random House LLC for permission.

The excerpt from "Bushed" by Earle Birney is from *The Collected Poems of Earle Birney*. Reprinted with the permission of Wailan Low, literary executor.

The excerpt from "Seine" is from *Soul Mouth* by Marilyn Bowering, published by Exile Editions, 2012. Reprinted with permission of the publisher.

The excerpt from "The Horses" is from *Collected Poems* by Michael Longley. Published by Jonathan Cape in Great Britain in 2006 and by Wake Forest University Press in the United States in 2007. Reprinted by permission of The Random House Group Limited and by permission of Wake Forest University Press.

The excerpt from "What Happens When We Leave" is from *From Darkening Porches* by Jo McDougall. Copyright © Jo McDougall. Reprinted with the permission of The Permissions Company, Inc., on behalf of the Univeristy of Arkansas Press, www.uapress.com.

"Contact" by Robert Currie is from *Running in Darkness*, published by Coteau Books, 2006. Copyright © Robert Currie.

The excerpts from "A Tale of Two Gardens," "Epitaph for No Stone," and "The Balcony" by Octavio Paz, translated by Eliot Weinberger, are from *The Collected Poems 1957–1987*, copyright © 1986 by Octavio Paz and Eliot Weinberger. Reprinted by permission of New Directions Publishing Corp. and Pollinger Limited (www.pollingerltd.com) on behalf of the Estate of Octavio Paz.

The excerpts from the poems "After Paradise," "The World: Love," "From the Rising Sun: VII: Bells in Winter," and the prose poem "To find my home..." are from *New and Collected Poems: 1931–2001* by Czesław Miłosz. Copyright © 1988, 1991, 1995, and 2001 by Czesław Miłosz Royalties, Inc. Reprinted by permission of HarperCollins Publishers.

The excerpts from "Oda al libro" ("Ode to the Book") by Pablo Neruda are from *Odas elementales*. © 1954 Pablo Neruda y Fundacion Pablo Neruda. Reprinted with permission.

Excerpts from: "No Woman No Cry" (written by Vincent Ford) © 1974 Fifty-Six Hope Road Music Ltd & Blackwell Fuller Music Publishing LLC; "Get Up, Stand Up" (written by Bob Marley/Peter Tosh) © 1973 Fifty-Six Hope Road Music Ltd & Blackwell Fuller Music Publishing LLC; "Talkin' Blues" (written by Carlton Barrett/Leon Cogill) © 1974 Fifty-Six Hope Road Music Ltd & Blackwell Fuller

Music Publishing LLC. Copyright renewed. All rights reserved. Used by permission. All rights administered by Blue Mountain Music Ltd.

Excerpts from *kipocihkân* by Gregory Scofield, Nightwood Editions, 2009, www.nightwoodeditions.com. Used with permission from the publisher.

<u>Previous publication of the Anne Szumigalski Memorial Lectures:</u>

Tim Lilburn, "Poetry's Practice of Philosophy," *Prairie Fire* 23, no. 3 (autumn 2002): 33–40.

Anne Carson, "Every Exit Is an Entrance (A Praise of Sleep)," *Prairie Fire* 25, no. 3 (autumn 2004): 6–21. This lecture also previously appeared in *Decreation: Poetry, Essays, Opera* (New York: Alfred A. Knopf, 2005): 17–42.

George Elliott Clarke, "Frederick Ward: Writing as Jazz," *Prairie Fire* 26, no. 4 (winter 2005-6): 4–31. A version of this lecture was also published in George Elliott Clarke, *Directions Home: Approaches to African-Canadian Literature* © University of Toronto Press, 2012: 190–206. Reprinted with permission of the publisher.

Mark Abley, "The Angel of the Big Muddy," *Prairie Fire* 28, no. 3 (autumn 2007): 4–19.

Margaret Atwood, "Why Poetry?" *Prairie Fire* 29, no. 2 (summer 2008): 7–11.

Don McKay, "Ediacaran and Anthropocene: poetry as a reader of deep time," *Prairie Fire* 29, no. 4 (winter 2008-9): 4–15. A version of this lecture was also published in Don McKay, *The Shell of the Tortoise*, published by Gaspereau Press, 2011: 9–24. Reprinted with permission of the publisher.

Marilyn Bowering, Re-Discovering Ancient Springs: a consideration of metaphorical space," *Prairie Fire* 30, no. 4 (winter 2009–10): 4–15.

Anne Simpson, "Poetry and Community," *Prairie Fire* 31, no. 4 (winter 2010–11): 4–11.

Glen Sorestad, "Pristine and Startled: Ways of Seeing," *Prairie Fire* 32, no. 4 (winter 2011–12): 48–60.

Robert Currie, "Coming (back) to Poetry," *Prairie Fire* 33, no. 4 (winter 2012–13): 9–19.

A.F. Moritz, "A Garden Is Not a Place: Poetry and Beauty," *Prairie Fire* 34, no. 4 (winter 2013–14): 4–20.

Lillian Allen, "Black Voice: Context and Subtext," *Prairie Fire* 35, no. 4 (winter 2014–15): 22–33.

Gregory Scofield, "Conversation with the Poet / *Who didn't know my aunty*," *Prairie Fire* 36, no. 3 (autumn 2015): 4–19.